The Machinery of Government

AN INTRODUCTION TO PUBLIC ADMINISTRATION

Contents

To Leslie and Winifred Sallis for all their help and encouragement over the years

Preface

This book has been written primarily for students studying for the Business Education Council's National Level Awards and who are taking the Public Administration and Public Sector Studies Board double module *An Introduction to Public Administration*. The book should prove useful to students studying for BEC Higher National Level Awards, those studying for GCE 'A' level in Government and Political Studies, and first-year degree students who require knowledge of how the British political and administrative system works.

The book covers the General and Learning Objectives for the module as laid out in the BEC 'Red Book', *BEC National Awards: Course Specification* (reprinted in January 1979). However, the order of the objectives has not been followed exactly in writing the book. It was felt that students would better grasp the workings of the machinery of government if certain objectives were grouped together, so, for example, manpower has not been treated as a separate topic, but is discussed in the chapters dealing with the civil service and local government.

One of the difficulties in writing a textbook on public administration is the problem of topicality. Either an author can concentrate on principles and models, hoping to ward off the effects which time and changing events have on the process of government and its interpretation, or current material can be included to provide illustrations and to highlight the issues of the day. The danger here is that sections of the book can become dated. Despite the dangers, this book takes the latter approach because it is felt that institutional and administrative problems can be made clear only through an understanding of the political issues which surround them. It is hoped that the student will update the book for him or herself by being interested in and aware of current issues. A number of the assignments included in the book encourage this. The way in which we live as a society and the arrangements which we make for pursuing and reconciling our individual and society goals and aspirations are the stuff of public administration, and this can be grasped only by having a lively and topical interest in events as they unfold.

In writing this book I am indebted to my friend and ex-colleague, Chris Townsend of Acton Technical College, for originally stimulating my interest in public administration and for many interesting discussions over the years. I also wish to thank Derek Smith, Principal of Acton Technical College, for many invaluable conversations about the practical and often frustrating aspects of administration. Susan Lomax and Pat Sallis performed an invaluable task in typing the manuscript, which would never have been completed without the help of Steve Bateman of IBM. Simon Lake and Isabel Park of Holt-Saunders Ltd proved exceedingly helpful in the production of the book and extremely patient in waiting for the appearance of the manuscript. All the views expressed in the book are mine alone.

E.J. Sallis

1
Political Concepts

1.1 THE NATURE OF GOVERNMENT

The modern world is divided into about 150 states, each of which claims sovereignty over a particular piece of territory and the population within its boundaries. All states have government. The actual forms of government vary enormously, depending on the size, wealth, power, history and population of the particular state. Some, like Saudi Arabia, are absolute monarchies; others, like Pakistan or Argentina, are governed by military dictatorships. The Papal State and Iran have rulers who are first and foremost religious leaders (these governments are known as theocracies). About one half of the world's population live under political systems that claim their inspiration from Karl Marx, and their governments are usually labelled communist. Other states, including those of Western Europe and North America, have governments of a democratic character. Despite the diversity of systems there are certain universal characteristics of government:

1. There are in all states *rulers* – those who exercise power and make decisions – and there are those who are *ruled and governed* – those who have to obey.
2. In all states there is some *legitimizing doctrine* on which the *authority* of the rulers is said to rest. In most modern states the source of authority is set down in a constitution.

3. All states are, in the phrasing of Max Weber, 'the monopolist of the legitimate means of violence'. That means the governments of states possess the physical means to *enforce* their authority within their boundaries and, often, beyond it. Though the *authority* of governments to rule may be said to stem from the constitution, their *power* to do so stems from their possession of police and paramilitary forces, the armed services, the courts and the institutions of punishment. In many states, conflicts over who shall rule and the nature of the society are fought out through armed struggle and civil war, and *coups d'état* are the means used to change the government.
4. All states require a *bureaucracy* and an *administrative system* if government is to function and the policy decisions of rulers are to be implemented. Government officials are responsible for providing services and administering the taxation system through which governments are largely financed.
5. All states, to a greater or lesser extent, exercise a degree of control over the means of *mass communications*. The degree of direct control is usually in direct proportion to the degree of control which a government wishes to exercise over its subjects or citizens.

To describe the common features of governments does not explain the reasons for their existence. To explain the present system of government of any one state its political history must be examined. But, in general terms, it can be said that governments exist to protect some or all of the members of society from external aggression, from disorder from within and from the consequences of disasters, whether economic or natural. In many states the form of government is organized in the interests of a small and usually wealthy and privileged class, with the rest of the population being as much controlled as protected by the government.

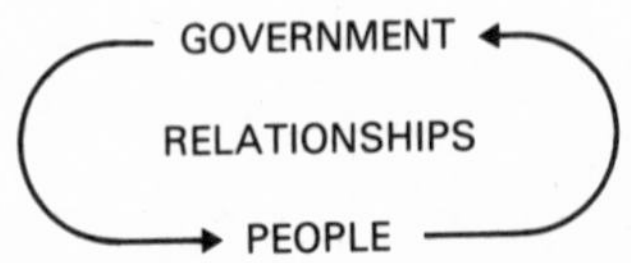

Figure 1.1 *The relationship between the government and the people. From Crick, B. & Porter, A. (1978) Political Education and Political Literacy p. 15. Harlow: Longman. Reproduced with the permission of The Hansard Society for Parliamentary Government.*

In all states, therefore, some individuals have power while others obey. An interesting question about the nature of government in any particular state is the nature of the *relationship* between the government and the people (Fig. 1.1). This relationship can be one of *tyranny,* where rulers use naked force, violence, terror and oppression to coerce their population into obedience. Examples of such tyrants are numerous – so numerous, in fact, that throughout history tyranny can be said to be the most common form of rule. Hitler's Germany, Stalin's USSR, Idi Amin's Uganda and Pol Pot's Kampuchea are but a few modern examples. But the relationship between governors and governed can also rest on *consent,* where the government owes its existence to the people and is responsive to their needs and wishes. This is one basic ingredient in *representative democracy.*

Governments may be classified in many ways. One useful classification is by the numbers involved in ruling (Table 1.1).

Table 1.1 *The numbers involved in ruling*

Type of Government	*Numbers*
Autocratic government	Rule by one man – a dictator, monarch, emperor, tyrant, despot, etc.
Oligarchic government	Rule by a few – an élite, a ruling class, a military junta, etc.
Democratic government	Rule by the many – the citizens, the people, the mass, etc.

Democratic government is of two types:

1. *Direct democracy,* which exists when all citizens or members of a group have a direct role in the process of decision-making. In modern states with large populations this type of democracy is clearly impossible, except where people's views can be sought on specific issues via referenda. Even in clubs, societies and voluntary organizations it is rare to find direct democracy. Normally a committee of members responsible to the total membership makes decisions.
2. *Representative democracy,* which is the common form of democracy where citizens elect representatives to make decisions on their behalf. The representatives are *accountable* to the electorate through a system of periodic elections. The British system of electing Members of Parliament is an example of representative democracy.

1.2 POWER AND AUTHORITY

In order to understand the nature of government it is necessary to grasp two important concepts:

1. *Political power.* This is the ability of government to achieve particular courses of action. It may be exercised by the use of force or through legal processes. The army, the police force and the legal system are the institutional means by which power is exercised.
2. *Authority.* This goes hand in hand with power. Rule can be exercised by force, but it is more usual for governments to justify their use of power by an appeal to some authority in order that they may be seen to have a right to rule (legitimacy). Authority is, then, the *right* to exercise power.

The German sociologist, Max Weber, argued that there were three sources of authority: traditional authority, rational or legal authority and charismatic authority.

Traditional authority

This is where the exercise of power and respect for the laws and rules of society are justified by reference to history, customs and traditional ways of doing things. In Britain the positions of the Monarchy and the House of Lords, limited though their power is, are legitimized by reference to their long historical existence.

Rational or legal authority

This is where the exercise of power is legitimized by law or by the individual's acknowledged skill and expertise. Most authority in British politics is of the rational or legal kind. Government Ministers, for example, can exercise only those powers for which they have legal sanction.

Charismatic authority

This is where an individual's authority comes from his or her presence or strength of personality (charisma). Many leaders, as different as

Hitler and Martin Luther King, have been able to mobilize people simply by having this type of personality.

1.3 THE CONCEPT OF POLITICS

In the previous section the nature of the relationship between the government and the people was discussed. One aspect of that relationship is the means by which disputes in society, either between the government and the people or between different sections of society, are dealt with.

Disagreements, disputes and conflicts can be fought out and attempts made to solve them by a variety of means – through the use of violence, force, coercion, corruption, revolution, *coup d'état,* terrorism and various means of passive resistance. One other means of conflict resolution is political activity. In the history of mankind, politics has been a 'minority sport' and continues to be so in many states. The conditions of its existence require a tolerance of and respect for other points of view, and an acceptance of the view which legitimately wins the day, even if that point of view is not one's own. Politics can take place only in an atmosphere or a culture in which it is assumed that there will be differences of views, and differences which will be strongly and vigorously expressed. Politics exists because human beings, individually or in groups, have different interests, and disagree about what should be done, when it is to be done, where it is to be done, and how it should be done. On occasions the government in a *political* society will be the arbitrator in disputes, as well as a participant on other occasions. It will also have a role in protecting minority views and defending views which are not its own. In such a society the government must be prepared to enter into a public dialogue on its policies and purposes. As J.D.B. Miller has said of political activity, in his book *The Nature of Politics:*

> The essence of a political situation, as opposed to one of agreement or routine, is that someone is trying to do something for which there is no agreement: and is trying to use some form of government as a means and as a protection. Political situations arise out of disagreements.

Political activity may take place via party politics, in which organized political parties with definite philosophies and policies compete for power at a national or local level, but it can take place in a non-party context, where individuals or groups compete for influence and control within organizations of all types, e.g. trade unions, clubs, business organizations, etc.

There are a multitude of reasons why political disputes take place, and there are many different explanations of their origin. For example, the Marxist view of politics concentrates on the fact that different groups or classes in society have different and opposing economic interests, and that these differences lead to disputes about the allocation, distribution and control of wealth. However, political disputes are not only about economic concerns, although these are a major cause of conflict. Political activity can result from conflicts about basic values and beliefs – religious, moral and social – about how we should treat others and the means necessary to secure desirable ends, such as the elimination of poverty or homelessness. Basic moral values are at the heart of the great political doctrines and constitute their basic beliefs. Socialists, for example, believe that greater equality in society is a desirable end, as it will lead to greater fraternity and the elimination of social differences. Conservatives, on the other hand, argue that inequalities can be justified and that the pursuit of equality frustrates the individual's freedom to pursue his or her own goals.

1.4 BUREAUCRACY AND ADMINISTRATION

The term 'bureaucracy' is a term often employed to describe public bodies which implement the policies which have been formulated by politicians. In Britain it can be used to describe the civil service, the local authorities and the wide variety of semi-governmental bodies which have become known as QUANGOs (quasi-autonomous non-governmental organizations).

The word 'bureaucracy' has a wide variety of meanings and, as it is widely used to describe public administration, it is necessary to understand them. The word is often employed as a term of abuse and is associated with the notions of *organizational inefficiency* – 'red tape', complex and time-consuming procedures – and indifference to the individual needs of clients and the general public. Most people have their own personal stories of trivial delay or frustration associated with relatively minor matters (or perhaps major matters) when dealing with public authorities – matters which are the stuff of complaints to MPs, local councillors, complaints boards and 'ombudsmen'.

'Bureaucracy' is a term which can also be used as a description of *rational organization.* By this definition a bureaucracy is an organization in which appointed officials carry out their work in accordance with sets of rules, as against organizations where corruption, nepotism and bribery are the means by which public resources are allocated. In this sense Britain's public administration is bureaucratic, although until the reforms of the civil service in the 1850s corruption in government was commonplace. In order to preserve the integrity of public administration it is necessary to have, among other things, a close accountability of the public bureaucracies to elected representatives and an open approach and access to official information. These latter points will be discussed in detail in the final chapter of the book.

The word 'bureaucracy' is also used to describe the *structure* of certain organizations. Following the sociologist Max Weber, bureaucratic organizations are usually said to have the following features:

1. A set of written rules in accordance with which the organization operates.
2. A hierarchical structure, with each level of management accountable to the level above it for the carrying out of its responsibilities.

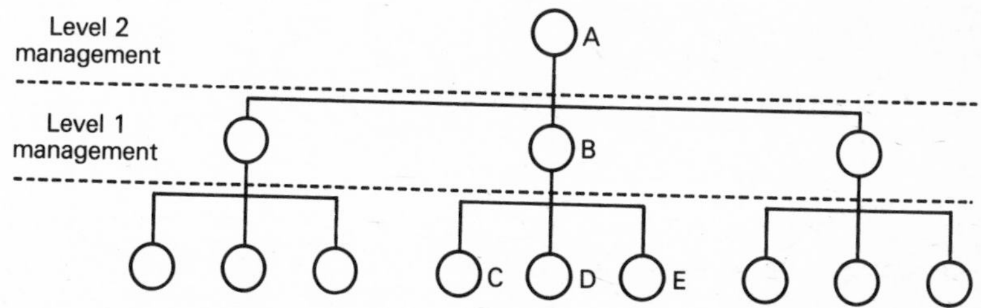

Figure 1.2 *A hierarchical organizational structure*

In Fig. 1.2 Manager *B* is *responsible for* a section of work performed by *C, D* and *E.* For the performance of these responsibilities *B* is *accountable* to his superior, Manager *A.*

3. Each specialist position in the hierarchy is filled by trained personnel. The holding of public offices usually demands knowledge of relevant academic disciplines, e.g. engineering, law, public administration, etc. The British civil service (although not local government) is unusual in this respect, as the top posts are *not* staffed by technical specialists, but by 'generalist' administrators.

4. Organizational management is based on written documentation and files.
5. Officials within the organization do not have other jobs or interests. Their occupation is, in a sense, a 'vocation'. Officials have job security once they have shown themselves to be competent. The job will usually be a 'career', as the individual will move up the hierarchy in the course of his or her career.
6. The entry and promotion of officials are based on merit.

1.5 CONSTITUTIONS

In order to legitimize political rule, most modern states have sets of rules which regulate the relationship between the government and the governed; these sets of rules are known as constitutions. A constitution is a document which lays down the ground rules for the government of society. A typical constitution will usually contain some, or all, of the following elements:

1. A statement of the basic or fundamental goals of the society. For example, the constitution of the USA describes these as 'life, liberty and the pursuit of happiness'.
2. The sources of sovereign power and authority. In the constitution of the USSR (1936) such power is vested in the 'working people of town and country'. In the South African constitution it is 'Almighty God'.
3. The forms of government and the duties of office holders and institutions. In the USA's constitution the powers of the President and the Congress are specified, together with other offices and duties, for example 'the Vice-President is President of the Senate'.
4. The rights of citizens. Again, in the USA's constitution 'Congress shall make no law respecting an establishment of religion, or prohibiting the free exercise thereof; or abridging the freedom of speech, or of the press, or the rights of the people peacefully to assemble, and to petition the Government for a redress of grievances'.
5. The mechanism by which a constitution may be amended.

It is important to note that studying constitutions can have its pitfalls. Constitutions are not necessarily guides to the political practice of a state. An example is Stalin's 1936 Constitution of the USSR, which has an impressive list of guarantees of civil liberties – freedom of speech, the press, assembly, etc. At the time Stalin was not only denying civil rights but was systematically condemning millions of Soviet citizens to their deaths. A western example of how constitutions may not guarantee rights in practice can be seen by looking at the position of blacks in the USA. It took black Americans more than 200 years to obtain equal civil rights despite a constitution which guaranteed freedom for all.

The 'Constitution' of the United Kingdom

The UK does *not* have a constitutional document. Most modern states have found such a document necessary in order to reconstruct their political systems and society in the aftermath of a dramatic break in their political history as a result of wars, revolutions or *coups d'état,* or after a period of colonization. British political history has been one of evolution and so the dramatic necessity to codify the rules of political conduct has not arisen.

The lack of a constitutional document has given rise to a great deal of discussion about whether the UK has a constitution in any real sense and, if it has, what actually constitutes it. Professor Finer has defined a constitution as:

> codes of rules which aspire to regulate the allocation of functions, powers and duties amongst the agencies and offices of government and define the relationships between these and the public.
>
> S.E. Finer, *Five Constitutions* p.15

If this definition is accepted then the UK can be said to have a constitution. Its sources can be found in statute law, common law, customs and conventions, European Community law and the European Convention on Human Rights.

Statute law

Various Acts of Parliament, such as the Habeas Corpus Act 1679, the Parliament Acts 1911 and 1949 and the European Communities Act 1972, are concerned with fundamental questions about the nature of the liberty of the subject or the institutions of government. What is different about these British constitutional documents is that these British laws have *no* special status in law and do not require special procedure to amend or alter them. It is as easy to abolish an Act like Habeas Corpus, which protects a citizen from unlawful imprisonment, as it is to abolish the Milk Marketing Board.

Common law

There are two sources of common law which are relevant here. First, there are the decisions of judges which have developed as authoritative expositions of the law. This includes, for constitutional purposes, such writs as mandamus, certiorari, prohibition and habeas corpus (see Chapter 12 for a full explanation of these writs) which affect the carrying out of duties by public officials. The second source is the interpretation of statute law, that is, the interpretation by judges of the meaning of laws made by Parliament.

Customs and conventions

It is often erroneously said that the UK has an 'unwritten constitution'. We have seen that many of its sources can be found in Acts of Parliament or the Law Reports. However, an important source of 'the rules of the political game' is to be found in practices developed over time, known as *conventions*. These are not law, since they have never been enacted by Parliament, but are usually regarded as being binding. Examples are numerous: that a government should resign if defeated on a major issue in the House of Commons; that a minister should resign if his department makes a major error of judgement to which he is a party (individual ministerial responsibility); that the Prime Minister is the Head of Government. The conduct of Parliament is largely conventional, as is the position of the Prime Minister and the Cabinet. In order to decide what is or is not a convention, it is necessary to look at history, usage and authoritative textbooks, such as Erskine May's *Parliamentary Practice*.

European Community law

A new source of constitutional law was provided by the UK's entry into the European Community in 1973 and the acceptance of the Community's constitution, the *Treaty of Rome*. Under the Treaty, Community directives passed by the Council of Ministers become law in the UK. Here we have an interesting example of how the lack of a constitutional document can cause confusion. In conventional terms Parliament is the supreme legislative body in the UK. This idea of the sovereignty of Parliament is bound round with other conventions, for example that Parliament cannot bind its successor and that treaties entered into do not have the force of law. But all these conventions are in direct opposition to the Treaty of Rome which, in certain areas, binds member states. What happens in practice is that the conventions will alter. As Lord Denning, Master of the Rolls, has said in a case affecting the EEC, 'Legal theory must give way to practical politics'.

The European Convention on Human Rights

The UK is a signatory, together with 15 other nations, to the European Convention on Human Rights, which was drawn up in 1950. The UK has ratified the Convention but it has not ratified all the protocols (amendments). Under the Convention, nations have agreed to submit to international control all their actions which concern basic human rights and freedoms. It is possible for individuals to complain to the European Commission for Human Rights about alleged violations of the Convention. This can happen only after ordinary legal remedies have been exhausted, and the procedure before the Commission is a lengthy one. As the Convention has not been incorporated into English law, a decision of the court can be enforced only by the goodwill of the Government. The British Government has been in breach of the Convention on a number of occasions, particularly over actions in Northern Ireland. The Northern Ireland (Emergency Provisions) Act 1973 allows, among other things, trial without jury for serious offences and is in contravention of the Convention. Similarly, the law banning homosexuality in Northern Ireland contravenes the Convention.

The Need for a Bill of Rights

In British law there are few positive rights for the citizen and so, unlike the law in other countries such as the USA, British law does not guarantee essential freedoms. Most British freedoms are based on a negative concept, that is, the citizen can do anything unless the law forbids it. This gives rise to problems, as the ordinary law can be used to diminish areas of freedom and the citizen has no means of redress. There is no equivalent to the Supreme Court, which can challenge the constitutionality of an Act or of actions by public officials.

Rights can be found in certain laws, such as Habeas Corpus or the Sex Discrimination Act, but they provide a patchwork rather than a comprehensive statement of rights. There have been a number of calls in recent years for the introduction of a Bill of Rights which would provide a guarantee of basic freedoms. Such a law would need a special status and would have to give the courts the power to declare Acts of Parliament unconstitutional. Opponents of the notion argue that such a Bill of Rights would remove the flexibility and adaptability of the British constitution: could the USA have joined a body like the EEC under its constitution? It is also argued that it is not law which guarantees freedom, but the vigilance of the population of the nation and the maintenance of a culture in which freedom can flourish.

1.6 SEPARATION OF POWERS

The main branches of government are usually classified under three headings:

1. *The executive.* This branch of government makes and implements policy. In the UK executive power is held by the Prime Minister and the Cabinet.
2. *The legislature.* This is the arm of government which passes law. In the UK this role is exercised by Parliament.
3. *The judiciary.* This is the arm of government which adjudicates or pronounces on law. This role is exercised by the courts.

It was argued by the French political theorist Montesquieu in the eighteenth century that political liberties were best protected if these functions had separate powers and personnel. Each branch of government can then act as a check on and balance to the power of the other branches. A law, for example, could be made only if the other two branches approved. The executive could refuse to sign it and the courts could rule it unconstitutional . Such a situation can occur under the constitution of the USA. The separation of powers prevents the power of government from being exercised by one person or group of people and would be an antidote to Lord Acton's dictum that 'all power tends to corrupt and absolute power corrupts absolutely'.

In the UK there is only a limited separation of powers. In fact certain conventions of the constitution, such as the responsibility of individual ministers to Parliament, are in direct contradiction to the doctrine. The major area of separation is between the judiciary and the other two branches of government, as the independent role of the judiciary is established by convention. But even despite this separation the head of the judiciary is the Lord Chancellor, a political appointee and a Cabinet Minister, who acts as 'speaker' in the House of Lords. Courts in the UK do not have the power to overturn or declare unconstitutional Acts of Parliament, as do US courts. The UK doctrine of the supremacy of Parliament is in direct opposition to the idea of the separation of powers.

ASSIGNMENTS

A1.1 Define the following concepts:

(a) power;
(b) authority;
(c) sovereignty;
(d) legitimacy;
(e) the state;
(f) the rule of law.

A1.2 Imagine that you are the founding member of a social club and that you have been asked to write its constitution. Draw up the constitution, making certain that it contains sections on at least the following:

(a) the objectives of the club;
(b) the duties of office holders;
(c) the rights and duties of members;
(d) the form of elections;
(e) the circumstances in which members may be disciplined.

A1.3 It is often argued that the United Kingdom needs a constitution or a Bill of Rights. Give:

(a) your opinions about what might be contained in it and why;

(b) the advantages and disadvantages it would have for the citizen over the present 'unwritten' constitution. You should state what rights it might protect which are at present unprotected.

(You should consult your college library when carrying out this assignment to obtain copies of the *European Convention on Human Rights* and S.E. Finer's *Five Constitutions*.)

A1.4 Using Max Weber's classification of sources of authority, comment on the authority exercised by the following office holders:

(a) a policeman;
(b) the Queen;
(c) the Prime Minister;
(d) Adolf Hitler;
(e) a judge;
(f) your lecturer;
(g) a Member of Parliament.

2
Process of Participation in Politics

2.1 PARTICIPATION: THE CONCEPT

In recent years 'participation' has become a vogue word and there are demands from many sections and groups for increased participation in the processes and institutions of British society. These demands have included calls for greater involvement and industrial democracy at places of work and for community involvement in planning and the provision of the whole range of public and social services. Examples of the 'participation movement' can be seen in the growth since the Second World War of major new pressure groups such as Shelter, CND and Friends of the Earth. Another expression of the mood was the brief but explosive period of student protest in the universities and colleges in the late 1960s, much of which was concerned with demands for greater involvement in the running of those institutions. In industry there have been demands for worker participation to counteract the 'alienation' felt by many people at work and this was reflected in the publication in 1977 of the Bullock Committee report *Industrial Democracy,* which called for a major shift of power in British industry.

Demands for increased participation can be seen as a response to the growing size and remoteness of government and to the alienation from their employment felt by many people. In the public sector there has been a feeling on the part of many commentators that controls via the normal channels of representative democracy have been insufficient to guarantee the involvement of ordinary electors in the decision-making process. This was argued to be the case, for example, in the process of town and country planning. The Skeffington Committee on People and Planning, which reported in 1969, recommended elaborate and extended procedures so that members of the public could be informed about and participate in the planning process. The Report argued that local authorities should actively seek out public views by appointing community development officers who would interview those members of the public not represented by established pressure groups and organizations. These views could then be fed into the local authority's planning processes.

It needs to be asked what precisely is meant by participation. Too often the word is used to cover consultation or the mere provision of information about decisions which have already been made. Participation has been defined as 'the act of taking part or having a share with others in some action' (G. Parry, 'The Idea of Political Participation' in G. Parry (Ed.), *Participation in Politics*). But what precisely does 'taking part' mean? It certainly does not mean being presented with information, and merely being consulted is probably at best only pseudo-participation.

In order for the citizens of a democracy genuinely to participate in the decision-making process they need to possess a degree of *power*. They need at least enough power to *influence* decisions, or they need the power which comes from being *a party* to the making of decisions. Both situations involve their *inclusion* in the decision-making process, and such situations can exist only if there is a climate or a political culture in which the government rests on consent and where protest and dissent are seen as a legitimate part of the political process. In order for government to be participatory it has to be open and has to be prepared to receive and to seek views, many of which will differ from its own. In this chapter and in the subsequent two chapters the channels and methods of participation available to the citizen to influence political decision-making will be examined.

2.2 PUBLIC INVOLVEMENT IN POLITICS

The idea of democracy implies rule by the people, and so it must be asked in what sense, if any, the people rule or participate in the governing of the country. Clearly, in a representative democracy there can be only a small number of decision-makers, but in theory at least this does not prevent extensive participation in the process leading up to the making of decisions.

In Britain only a small number of people are political decision-makers. There are 635 MPs and about 25 000 local councillors. If to this number we add senior civil servants and local government officers, chairmen and senior managers in the nationalized industries and other public bodies, and the leaders of pressure groups and major business organizations, the number of people who have a share in decision-making is probably less than 50 000.

Despite the clamour in recent years for increased participation, Britain's political system is *élitist.* This means that only a small minority of the population actually make the decisions. This minority, though not homogeneous, do possess close links and contacts, and many have similar views and interests. Many of them have originated from the same privileged backgrounds. A term often used to describe this minority is the *establishment.*

There is not, however, a single élite or establishment in Britain. Instead there are changing or circulating élites, or what Anthony Sampson, in his book *New Anatomy of Britain,* describes as 'rings of establishments', which are connected but which do not constitute a single establishment. Though members of various élite groups do have some views and assumptions in common, it must be remembered that there are often sharp disagreements and conflicts between élite groups. On matters of economic policy, for example, disagreement is common between leaders of the Trades Union Congress and leaders of the Confederation of British Industry.

Table 2.1 *Involvement in national politics*

	Estimated number	*Estimated percentage of the electorate*
Electorate 1970	39 342 000	98
Voters 1970	28 345 000	72
Organization members	24 000 000	61
Receiving weekly cash benefits	18 600 000	47
Party members, all categories	8 000 000	20
Official posts in organizations	5 500 000	14
Very interested in politics	3 500 000	9
Political activists	2 750 000	7
Individual party members	2 000 000	5
MPs, senior civil servants	4 000	0.0001

The existence of a political élite means that, while it can be argued that Britain has a representative democracy in terms of government *of* the people, *for* the people, it is not government *by* the people. It is true to say that there is an inverse relationship between the exercise of political power and the number of people participating in decision-making. This can be seen from Table 2.1, which is taken from Richard Rose's book *Politics in England Today* (1974).

Britain's democracy is not unique in having a ruling élite or ruling élites. All similar Western democracies do. The important matters are the way in which decisions are made, the existence of and freedom given to the communication and acceptance of alternative views and ideas, and the degree to which decision-makers are *accountable* to the citizens. It is important that government should be not only representative but also responsible government. If Britain can, in any sense, be said to be government *for* the people, then those who possess and exercise political power must submit their actions to public scrutiny and approval. This is the meaning of *public accountability*. The important questions to ask in this context are:

1. How easy is it for individuals or groups to have their views listened to by those in power?
2. How regularly and efficiently are the views of the public sought by decision-makers?
3. How easy is it for the ordinary citizen to participate in the decision-making process at national or local level if he or she wishes to do so?
4. How regularly are elections held so that those in power make themselves accountable to the electorate and the electorate can replace them if dissatisfied with their performance?

2.3 PLURALISM

In the last section we outlined the élitist nature of British political life and mentioned the fact that decision-making is dominated by a small minority or, to be precise, minorities. But the existence of élites should not lead us to conclude that there is not considerable influence and power exercised by groups outside the ruling élite. The influence of the trade unions, particularly over Labour governments, is evidence of this.

Although decision-making powers are exercised by a few, the power of influence is not exercised by one group, but is shared among many.

In this sense politics may be said to be *pluralist*. It is often argued that theories of élitism and pluralism are diametrically opposed, élitism emphasizing the concentration of power and pluralism its disposal. But it is also the case that they are answers to different questions. Elitism is concerned with the exercise of *decision-making powers* while pluralism is concerned with the *power of influence* over the decision-makers, and seeks to answer the question 'who influences policy?', concluding that it comes from a variety of sources and through a variety of channels. In this sense power to influence decisions is widely, if not evenly, spread in society. Pluralism will be explored in more detail in the discussion of pressure group activity in Chapter 4.

2.4 CHANNELS OF PARTICIPATION

A citizen may participate in decision-making via a number of different channels, both at local and at national level (see Fig. 2.1).

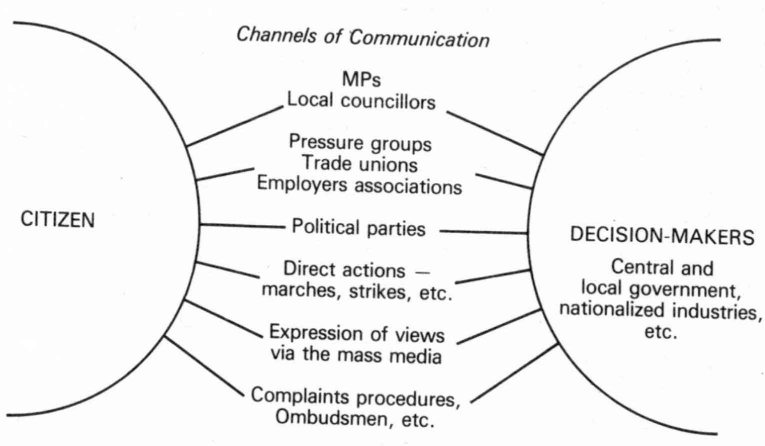

Figure 2.1 *Channels of political communications*

Standing for public office

The most well known means of participating is standing for public office, such as that of local councillor, member of Parliament, or member of the European Parliament.

Elections

As the number of elected representatives is small, most people participate in politics through registering their votes at periodic elections. Although this is the most important means of ensuring the democratic accountability of government, only some 75 per cent of the electorate exercise their right at general elections (see Table 2.2), and only a minority, 30 to 40 per cent, at local elections.

In the referendum on Britain's continued membership of the EEC held in June 1975 the turnout was 64.5 per cent, and in the first direct elections to the European Parliament in June 1979 it was 32.7 per cent.

Table 2.2 *Turnout at general elections since 1945*

Election	*Electorate*	*Total vote*	*Percentage turnout*
1945	33 240 391	25 085 978	72.7
1951	35 645 573	28 595 668	82.5
1955	34 858 263	26 760 498	76.7
1959	35 397 080	27 859 241	78.8
1964	35 892 572	27 655 374	77.1
1966	35 964 684	27 263 606	75.8
1970	39 342 013	28 344 798	72.0
1974 (Feb.)	39 798 899	31 333 226	78.7
1974 (Oct.)	40 072 971	29 189 178	72.8
1979	41 093 264	31 220 010	76.0

Source: Butler, D. & Sloman, A. (1980) *British Political Facts 1900–1979* 5th edition. London: Macmillan. Reproduced with permission.

Societies and groups

A high proportion of the adult population are members of voluntary organizations, professional associations, clubs, societies and groups of all kinds. Many of the groups have a political role in that they either have a right to be consulted in various areas of decision-making, or they may demand to be consulted if they feel it is in their members' interests.

Membership of political parties

The individual citizen can participate directly in political activity through membership of a political party. As will be shown in Chapter 3, membership of the main parties has been falling in recent years, and again, as in all organizations, only a minority of members play an active role.

Advisory bodies

Many individual citizens participate in public administration through membership of various advisory, consultative and governing bodies. These include school and college governing bodies, local community health councils, community relations councils, nationalized industry consumer bodies, etc. Nominations to these bodies are often made by political parties or interested pressure groups, and the membership of these bodies therefore contains a high proportion of people already active in other organizations. For example, school and college governing bodies contain a high proportion of local councillors.

Complaints procedures

If individual citizens wish to complain about the operation of public bodies or their actions, there is an elaborate mechanism for the redress of grievances. The role of complaints procedures is explained in Chapter 12.

2.5 ELECTIONS IN THE UK

The major means of political participation is through elections. In the United Kingdom an individual citizen may exercise his or her vote in the following elections: elections for MPs; elections for county councillors; elections for district or borough councillors; parish council elections; elections to the European Parliament; referenda.

Elections for Members of Parliament

General elections for all members of the House of Commons must be held at least every five years. The timing of elections rests with the Prime Minister. If an MP dies or retires a by-election is held.

Elections for county councillors

Elections for county councillors are held every four years (see section 10.6).

Elections for district or borough councillors

Elections for district, metropolitan district or London Borough councillors are held every four years (see section 10.6).

English parish and Welsh community elections

Most English parishes and Welsh communities have an elected council which is elected every four years. In smaller parishes and communities where there is no council a meeting of all the electors takes place either annually or bi-annually.

Elections to the European Parliament

The first elections for Members of the European Parliament were held on 7 June 1979.

Referenda

So far these have been held only on issues of major constitutional importance. The first and only nationwide referendum was held in June 1975. The question put to the electorate was 'Do you think the United Kingdom should stay in the European Community (the Common Market)?'. Of those who voted, 64.5 per cent voted 'YES' to the question.

Various parts of the United Kingdom have had their own referenda on constitutional issues. In March 1973 a referendum was held in Northern Ireland on the issue of whether the province should remain part of the United Kingdom or join the Republic of Ireland. The referendum was boycotted by Catholic workers, but of the 58.7 per cent of the electorate who voted, 591 820 voted for the province to remain part of the United Kingdom and 6463 voted for it to join the Republic of Ireland.

In March 1979 the electorates of Scotland and Wales voted on the issue of whether they wished to have devolved government in those countries. (For details of results see 'devolution' in section 7.13).

2.6 THE FRANCHISE

People can vote in elections in the United Kingdom providing they are 18 years or over, are citizens of the United Kingdom, the Republic of Ireland or the Commonwealth, and are resident in the United Kingdom, and have their names on the electoral register. There are a number of people who are not qualified to vote:

1. Aliens (except for citizens of the Republic of Ireland).
2. Certain mental hospital patients.
3. Peers and peeresses in their own right, who are excluded because they have direct representation in Parliament in the House of Lords. However, they are enfranchised to vote in local elections.
4. Prisoners.
5. Those convicted of corrupt and illegal electoral practices. They suffer temporary disqualification. Illegal electoral practices include bribery of voters or spending more than the stated electoral expenses.

Each elector can vote only once in an election. Before the Representation of the People Act 1948, there was a system of plural voting. Additional votes were given to university graduates and those owning their own businesses. Plural voting was abolished by the 1948 Act, although the issue of its desirability in local government elections has since been raised. It is argued that local businesses which are major ratepayers should be enfranchised, although this would breach the principle of one man one vote.

2.7 QUALIFICATIONS FOR OFFICE

The following people are *not* eligible to stand for election to the House of Commons (for local councillor franchise see Chapter 10):

1. Those aged under 21 years of age, despite the fact that the voting age and the age of majority is 18 years.
2. Aliens, except citizens of the Republic of Ireland.
3. Peers and peeresses in their own right.
4. Clergymen of the Church of England, the Church of Scotland, the Roman Catholic Church, the Presbyterian Church of Scotland, and the Church of Ireland.
5. Bankrupts. (The disqualification for bankrupts normally lasts for five years after discharge.)
6. Mental hospital patients who have been certified under the Mental Health Act 1959.
7. Those holding office under the Crown. The House of Commons Disqualification Act 1957 disqualifies holders of office or places of profit under the Crown. In this category are civil servants, members of the armed forces, judges, members of police forces and others, such as members of the boards of various QUANGOs or public corporations. This ban applies to both part-time and full-time appointments, and to members of the European Parliament. In 1979 Mrs Shelagh Roberts, European Parliament Member for London South-West, was disqualified for holding a part-time office under the Crown. After she had resigned the post she was re-elected at a by-election caused by her disqualification.
8. Prisoners in United Kingdom or Republic of Ireland jails serving a sentence of more than one year under the Representation of the People Act 1981.

There is not always a great deal of logic to many of these disqualifications. Peers and Church of England clergymen, it can be argued, are rightly debarred, as they have representation in the House of Lords, but Roman Catholic clergymen do not. Between 1967 and 1981 imprisonment was not a disqualification, unless a person had been convicted of treason. Until the Criminal Law Act 1967 conviction for a felony (serious crime) was a disqualification. Under this Act felony as a category of crime was abolished and, although it was replaced, electoral law still debarred only felons from office. This loophole allowed prisoners to stand and to be elected to office. Any MP so elected could not sit or vote in the House of Commons. In April 1981 the IRA hunger striker, Bobby Sands, was elected for Fermanagh and South Tyrone at a by-election. He was serving a sentence for terrorist offences in the Maze Prison and subsequently died in prison from fasting as a protest about the lack of political status given to IRA prisoners. His election was seen as a major propaganda victory for the IRA. This loophole was closed in 1981 with the passing of the Representation of the People Act, which debarred prisoners serving sentences of a year or more.

2.8 THE ELECTORAL SYSTEM

'First past the post'

The system of voting used for most elections in the United Kingdom is the *simple majority* or *first past the post system*.The exception is Northern Ireland, where the single transferable vote system is used for local government and European Parliament elections. (The single transferable vote system is described later in the chapter.)

The country is divided into 635 geographical areas known as constituencies. (The number of constituencies has been as high as 707 in 1918 and as low as 615 in 1922.) Each constituency elects one Member of Parliament. The constituencies have, in theory, roughly equal electorates, and a permanent Boundary Commission reports to Parliament on necessary boundary changes to maintain the balance. Nevertheless, there are considerable anomalies. in 1981 there were 11 constituencies with electorates of over 100 000 and 14 with under 40 000 electors. For example, Buckingham had 110 000 and Basildon 108 000 electors, while at the other end of the scale Gateshead West had 29 000 and Glasgow Central only 19 000. In addition, not all of the countries making up the United Kingdom are similarly represented. There is one MP for every 66 000 electors in England, one for every 53 000 in Scotland and one for every 57 000 in Wales.

The first past the post system is the simplest of all electoral systems. Each registered voter can exercise one vote in the constituency in which he or she is registered. At the polling station the voter marks a cross against a candidate's name on a ballot paper. Voting is secret. The candidate who gains a majority of votes cast wins the seat in Parliament for that constituency. But winning a majority does *not* mean winning a majority of votes cast: in reality it means coming first.

Consider the following example:

A. Brown (Conservative)	20 000
E. Jones (Labour)	16 000
S. Smith (Liberal)	10 000

A. Brown would be elected as the MP, since he or she gained the most votes, even though 57 per cent of the electorate did not vote Conservative. The first past the post system has been heavily criticized, especially by the Liberal Party, one of whose main policies is to replace it by a proportional representation system of election which gives seats in proportion to votes cast.

The present system favours the two main parties and gives them more seats than they would be entitled to if seats were distributed in proportion to votes cast. Table 2.3 demonstrates how the present system discriminates against the Liberals.

Table 2.3 *Election results 1979*

Party	*Number of seats in the House of Commons*	*Percentage of seats won*	*Percentage of votes cast*
Conservative	339	53.4	43.9
Labour	268	42.2	36.9
Liberal	11	1.7	13.8
Others	17	2.7	5.4
Total	635	100.0	100.0

As can be seen from the table, the Liberal Party is badly affected by the present system. Except in a small number of constituencies, its supporters are spread throughout the country in such a way that, while its candidates may come second and third, they rarely come first. Under the first past the post system only candidates who come first win. In 1979, if seats in the House of Commons had been given in strict proportion to votes cast, then the Liberal Party would have gained 88 seats, and not the 11 it actually won.

Other examples of the anomalies thrown up by the system can be seen by looking at the February 1974 election, in which the Labour Party gained a smaller proportion (37.2 per cent) of the vote than the Conservative Party (38.1 per cent). A similar, albeit reverse, situation occurred in the 1951 election, where Labour gained 231 067 *more* votes than the Conservatives but 26 *fewer* seats.

Although the British electoral system can be described as 'one man, one vote', it cannot be described as a 'one man, one vote, one value' system. Electors in marginal constituencies where party strength is finely balanced are the key to winning or losing an election. A Conservative voter in a strong Labour constituency may feel that his or her vote matters little – a feeling which is correct. The reasons for the distortions produced by the first past the post system are:

1. Despite the periodic redrawing of boundaries by the Boundary Commission, constituencies are of unequal size due to population movements.
2. Scotland and Wales are overrepresented, while Ulster is deliberately underrepresented. In 1978 a Speakers Conference on Electoral Law recommended that Northern Ireland's representation should be increased to 17 from its present 12 MPs. An Act to this effect was passed in March 1979 but will not come into effect until the boundary change of the mid-1980s.
3. Party support is unevenly distributed and this favours the two major parties. Labour and Conservative have areas of concentration of their support. Liberal support is in the main too thinly spread across the country for them to win more than a handful of seats under the present system.

2.9 ALTERNATIVE VOTING SYSTEMS

In other Western democracies a variety of electoral systems are used. Most of them are designed to try to match representation to the actual votes cast and most of them do so more effectively than Britain does. There are a wide variety of possible alternatives to the British first past the post system, some of which are discussed below.

The second ballot system

This is the system used in France. Its purpose is to eliminate the winning of seats on a minority of votes in a constituency. In Britain, in the 1970 election 38 per cent of MPs were returned on a minority vote, that is, more people voted for other candidates than for the candidate who won. The second ballot system requires two elections. If no candidate wins an overall majority on the first ballot then the candidate(s) with the least number of votes is (are) withdrawn and only the leading two candidates remain on the ballot for the second election. In such a system the leading candidate does not necessarily win the second ballot and there is plenty of opportunity after the first ballot for deals to be made between the two leading candidates and the unsuccessful ones.

A good example of the effect of the second ballot system can be seen in the 1980 election for a Labour Party leader. The Parliamentary Labour Party used the second ballot system for this election, although it has now been replaced by a wider electoral college system (see section 3.4).

First Ballot Result

Candidates	*Votes*
Dennis Healey	112
Michael Foot	83
John Silkin	38
Peter Shore	32

Peter Shore and John Silkin were then eliminated and the second election took place a week later, with the majority of the votes of the third and fourth candidates going to Michael Foot.

Second Ballot Result

Candidates	*Votes*
Michael Foot	139
Dennis Healey	129

Alternative vote system

The alternative vote system works on a similar principle to the second ballot system, except that only one election is necessary. Voters show their first and second choices on their ballot paper. If no candidate wins a majority on first preferences then the last candidates are withdrawn and their second preferences are distributed to the leading two. Again, the purpose is to make certain that candidates win with a majority of the vote.

Proportional representation

There are a number of voting systems which attempt to equate accurately the number of votes cast with the number of seats won in Parliament. Two will be discussed here: the party list system and the single transferable vote system.

The party list system

This system is used in a number of countries, including Israel, Belgium, Italy, Greece and West Germany. Multi-member constituencies are employed, each political party draws up a list of candidates and the electors vote for the party list which they prefer. Seats are then allocated to parties in proportion to votes cast. The parties fill their seats from the lists by taking their candidates in the order of the published lists. The drawback of the system is that it removes the elected representative from the electors. Candidates cannot represent geographical areas, as electors cannot vote for particular individuals to represent them. It means that political parties at a national level decide who the candidates are, not local parties as in Britain.

The single transferable vote system (STV)

This is the system favoured by the Liberal Party and is the one used for local council and European Parliament elections in Northern Ireland to ensure a fair representation of the Catholic minority. It is also the voting system used in the Republic of Ireland.

Large, multi-member constituencies are employed. For example, in the European Parliament elections in Northern Ireland in June 1979 the whole of Northern Ireland was a single constituency which elected three members to the European Parliament. If used in British parliamentary elections, between four and seven members per constituency would probably be necessary.

Voters mark their ballot papers 1, 2, 3, 4, etc. against the candidates, according to their preferences. Once the votes have been cast the electoral officer establishes a quota. This is the minimum number of votes required to establish election of a candidate.

$$\text{Quota} = \frac{\text{number of votes cast}}{\text{number of seats} + 1} + 1$$

Initially, if a candidate gains the quota on first preferences he or she is elected. Since votes over this number are superfluous, the surplus votes are distributed in accordance with the second preferences on the ballot papers. Votes are transferred to candidates until the required number of candidates achieve the quota. The advantages which STV would have over the present system in Britain are:

1. It would widen the choice available to electors. Larger constituencies electing more members would allow electors to vote for individuals within parties and to cross party boundaries if they wish, e.g. giving their first three preferences to Labour candidates and their fourth to a Liberal in a four-member constituency.
2. All electors' votes have an equal value. It would allow Liberal candidates or minority candidates to have seats in proportion to votes cast and would prevent the kind of results shown in Table 2.4 after the 1978 local elections in London.

Table 2.4 *Results of some 1978 London borough local elections*

London Borough	*Conservative* %	*Seats*	*Labour* %	*Seats*	*Liberal* %	*Seats*	*Others* %	*Seats*
Hounslow (60)	47.6	24	47.0	36	2.4	0	3.0	0
Waltham Forest (57)	45.2	21	43.5	36	3.3	0	8.0	0
Hackney (60)	28.4	1	59.9	59	3.0	0	10.7	0
Islington (52)	38.2	2	49.0	50	2.8	0	10.0	0
Tower Hamlets (50)	14.8	0	55.6	43	10.5	7	19.1	0

3. It would preserve the connection between MPs and geographical constituencies.
4. It has been argued that it would lead to more consensus politics and great continuity in policy, as third parties like the Liberal would hold the balance of power in the possibly inevitable coalitions which would occur after the introduction of an STV system. The minority party's involvement in government could prevent the see-saw of policy which happens under the present system.

The introduction of proportional representation is opposed by the Conservative and Labour parties not on the grounds of equity but simply because it would lead to coalition governments. They argue that the electorate of the country want strong government and the manifesto of their party implemented. They argue that the inclusion of minority parties in government would give them an influence not justified by their electoral support.

ASSIGNMENTS

A2.1

Election Results

Party	28 February 1974 No. of seats	% of vote	10 October 1974 No. of seats	% of vote	3 May 1979 No. of seats	% of vote
Conservative	296	38.1	276	35.7	339	43.9
Labour	301	37.2	319	39.3	268	36.9
Liberal	14	19.3	13	18.3	11	13.8
Others	24	5.4	27	6.7	17	5.4
Totals	635	100.0	635	100.0	635	100.0

Answer the questions below. Some of the questions relate directly to the table while others are based on the implications of the results:

(a) Give criticisms of the present electoral system as it affects the Liberal Party.
(b) Imagine that you are a member of one of the larger parties. Present your arguments in favour of the present system.
(c) Outline how an alternative system of voting could provide greater representation for the minority parties.
(d) What, in your opinion, would have been the effect on the balance of parties in the House of Commons if a proportional system of representation had been used for these three elections?
(e) How accurate is it to describe British politics as a 'two-party system'?

A2.2

Which of the following people are entitled to vote in a British general election?

(a) Citizens of the European Community
(b) Citizens of the Republic of Ireland
(c) Members of the House of Lords
(d) People aged over 18
(e) Citizens of Commonwealth countries not resident in

the UK

(f) Citizens of Commonwealth countries resident in the UK
(g) British citizens resident abroad
(h) Members of the British armed forces stationed abroad

A2.3 List the main channels through which an ordinary citizen can participate in decision-making at:

(a) a local level;
(b) a national level.

A2.4 Has the introduction of referenda into British politics made Britain a more democratic country? Are there dangers in the use of referenda?

3
Political Parties

3.1 PARTY POLITICS

Politics in Britain is party politics. In all elections – local, national and European – the overwhelming majority of the electorate vote for party candidates. The whole system of British government is built around the existence of competing political parties – political parties which mobilize support in order to elect MPs and local councillors. Once elected, MPs and councillors are expected to support their party's policies.

Political parties are based on particular interests and represent competing views or philosophies about the type of society they feel to be the most desirable. Inevitably party views on particular issues occasionally overlap, but British political parties do have distinctive policies and views. Nevertheless, the major parties – Conservative and Labour – do contain within them people with a wide range of viewpoints and so each party is to an extent a coalition of views. Although the majority of the electorate vote for one of the two major parties, the electorate is in fact offered a very large choice, since a large number of minor parties, especially at the political extremes, offer themselves for election. The extent of that choice is shown below.

Political parties in the UK
(*Represented in Parliament January 1982)

Marxist

Communist Party of Great Britain
Communist Party of England (Marxist-Leninist)
Socialist Workers Party
Workers Revolutionary Party
International Marxist Group
Socialist Party of Great Britain

Democratic socialist

Labour Party*
Social Democratic Party*

Liberal

Liberal Party*

Environmentalist

Ecology Party

Nationalist

Plaid Cymru* (Welsh nationalist)
Scottish National Party*
Social Democratic and Labour Party (Northern Ireland)

Conservative

Conservative Party*

Unionist (Northern Ireland)

Official Unionist Party*
Democratic Unionist Party*

Extreme right wing/fascist

National Front
New National Front
British Movement

Revolutionary nationalist (Northern Ireland)

Sinn Fein (Republican clubs)
Provisional Sinn Fein
Irish Republican Socialist Party

3.2 LEFT AND RIGHT IN BRITISH POLITICS

The terms 'left' and 'right' are part of the currency of politics. It is important, therefore, to understand their meaning. They are in daily usage, but they are not precise terms and there is confusion about their use.

The usual meanings of the terms 'left' and 'right' are given in Fig. 3.1, with the Communists on the extreme left through to Fascist groups on the extreme right. However, to many members of political parties this is a distorted picture of politics, for two reasons.

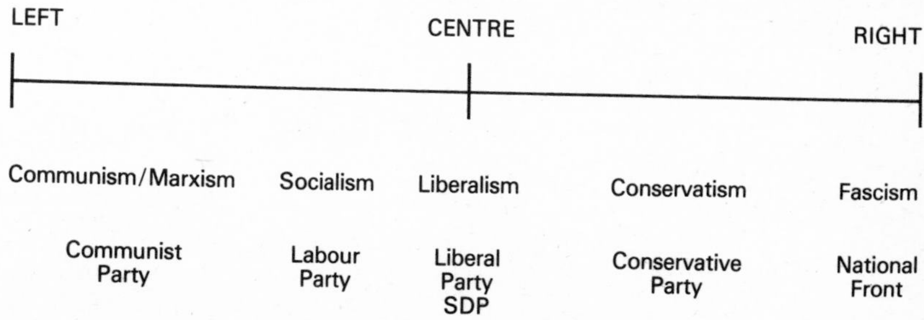

Figure 3.1 *The traditional left/right continuum*

First, it presents all politics as a battle between two sides – left and right – and allows no distinct place for other forms of politics such as nationalism or the radical forms of liberalism. Many liberals and social democrats see their parties as radical parties with definite ideas about political change, and not just as parties holding the centre ground.

Second, on either side of the continuum there is a very marked difference between the groups at the extremes and those parties towards the centre of politics. Broadly, those parties at the extremes – Communist and Fascist – share authoritarian views and believe in the importance of extra-parliamentary means of gaining power. Those in the centre share common views on the importance of parliamentary democracy and individual liberty. It has been claimed that in many respects, as far as these broad issues are concerned, the Conservative, Labour, Liberal and Social Democratic Parties are on one side of the spectrum, while the Communists and Fascists are on the other, despite the marked difference of views of the latter two groups.

3.3 A 'TWO-PARTY SYSTEM' OR A REALIGNMENT OF BRITISH POLITICS?

In the 1979 General Election 75 per cent of the votes cast went to either the Conservative Party or to the Labour Party and, because of the way in which the first past the post system works, this gave them 95.6 per cent of the seats in the House of Commons. Electoral support for the two major parties has declined since the war. In 1951 the 'two-party system' reached its peak, with 96.8 per cent of the vote going to the two main parties. Since then their support has declined, with votes going in the main to the Liberal Party and to the two nationalist parties – the Scottish National Party and Plaid Cymru. In Northern Ireland, as a result of the direct rule imposed on the province in 1972, the Ulster Unionists, who previously had been aligned with the Conservative Party, broke their allegiance with that party.

The workings of the electoral system have made it difficult for third parties to break the monopoly enjoyed by the Labour and Conservative parties, despite the decline in popular support for them. In the February 1974 election the Liberal Party gained 19.3 per cent of the vote but only 14 Parliamentary seats. It is generally recognized that a third party requires about 30 per cent of the popular vote in order to 'break through' the monopoly of the main parties and have seats in the

Commons roughly in proportion to the vote it receives.

A major change in the British 'two-party system' came about in 1981 with the formation of the Social Democratic Party. This was formed by former members of the Labour Party who were disillusioned by the increasingly leftward shift in the policies of Labour as a result of the growing influence of left-wing activists, including minorities with Marxist views. At the time of writing (December 1981) it is too early to state what effect the new party will have on the Labour Party or on British politics in general. The SDP are the third largest party in Parliament, with 26 MPs (24 ex-Labour, one ex-Conservative and one by-election win, and they have a membership of 22 in the House of Lords), but only one of these MPs was elected as a Social Democrat and the others have not put themselves to the test of re-election. What is clear is that the evidence of public opinion polls indicates that a large number of the electorate have expressed a willingness to shift their support to the SDP. Public opinion polls express a mood at a particular time and do not necessarily indicate what will happen at a general election, when many of the electorate swing back to traditional allegiances. In February 1981 a National Opinion Poll survey showed that 40 per cent of those polled were in favour of a new Centre/Social Democratic Party, and in March 1981 a Gallup Poll found that 41.6 per cent of its sample of electors were prepared to give their vote to a Social Democratic/Liberal alliance.

In the first by-election which the SDP contested, in Warrington in July 1981, one of the SDP leaders, Roy Jenkins, gained 42 per cent of the vote. The Labour Party retained the seat but the majority was cut from over 10 000 to 1759. The Conservative candidate lost his deposit. In October of that year a Liberal/Alliance candidate, Bill Pitt, won a by-election in Croydon North-West, a former Conservative seat; and in November 1981 Shirley Williams won the Crosby by-election for the SDP. Crosby was also a former Conservative seat. In all three of these by-elections in 1981 the SDP/Liberal Alliance gained between 40 and 49 per cent of the votes cast. If the Social Democratic Party is to win seats at a general election it must break through the 30 per cent barrier. To do this an electoral pact or alliance is required with the Liberal Party so that neither party will run candidates against each other and split the 'moderate' vote.

The decline in support for the two main parties has come about for a number of reasons. First, there is the relative lack of success which both parties have had in solving Britain's economic problems.

Second, both political parties have moved towards their extremes. In the 1950s the term 'Butskellism' was coined (after the affinity of views of the Conservative R.A. Butler and the Labour leader Hugh Gaitskell). It described the consensus on many major issues which existed between a majority of MPs in both the main parties. This 'consensus politics' has broken down, and in the 1970s and 1980s has been replaced by a more 'ideological' and doctrinaire style of politics. Michael Foot, the Labour leader, was at one time leader of the Tribune Group, which is on the party's left wing, while Margaret Thatcher is on her party's right wing. Much of this move towards extremes reflects both the country's poor economic performance and the consequent need for a more radical approach to the economy. It also represents the increasing influence over policy of party activists, whose views are often more extreme than those of parties' electorates.

Third, though this is questionable, some observers have linked the decline in support for the two main parties with the decline of 'class politics' in Britain. The Labour Party has traditionally drawn its support from the working class, while the Conservative Party is seen as the middle-class party, although its electoral support is drawn equally from the middle and the working classes. The argument is advanced that fewer of the electorate now see themselves in class interest terms and tend to vote on the basis of 'issues' or according to how they believe a party's manifesto will affect them, especially their living standards. Thus, in the 1979 election, the Labour Party lost many working-class voters to the Conservatives due to the latter's pledge to sell council houses to tenants.

Both the Conservative and the Labour Parties have lost membership over the years, although they still remain 'mass' parties. It is difficult to be precise about actual membership, as neither party keeps accurate membership figures. It is estimated that the Conservative Party's membership has fallen from 2.8 million in the early 1950s to 1.5 million today, whereas the Labour Party's individual membership in the same period has fallen from the million membership mark to a figure claimed by the Party in 1981 to be 358 000. There are some 6 million trade union members affiliated to the Labour Party who pay a political levy with their union dues. This figure includes many who vote for other parties but who, for a variety of reasons, do not opt out of the political levy.

The decline in membership has meant that in many local constituency parties of both the Labour and the Conservative Parties small numbers of extremists among the activists can have influence out of all proportion to their electoral strength. This has happened particularly in the Labour Party, where certain local parties have ousted or tried to oust sitting 'moderate' MPs. Dick Taverne, MP for Lincoln, fought a by-election against his own party in 1973, and Reg Prentice, former

Labour MP for Newham North-East (now a Conservative MP), was another sitting member who failed to be reselected by his local party. At the 1980 Labour Party Conference constituency parties were given the right to make all sitting Labour MPs submit to annual reselection. The effect of this measure may have the effect in certain constituencies of 'moderate' MPs being replaced by more left-wing candidates.

3.4 THE LABOUR PARTY

History

The Labour Party came into existence in 1906, and had its origins in the Labour Representative Committee which was formed in 1900 to provide a distinct Labour group in Parliament. It was sponsored by the trade unions, co-operative societies and a number of socialist groups. The original purpose of the LRC was to provide a pressure group for Labour interests inside Parliament. After 1906, when 26 MPs were elected, the name was changed to the Labour Party and a party organization inside Parliament was established. Initially a party leader was not elected and instead there was an annual election of a chairman. Policy was determined at an annual conference and it was here that a National Executive Committee was elected, on which sat representatives of sponsoring organizations. During its first few years of existence Labour policy was little different from that of the Liberal Party, which they largely supported in Parliament. The party had its first experience of government office in a minor capacity during the wartime coalition formed in 1916.

After the war the party was reorganized. It was put on a national footing, with the creation of constituency parties and with individual as well as trade union memberships. The party gained a socialist constitution in 1918, and an aspect of its socialism is laid out in the famous Clause IV – 'to secure for the producers by hand and by brain the full fruits of their industry, and the most equitable distribution thereof that may be possible upon the basis of the common ownership of the means of production and best obtainable system of popular administration and control of each industry and service'.

The first Labour Government was formed in 1924. It was a minority government and it had Liberal support. It lasted ten months and had as its main achievement Wheatley's Housing Act, which helped to establish a system of public housing. The Prime Minister was Ramsay

Macdonald. The second Labour Government, also under Macdonald, was formed in 1929. This was also a minority government, although this time the Labour Party was the largest in Parliament. It lasted until 1931. During its period of office the Government faced the problems of mass unemployment during the height of the economic depression of the period. The Government lacked a clear policy to deal with the crisis. An international financial crisis occurred in the summer of 1931 and its repercussions brought the Government down. King George V helped to organize a secret deal between Macdonald and the Conservative and Liberal parties to form a national government. Macdonald and 13 Labour MPs joined the Government and Macdonald became Prime Minister. The rest of the Labour Party refused to follow him. At the 1931 election the party lost a great deal of support. The Labour Party remained in the doldrums during the 1930s and the power within the party moved from the Parliamentary Party to the trade unions and the party outside Westminster.

In 1940 the Labour Party joined Winston Churchill's wartime coalition government and Clement Attlee, Labour's leader, became Deputy Prime Minister. Ernest Bevin, leader of the Transport and General Workers Union, became Minister of Labour and was responsible for the wartime direction of labour. The Labour Party withdrew from the coalition after the end of the war in Europe. At the 1945 General Election the Labour Party won a major victory with a majority of 146 seats.

The Labour Government had a clear mandate for carrying out substantial reforms. Among its legislative achievements were measures which considerably developed the 'welfare state'. The wartime proposals of the bipartisan Beveridge Report were put into practice and included comprehensive social security benefits and national insurance, and legislation to create the National Health Service. In industry the Government carried out a major programme of nationalization, including the railways, iron and steel, the Bank of England, areas of road and air transport, and coal. The Labour Government in foreign affairs helped to establish NATO in alliance with the USA to counter what it saw as the threat posed by the Soviet Union. The party narrowly won the 1950 election but lost office in 1951.

The 1950s were a period of internal dissent during which the party was out of office. There was considerable internal conflict between the moderate leadership of Hugh Gaitskell and the left of the party, led by Aneurin Bevan. Gaitskell wanted to drop Clause IV and had a strong belief in the western alliance and Britain's nuclear deterrent. Bevan was partially committed to unilateral nuclear disarmament. The issue came to a head at the party conferences of 1959 and 1960. Initially the party voted for disarmament, leading to Gaitskell's famous 'fight, fight and fight again' speech, but the decision was reversed the following year. Gaitskell died in 1963 and was succeeded by Harold Wilson as leader.

Wilson gave the Labour Party the image of a radical party committed to technological change in the form of the 'white heat of technology'. The party narrowly won the 1964 election with an overall majority of four seats. In the 1966 election it had a more decisive victory, with an overall majority of 96. Initial attempts at overall economic planning, with Deputy Prime Minister George Brown's National Plan of 1965, were quickly abandoned in 1967, when external payments forced a devaluation of sterling. The party lost the 1970 election and was out of office until 1974.

Re-elected in February 1974 the Government was a minority one and a second election was held in the October, when the party gained an overall majority. The major plank of its platform was the control of inflation via an agreement with the trade unions known as the 'Social Contract', the architect of which was Jack Jones, leader of the Transport and General Workers Union. A referendum on the issue of Britain's remaining in the EEC, which it joined in 1973, was held, and the result was an overwhelming 'yes' to continued membership. The effects of the oil crisis and the fall in world trade coupled with spiralling inflation led to a series of pay policies and cuts in public expenditure. In 1978 Harold Wilson resigned the leadership and was succeeded by James Callaghan. Through a series of by-election defeats the Government lost its overall majority and in 1977 a pact for Parliamentary support with the Liberal Party – the 'Lib-Lab Pact' – was formed. The Government was defeated on an issue of no confidence in 1979 and lost the subsequent election.

In 1980 Callaghan resigned the Labour leadership and was succeeded by Michael Foot, who narrowly defeated Dennis Healey in the leadership contest. The period since 1979 has been marked by deep internal divisions, particularly between the left and right wings of the party. The left, led by Tony Benn, and a majority of the party's National Executive Committee have sought to make the Parliamentary Labour Party more accountable to the party outside Westminster. This has been accompanied by campaigns for the NEC to control the content of the election manifesto, for the party leader to be elected by constituency parties and trade unions as well as by the PLP, and for MPs to undergo annual reselection conferences in their constituencies. The victory for the last two measures at the 1980 Blackpool conference led to a group of 'moderates', led by David Owen MP and William Rodgers MP, together with Shirley Williams and Roy Jenkins, leaving the party and forming the Council for Social Democracy, later to become, in 1981, the Social Democratic Party. In 1981 the 'moderates' within the party formed the Labour Solidarity Committee with the aim of reversing the Blackpool decisions and challenging the left. The left, led by Tony Benn, has argued for withdrawal from the EEC, unilateral nuclear disarmament, import controls and further measures of public ownership.

Structure and membership

The Labour Party had its origins in a coming together of organized labour (in the form of trade unions) with socialist and co-operative groups. This combination continues today, with the trade unions playing a major role in the party's affairs and providing the bulk of its membership and income. The role of the unions can be shown dramatically in the membership figures. Although these are inaccurate, it is clear that the party has over 350 000 individual members and some 6 400 000 members who pay a political levy with their union dues. It is certain that many union members are unaware that they are paying the levy or find it easier not to 'contract out' of the payment. It is interesting to note that from 1927 to 1946 union members had to 'contract in' to the payment of a political levy and when the law was changed in 1946 to 'contracting out', membership rose from 2.6 million to over 4.3 million. Many union members actually vote for other parties. The significance of union membership becomes clear at the party's Annual Conference because affiliated unions exercise 'block votes' on behalf of their members and effectively dominate the conference and its decisions as a result. Under the new rules for electing Labour's leaders the trade unions have 40 per cent of the votes in the electoral college which elects the leader.

The Annual Conference and party leadership

The Annual Conference is given the role of the final arbitrator of party policy. The role of the Conference has been a subject of continuing debate, especially about the degree of influence or control which it should have over the decisions of the Parliamentary Labour Party. Labour prime ministers and leaders, feeling the need for flexibility of action, have taken the view that Conference decisions should be advisory. The contrary view is taken by the left wing, who believe they should be mandatory. The fact that until January 1981 the leader of the party was chosen only by the PLP gave party leaders an independence from Conference and from the party's executive body, the National Executive Committee. A dramatic change in the relationship between the Conference, the PLP and the leader came about as a result of the 1980 Conference decision concerning the election of the leader and deputy leader, and this has shifted power from the PLP to the unions and the constituency parties (see Fig. 3.2).

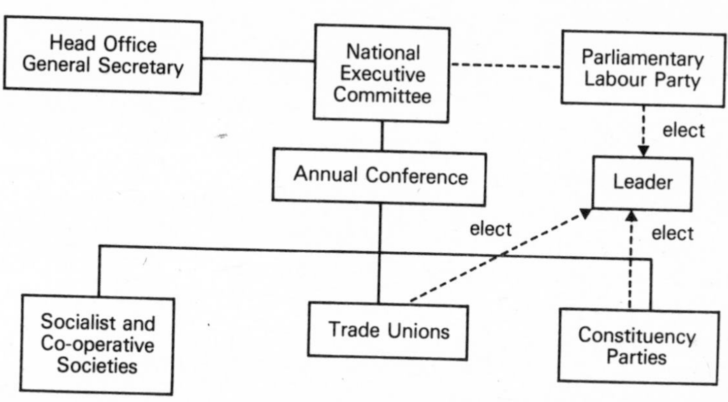

Figure 3.2 *The structure of the Labour Party*

The leader of the Labour Party leads the Labour MPs in the House of Commons and is the person called to be Prime Minister by the Monarch in the event of a general election victory. As the leader needs the loyalty of MPs it had been they who elected him or her. However, the system came under attack, especially from the party's left wing, who in the 1970s had been gaining strength in the constituencies. They were calling for greater accountability of MPs to their constituency parties. At a special conference at Wembley in January 1981 a new leadership formula was produced. The leader is elected by an electoral college where 40 per cent of the votes are cast by the trade unions, and 30 per cent each by the constituency parties and the PLP. The effect of this change is not yet entirely clear. Theoretically, the decision could be taken to elect as leader a person who does not have the overwhelming support of the PLP. The Labour Solidarity Committee is committed to altering the formula, with greater representation going to the PLP. The 1980 Annual Conference decision has shifted policy-making power to the Conference and away from the party leadership.

Groups within the Labour Party

The Labour Party is a coalition of interests and to give voice to these different interests there are a considerable number of groups within the party which operate as internal pressure groups for particular opinions or views.

Tribune Group

This is a left-wing group established in 1965 by, among others, Michael Foot and Ian Mikado. It has its own newspaper, the weekly *Tribune*. It is against Britain's nuclear weapons, believes in greater public ownership and planning of the economy, and is anti Britain's continued membership of the EEC. It has a membership of about 70 MPs as well as a number of local groups.

Labour Solidarity Campaign

This is a right-wing group which is the successor to the Manifesto Group. The latter group was formed to counter the influence of the Tribunites and to emphasize the importance of the mixed economy to political freedom. The Solidarity Campaign was formed in 1981 and has strong backing from Labour MPs. It is led by Denis Healey and Peter Shore. Its task is to counter the 1981 campaign by Tony Benn for the deputy leadership of the party and to reverse the 1980 Annual Conference decisions about the compulsory re-selection of MPs and the new method of electing the party's leader.

Campaign for Labour Victory

This was formed in 1977 to provide an organization for 'moderates' at grassroots level.

Fabian Society

This was founded in 1884 by George Bernard Shaw and Sidney Webb. It is an intellectual and research organization. Its motto is the 'inevitability of gradualness'. Many Labour policies have been the result of its publications.

Campaign for Labour Party Democracy

This is a left-wing group closely associated with Tony Benn and the campaign to make the Parliamentary Party and future Labour governments more accountable to the party's grassroots. Formed in 1973, it has been in the forefront of the campaign for the compulsory re-selection of MPs.

Labour Party Young Socialists

This is the official youth section of the party. For the past ten years its activities have been closely linked to those of the Militant Tendency.

Militant Tendency

This is an organization on the far left of the party, many of whose members can be described as Trotskyist. (A Trotskyist is a follower of the Russian revolutionary Leon Trotsky, 1879–1940, who argued for 'permanent and international revolution'.) The group publishes the paper *Militant* and has some 60 full-time organizers and paper sellers. The group has had a policy which has come to be known as 'entryism', the aim of which is to 'capture' local constituency parties. The group was subject to investigation by the former Labour Party national agent, Lord Underhill, in 1975 and 1980. The NEC of the party has always refused to take any action on the activities of the group based on the Underhill reports, on the grounds that the Labour Party does not indulge in 'witch-hunts'.

Rank and File Mobilizing Committee for Labour Democracy

This was set up in 1980 as an umbrella group to bring together a number of left-wing groups in the party, particularly the Labour Co-ordinating Committee (set up in 1978), the Campaign for Labour Party Democracy, the Institute of Workers Control, and the Militant Tendency. There is a considerable duplication of membership and aims. The Labour Co-ordinating Committee has the intention of revitalizing inner party democracy and policy-making. These groups considered that the 1974–79 Labour Government failed to achieve much in the way of socialist measures, and to make certain that a future Labour government does not follow the same path they have championed Mr Benn's campaign for greater accountability of the Parliamentary Party to the Party Conference and for the compulsory re-selection of MPs.

The political thought of the Labour Party

The Labour Party is generally thought of as being a reformist socialist party. Like the Conservative Party, it contains people of a wide spectrum of views, from Marxists in the Militant Tendency on the extreme left, who wish to see an end to the capitalist system, to social democrats on the right wing, who firmly believe in the operation of the mixed economy and Britain's continuing position in the western alliance. The views of Labour Party members may and do overlap with those of certain Communists, Social Democrats, Liberals and Conservatives. Harold Wilson described the Labour Party as being a 'broad church'. Since the expulsion of the right-wing Social Democratic Alliance in the late 1970s for running candidates against MPs whom they saw as being ultra-left, and the resignations to form the Social Democratic Party, the range of views has narrowed, although it is still true to say that the party contains a wide range of views.

It must always be remembered that party dogma and beliefs are not always translated into action. It is not necessarily a guide to what Labour members believe in to look at what Labour governments have done. The practicalities of office have made Labour governments and Prime Ministers essentially pragmatic in their outlook and, if it has been considered necessary, Conference decisions have been ignored.

The Labour Party's 1979 election manifesto opened with the sentence 'Now, more than ever, we need Labour's traditional values of co-operation, social justice and fairness'. Ideas and values such as these have always been important to the Labour Party, and the following are the main themes running through Labour thought.

Equality

The socialist dream has always been for a 'classless society' in which social divisions based on income, wealth, birth and privilege would be abolished. As the socialist historian R.H. Tawney put it, in his book *On Equality* (1931), '. . . it is the mark of a civilised society to aim at eliminating such inequalities as have their source, not in individual differences, but in its own organisation.' This, in its most radical sense, is what is meant by equality. In practical policy terms the Labour Party has been egalitarian in the sense of promoting policies for comprehensive education, expanding the social services and in the public ownership of major industries. The argument for equality was probably most strongly put by Anthony Crosland, who was Labour Foreign Secretary from 1976 until his death in 1977, in *The Future of Socialism* (1956). In that book Crosland argued that inequalities in society could be justified only if it could be shown that they contributed to the common good.

Public ownership

This has been a theme which has caused considerable controversy within the party and is a major issue which distinguishes left from right. Nevertheless, the party's constitution in Clause IV is committed to the extension of public ownership. In Britain nationalization embraces all the major utilities as well as a proportion of the country's major transport and manufacturing undertakings. The Labour Government 1945–51, while being the architects of the public corporation, never introduced an important element of Clause IV – the 'popular administration' of the nationalized industries. Workers' control has never been an element in the thinking of Labour governments.

The welfare state

The Labour Party has been associated with and has been the main architect of the system of welfare benefits which has become known as the 'welfare state'. The party put the notion of the National Health Service into operation, as well as a comprehensive system of social security benefits. Similarly, the party has nurtured and stressed the advantages of comprehensive education and council housing.

In order to provide these benefits, which have been seen both as an antidote to the inequalities of capitalism and as a means of extending equality, a huge level of public expenditure and hence taxation has been seen as a necessity. In recent years one of the fundamental differences between the Conservative and the Labour parties has been their conception of the purpose of the state and the level at which public expenditure should run. Labour thinking is based on the necessity of advancing equality, demanding heavy state involvement in society and thus high levels of public expenditure and taxation.

The mixed economy

Socialists are by doctrine opposed to the free enterprise system of capitalism, believing instead in co-operative action and the public ownership of industry. Labour governments, however, have been interested in advancing the mixed economy, consisting of both public and private enterprise. It has been necessary to control the operation of the free enterprise sector of the economy rather than to take it over, especially in the 1950s and 1960s, when the free enterprise system was successful in producing a high rate of economic growth and increasing living standards.

3.5 THE CONSERVATIVE PARTY

Origins and history

Whereas an exact date can be given to the formation of the Labour Party, the same cannot be done for the Conservative Party. It has been claimed that its origins can be traced to the Civil War in the 1640s and the supporters of the King. However, the name 'Conservative' was not used until the 1840s. During the period between 1886 and 1922, when the issue of Irish home rule dominated British politics, the party was known as the Unionist Party. The original name of the party, Tory, by which it is still known, was first used in the 1680s as a term of abuse by opponents. (It meant an Irish brigand.) What is clear is that, despite different labels, there has been a broad continuity of conservative views in British politics since the seventeenth century. During this century the party, under a variety of labels – Unionist, National and Conservative – has been the dominant party of government.

The 'father' of the modern party is often said to be Benjamin Disraeli (1804–81). He is particularly remembered for his concept of 'one nation', in which he argued that it was the task of Conservatives to weld the nation into a cohesive whole and to reject class-based policies. To this end he extended the franchise to include industrial workers in 1867 and carried through other measures to improve social conditions, including a Factory Act and a Public Health Act. He believed in Britain's imperial role in the world, creating Queen Victoria Empress of India and securing for Britain a dominant share in the Suez Canal. The latter acts gave the party the image of the party of

Empire and provided the thrust for Britain's colonial extension in the late nineteenth and early twentieth centuries. The themes of Empire and opposition to Irish home rule were pursued by Disraeli's successors, Lord Salisbury and Arthur Balfour, although they did not share Disraeli's interest in social reform, preferring to maintain social order and hold back change. Two themes of conservatism, cautious but imaginative social reform and resistance to change, can be seen in the late nineteenth and early part of the twentieth century. These tensions were evident in the early years of this century between the party leader, Arthur Balfour, who was not interested in reform, and the former Liberal Joseph Chamberlain, who pushed for a policy of tariff reform giving Empire goods the preference in British markets, linked to schemes of social welfare. Chamberlain's radicalism did not capture the party and the Conservatives suffered a disastrous defeat in 1906 to the reforming Liberal Party.

The Conservatives' fortunes were revived in the 1920s with the steady leadership of Stanley Baldwin. He was a moderate on social issues; although he did successfully resist the General Strike of 1926 he refused demands from his party's right wing to take the kind of punitive action against the unions at the end of the strike which they would have wished. Out of office after the 1929 election, Baldwin joined forces with the former Labour Prime Minister, Ramsay Macdonald, to form the National Government in 1931 under Macdonald's leadership. The Conservative Party formed the bulk of the support for the National Government which held power throughout the 1930s. Baldwin became its Prime Minister in 1935, being succeeded in 1937 by Neville Chamberlain.

As a result of opposition from within his own party over his handling of the war, Chamberlain resigned in 1940 and the National Government formed a wartime coalition government with the Labour Party. Winston Churchill was its Prime Minister. Despite Churchill's wartime leadership, the Conservatives lost heavily to Labour in the 1945 general election. They were returned to power in 1951, initially under Churchill's leadership and from 1955 to 1957 under Sir Anthony Eden. Eden resigned after the failure of Britain's last imperial venture against Egypt, which had nationalized the Suez Canal. Harold Macmillan became Prime Minister in 1957. The Conservatives, in the 13 years of office from 1951 to 1964, oversaw a period of unprecedented economic growth and a substantial rise in living standards which were summarized by Macmillan as 'You've never had it so good'.

Out of office between 1964 and 1970, they were returned at the 1970 general election under the premiership of Edward Heath. Originally the party came to power with a programme of 'less government' known as the Selsden programme. However, the worsening economic situation, rising unemployment and the oil crisis of 1973 caused a 'U-turn' in policy, involving a substantial increase in government intervention in industry and the introduction of incomes policies to tackle inflation. The Government was brought down as the result of a confrontation with the National Union of Mineworkers over pay. The strike by the mineworkers caused the Government to put industry and commerce on a three-day week during the winter of 1973–74. In February 1974 the Prime Minister called an election over the issue of who ran the country. The election results were initially indecisive: the Conservatives gained the most votes, but because of the workings of the electoral system, gained five fewer seats than the Labour Party. The number of Conservative MPs fell from 330 elected in 1970 to 297. The Liberal Party, whose vote rose by nearly 4 million from 1970 but which gained only eight extra seats, had initial discussions with the Conservatives over a Parliamentary pact but the negotiations fell through and the Labour leader Harold Wilson formed a minority government.

After a further and more decisive defeat in October 1974, the Conservative Party forced Edward Heath to contest a leadership election, the outcome of which was a victory for Mrs Margaret Thatcher in February 1975.

In Opposition and in Government after 1979, the Conservatives took a new line of policy, generally known as 'monetarism'. Simply, in economic terms, this involves pursuing a policy by which the authorities should control the supply of money and attempts to finely tune the economy by fiscal means should be abandoned. In addition, the new Government came in with a commitment to limit the scale of government – 'To roll back the state', in Mrs Thatcher's words. This has involved cutbacks in public sector manpower and the privatization of areas of government activity.

The structure of the Conservative Party

The organization of the Conservative Party is divided into three distinct but linked parts – the constituency associations, the Central Office and the party in Parliament (see Fig. 3.3).

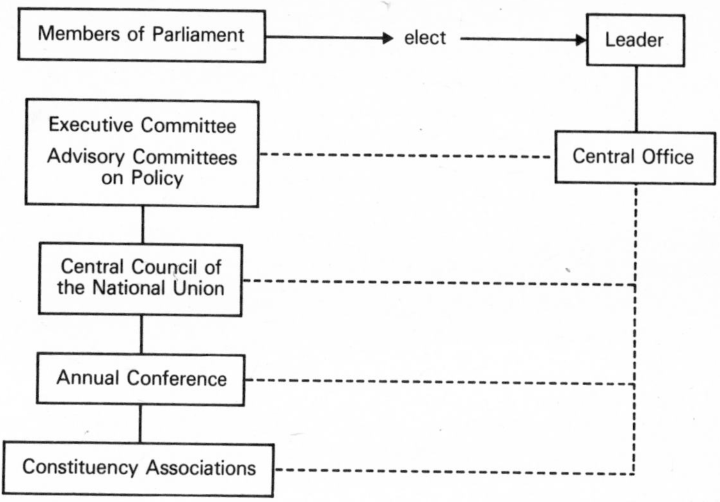

Figure 3.3 *The structure of the Conservative Party*

The constituency associations

The party locally is organized on a constituency basis. It is these local associations which recruit members, hold meetings and social events, organize election campaigns and choose the candidates for local and Parliamentary elections. About half the associations have a full-time paid agent, but the bulk of the work of campaigning and fund raising is carried out by volunteers.

The local associations are affiliated to the National Association of Conservative and Unionist Associations, which was founded by Disraeli in 1867. The National Union organizes consultation groups and the party's Annual Conference.

The Annual Conference differs in many respects from that of the Labour Party. Whereas the latter is, in theory at least, the party's policy-making body, this is not the case with the Conservative conference. Theirs is often accused of being 'stage-managed' by the party leadership. It is a forum of opinion of which Conservative leaders take note. A second point of difference is that only constituency associations are represented at the Conference. There is no equivalent of the trade unions with their block votes. Additionally, Conservative *representatives* are never given a mandate on how to vote, as are Labour *delegates*. At Conservative conferences representatives vote individually as they see fit.

Central Office

Conservative Central Office is headed by the party chairman. It is the bureaucracy or 'civil service' of the party. The control of Central Office is in the hands of the leader, and the chairman is responsible to her or him alone.

Members of Parliament

There are two organizations of Conservative MPs. Backbench MPs form the *1922 Committee,* which is an extremely influential organization within the party. Those MPs with governmental or 'Shadow Cabinet' responsibilities, depending on whether the party is in power or opposition, form the Conservative 'front Bench'. The Conservative leader is elected by MPs by a complex procedure under which, to win on the first ballot, a candidate must have an absolute majority of votes plus a 15 per cent lead over his or her nearest rival. If this does not occur a second ballot is arranged and candidates who did not enter the first ballot may stand. An absolute majority is sufficient for the second ballot. If this does not occur a third and final ballot is held, and entry is restricted to the three leading candidates on the second ballot. A system of alternative votes is used so that the second preferences of third and successive candidates can be transferred to the leading two to produce an absolute majority. This procedure was first used in 1965 to elect Edward Heath as leader. Before that date Conservative leaders 'emerged' as a result of complex behind-the-scenes discussions between senior Conservatives and (as leadership nominations usually took place when the party was in office) the Monarch, who has a constitutional duty to choose a Prime Minister. The 'emergence' of Sir Alex Douglas-Home as leader in 1963 over candidates more acceptable to the majority of MPs caused the system to be altered.

Conservative groups

The Conservative Party, being a mass party like the Labour Party, encompasses a broad spectrum of views from left to right. Various groups represent various positions on the spectrum.

The Monday Club

On the right of the party is the Monday Club. Formed in 1961, it is a membership organization with local branches. Some 40 MPs are members. It was formed to counter left-wing or reformist elements in the party. It takes a 'hard line' on moral and law and order issues and is committed to heavy defence spending. It has often called for tighter immigration controls.

The Bow Group

This is an intellectual and research group which at one time was associated with 'moderate' and 'reformist' views. However, though it does not express a collective view, its publications and statements have shown a rightward shift since the mid-1970s. In May 1981 it called for the resignation of the Secretary of State for Industry, Sir Keith Joseph, well known for his minimal government views, for having spent too much state money on the nationalized industries.

The Centre for Policy Studies

This was founded in 1974 by Margaret Thatcher and Sir Keith Joseph to provide research into social market economics. This is a view which sees the state as having a minimal role in economic life and where the free market has only limited interference from the government.

The Tory Reform Group

This was formed in 1975 to represent 'moderate opinion' within the party. It was formed from the Macleod Group, Pressure for Economic and Social Toryism, and the Social Tory Action Group. Unlike the more 'right-wing' groups, it favours stronger government action in the economy, particularly the use of incomes policies to control inflation.

The political thought of the Conservative Party

It is as difficult to categorize the political thought of the Conservative Party as it is to give a date to the party's origin. This is not only because the Conservative Party contains people with a wide range of views, but because a strong element in Conservative circles distrust doctrine and the advocacy of policies and convictions. This view has recently been subordinated since the election of Mrs Thatcher as leader, with her brand of 'conviction politics', but historically the anti-ideological stance represents the dominant view within the party. Traditionally, at least in this century, it has been the reforming parties – the Labour and Liberal Parties – which have stood for doing things. The Conservatives, though having produced manifestoes and ideas for legislation, have campaigned less for the implementation of party views but rather on their ability to manage government more successfully than their rivals.

Conservatism has tended to have underlying themes and predispositions of thought rather than programmes and worked-out doctrines. This is because traditional conservatism does not see politics as the most important aspect of life, and many Tory writers have at best seen it as a necessary evil, stemming from the disagreeable nature of mankind. As Quintin Hogg (later Lord Hailsham) put it in his *Case for Conservatism* (1947):

> For Conservatives do not believe that the political struggle is the most important thing in life . . . The simplest amongst them prefer fox-hunting – the wisest religion.
> The Conservative does not believe the power of politics to put things right in this world is unlimited.

What then are some of the themes of this traditional brand of conservatism? *Tradition* itself is an important theme. The belief in the traditional values, institutions and ways of proceeding, if they still serve a useful purpose, is important to Conservatives. Conservatives do not believe in preserving all traditional values or preventing change; rather they believe in gradualism and they are sceptical of changes until those changes can be shown to be beneficial. Linked closely to tradition is the respect for and maintenance of *authority, order* and the *rule of law*. Respect for traditional ways of doing things and traditional institutions such as the Monarchy and the House of Lords is important to Conservatives. The Conservatives place a high value on the respect for order and law and argue that it can never be right to break the law – even a bad law – because they fear that, once broken, law as a whole will be brought into disrepute and society could slide into anarchy.

Side by side with respect for authority go *leadership* and *strong government*. Conservatives see a necessity for both, although this does not mean that they believe in authoritarian government. Conservatives believe that strong government can be limited government and, though

Conservatives have exercised considerable control over the economy, they have usually argued for the necessity of limiting state action in this area.

Freedom and *free enterprise* are important Tory values. Tory freedom is based on the idea that the state must leave people free to pursue their own goals but that it has a role in providing them with incentives to work hard, set up businesses, and make profits. Hand in hand with Tory freedom goes the notion of the importance of *property* and property ownership. Together with the *family,* the Conservatives see *property* and its ownership as the basis of a democratic society. Conservative freedom produces inequalities, but in Conservative thought equality is not an important value, often being looked upon with suspicion and thought of as a goal which can be achieved only by coercion. Because of this a higher priority is given to private wealth, incentives and competition than to the provision of social services, the argument being that the provision of better social services can only follow the achievement of greater wealth.

Until the mid-1970s Conservatives in the main made a virtue out of non-ideological politics, moderation and steering a 'middle way' in government. Since the election of Mrs Thatcher in 1975, however, 'conviction politics' have come to the fore and a strand of ideological Conservatism has gained prominence. Non-ideological, traditional Conservatism, with its Disraelian concern for the less well off and for the creation of 'one nation', has been dubbed by Mrs Thatcher a 'philosophy of the wets'.

The new conservatism, whose major spokesman is Sir Keith Joseph, is a variant of nineteenth-century, *laissez-faire* liberalism. The belief is in free market economics and the importance of competition and enterprise in producing wealth. The role of government is seen as promoting this end even if its policies create social problems such as high unemployment. The major value is freedom, which is seen as wealth and profit. To this end, i.e. promoting capitalism, the Government has a major role in reducing public expenditure and the social services both so that individuals take on responsibilities formerly carried by the state and so that resources can be switched into the private sector and funds for industry are not 'crowded out' by public investment.

The 1979 Conservative election manifesto argued for the denationalization of a number of publicly owned industries, a reduction in income tax to provide greater incentives, a reduction in public expenditure, policies to promote the private sectors in health care and education, and the sale of council houses to promote 'a property-owning democracy'. The Conservative Party is committed to Britain's continued membership of the European Community.

3.6 THE LIBERAL PARTY

The Liberal Party, like the Conservative Party, has had a long history, and can be dated back to Whig groups of the seventeenth and eighteenth centuries. In the nineteenth century it developed as a party of constitutional reform and minimal government. Economic liberalism or *laissez-faire* was its dominant doctrine, and Liberals believed that the free market economy could best regulate itself without state intervention. The role of the state was essentially that of a 'night-watchman'. Liberalism in the nineteenth century not only came to mean economic freedom but also combined this with the personal liberty of freedom from oppression. This variety of freedom is often called negative freedom and is the liberty of the citizen from externally imposed constraints. Such a philosophy appealed particularly to the business community and to the new middle classes, and ties in well with current ideas of 'self-help'.

The great victory of the Liberal Party came in 1906 and during the life of this Government the party put forward policies which developed the other side of the concept of liberty, with a programme of social reforms. Positive freedom, or the freedom to be able to achieve things, came in the form of old age pensions, employment legislation, and measures which laid many of the foundations of the welfare state.

Throughout the philosophy of the Liberal Party the emphasis is laid on *the individual* and on his or her *liberty*. Large units, whether in government, business or the trade unions, are regarded with suspicion. In recent years Liberals have emphasized the importance of community politics, participation and local decision-making and have praised smaller units of government closer to the people.

Tolerance and *fairness* have gone hand in hand with individualism, and to this end Liberals have placed a high value on good race relations and reforms in the area of personal morality – abortion law reform (introduced by David Steel MP in the late 1960s), homosexual law reform, divorce law reform, etc.

Reform has always been, and continues to be, an important Liberal principle. Current Liberal policies include the introduction of proportional representation (from which the Liberal Party has much to gain), regional government and devolution, an extension of community politics, the replacement of the House of Lords by a democratic second chamber, the introduction of a fair incomes policy and the introduction of co-ownership and co-partnership in industry. The Liberal Party had an early commitment to the European Community.

As in other parties, there is a divergence of views in the party, perhaps an even greater divergence than in other parties. Although all Liberals believe in the importance of the individual and personal liberty, the party contains people who support *laissez-faire* and are sceptical about the benefits of additional state intervention, and at the other extreme the Young Liberals often take positions which are left-wing and interventionist.

The Liberal Party declined after 1920 because of a number of internal disagreements and was overtaken by the Labour Party as the party of reform. Various reasons for its decline have been given, and the growth of class-based politics and the rise of the trade unions certainly assisted the rise of Labour, which perhaps was more in tune with the mood of the times than was the individualism of the Liberal Party.

Table 3.1 *Liberal support at general elections since 1945*

Election	*Votes gained*	*No. of seats*	*Percentage of total votes*
1945	2 248 226	12	9
1950	2 621 548	9	11.8
1951	730 556	6	2.5
1955	722 405	6	2.7
1959	1 638 571	6	5.9
1964	3 092 878	9	11.2
1966	2 327 533	12	8.5
1970	2 117 035	6	7.5
1974 (Feb.)	6 063 470	14	19.3
1974 (Oct.)	5 346 754	13	18.9
1979	4 313 811	11	13.8

Source: Butler, D. & Sloman, A. (1980) *British Political Facts 1900–1979* 5th edition. London: Macmillan. Reproduced with permission.

Since 1960 the party has on occasions appeared to be making a come-back (see Table 3.1). There have been by-election successes at Orpington in 1962, Roxburgh, Selkirk and Peebles in 1965, Birmingham Ladywood in 1969, Rochdale, and Sutton and Cheam in 1972, the Isle of Ely, Ripon, and Berwick on Tweed in 1973, and Liverpool Edge Hill in 1979. But despite these and good election results in the 1974 general elections, the Liberals have not made the political break-through and remain largely a party of the Celtic fringe or of political protest at by-elections. The first past the post electoral system seriously hampers the party and has led many voters to see a Liberal vote as a 'wasted vote'. The Liberals formed a pact to support the Labour Government in 1977–78 to provide both stable government and a check to more extreme left-wing measures. The pact did not have any advantages for the party in the 1979 general election.

In 1981 the Liberals formed an electoral agreement with the new Social Democratic Party. The pact essentially provides that the two parties will not run candidates against each other. The two parties have similar views in a number of areas, including support for the EEC and NATO, co-ownership and industrial democracy, and the necessity of introducing proportional representation in order both to create a fairer electoral system and to break the monopoly of the two-party system.

ASSIGNMENTS

A3.1

(a) From copies of the last election manifestoes of the Labour, Liberal and Conservative parties, summarize the main policies of these parties. You should concentrate on their policies in relation to the social services, education, defence, housing, economic policy and the role of government.
(b) How do the policies of the Social Democratic Party differ from those of the other main parties, and what are the policies that they have in common with the Liberal Party?

A3.2

(a) Make a scrapbook from newspaper cuttings on a major issue of debate in both the Labour and the Conservative parties.
(b) Write a commentary on the issues that you have chosen, discussing how each party pursues its arguments. You should identify the main personalities involved in the issue.

A3.3

'Different political parties use political concepts to mean different things.' Define the following concepts from the point of view of a Socialist, a Conservative and a Liberal:
(a) equality;
(b) freedom;
(c) social welfare;
(d) rights;
(e) the role of the state.

4

Pressure Groups

4.1 TYPES OF PRESSURE GROUPS

Political activity in Britain is not confined to the operation of political parties within the established institutions of government. Public opinion is channelled, expressed and mobilized through organized groups which seek to influence and change government policy.

The term 'pressure group' is used to describe any organization which seeks to influence and change the policy of public authorities. (Occasionally pressure groups may operate to alter the policy of industry rather than that of government, e.g. Campaign for Real Ale.)

There is an enormous variation in the size and organization of pressure groups, from the Trades Union Congress with 11 million members in its affiliated trade unions and its large professional staff to, at the other end of the spectrum, a group of mothers campaigning for a pedestrian crossing outside a local school.

4.2 CLASSIFICATION OF PRESSURE GROUPS

Pressure groups can be classified into two main types: cause or promotional groups and sectional or interest groups.

Cause or promotional groups

These are pressure groups which seek to achieve a particular goal or the solution to a problem. Their ultimate purpose is to achieve their goal, and achievement is likely to lead to the winding up of the group. Examples of cause groups include: Abortion Law Reform Association (pro-abortion); Life (formerly Society for the Protection of the Unborn Child) (anti-abortion); Amnesty International; League Against Cruel Sports; Shelter; Campaign for Nuclear Disarmament; and Campaign for Homosexual Equality.

Sectional or interest groups

These groups represent a particular group or section of society who have common interests and purposes. They are usually formed to protect, safeguard or promote the interests of a particular group, trade or profession. Unlike cause groups, they may have a wide variety of goals to pursue and will remain in existence as long as it is in their members' interests for them to do so.

There are an extremely large number of such groups, including: the trade unions; the Confederation of British Industry; the Consumers Association; the Road Haulage Association; the Automobile Association; the National Union of Students; and the Indian Workers Association.

4.3 THE OPERATION OF PRESSURE GROUPS

There is an extremely wide variety and diversity of pressure groups in terms of aims, membership, size, resources and official recognition. Because of these factors it is impossible to describe how a 'typical pressure group' might operate. Different groups will use different means to achieve their aims. The following are some of the means by which pressure groups have sought to influence government.

Marches and demonstrations

These are popular means by which a group can attract the attention of the media and by which it can demonstrate the strength of its following.

Strikes and industrial action

While most industrial action is economic in its movitation (that is, aimed at achieving higher pay rises and/or better working conditions), some industrial action is overtly political. The General Strike of 1926 took on this character, as did the miners' strike in the winter of 1973–74, which led to the then Prime Minister, Edward Heath, losing an election called to gain a mandate for his stand against the National Union of Mineworkers. Similarly, the so-called 'Winter of Discontent', 1978–79, which consisted of a series of public sector strikes against the then Labour Government's pay policy, eventually led to the downfall of Mr Callaghan's government.

Publicity in the mass media

This may take the form of advertisements, but more usually it consists of some form of action or event which provides a news story.

Lobbies of Parliament and Government offices

Lobbying is a traditional form of demonstration designed to demonstrate the srength of a group and to enable group members to directly lobby their Members of Parliament.

Petitions

The collection of signatures provides another means of showing government the strength of support for a cause.

Violent actions

While most pressure groups would consider the other forms of action described here as legitimate, they would never resort to violence. However, some demonstrations become violent without this being the intention of the organizers, for example the Southall Riot of 1979 when a demonstration against a National Front meeting in a largely immigrant area led to violent clashes between police and demonstrators and to the death of one demonstrator.

A small number of groups have deliberately used violence to attempt to achieve their objectives. In Northern Ireland the Provisional Irish Republican Army has, since the late 1960s, fought an urban guerrilla war with the British Army and has instigated series of bombing campaigns in England.

Non-violent direct action

This covers such actions as sit-ins, sit-downs, hunger strikes, etc. This type of action was used by the suffragettes at the beginning of the twentieth century in their campaign to obtain votes for women. Their most notorious form of non-violent protest was for suffragettes to chain themselves to railings as a protest against their exclusion from the franchise.

Behind-the-scenes consultations

Although it is usually the outward demonstrations of pressure-group action, such as lobbies of Parliament and marches, which gain most attention in the media, it is important to remember that much of the lobbying by pressure groups is carried on behind closed doors, that is, through discussions with civil servants and Ministers. This is the most influential means of pressure, although it is the one which is virtually unknown to the general public.

4.4 LEGITIMATE AND NON-LEGITIMATE GROUPS

The mass media image of pressure groups is usually that of groups of protesters coming into headlong conflict with authority. The reality is far more complex and is often far removed from this picture. Pressure groups play an important role in the process of policy formulation in Britain, and it is for this reason that British politics is often described as *pluralist,* which means that there are various competing groups attempting to influence the process of government.

Pressure groups provide a major means through which the views of individuals are transmitted to government. In fact many pressure groups play an essential role in the successful operation of government, providing as they do knowledge and expertise in specialist areas. In order to understand the role played by pressure groups in relation to government, it is useful to follow the classification used by Professor Maurice Kogan in his book *Educational Policy-Making 1975* between *legitimate* and *non-legitimate* pressure groups.

Non-legitimate pressure groups

These are groups which the Government does not consult as a matter of course and whose views they do not seek when they are considering policy changes. Often the views of such groups are in conflict with the established political consensus. The prisoners' action group PROP has attempted unsuccessfully over a number of years to be seen as a legitimate representative of people in prison, while the National Union of Students is an interesting example of a group which was in direct conflict with the authorities during the student troubles of the late 1960s but which has moved to a position in which their opinions are seen as 'legitimate' by the Government. They are regularly consulted by Government during the process of educational policy-making.

The most extreme example of a non-legitimate group is the Provisional IRA. However, 'non-legitimate' is not necessarily the same as 'unlawful', but rather implies that there are no formal established links for consultation between Government and the pressure groups.

Legitimate pressure groups

These are pressure groups whose aims governments see as being 'legitimate', even though they may disagree with them. Such groups have established links and channels of communications with government, and may even have representation on government committees and advisory bodies. For example, the TUC and the CBI have an important role on the National Economic Development Council: they, together with the Government, make up the three parties in this important economic forum.

In a pluralist political system the interplay between government and pressure groups is essential, not only to represent views to government but to allow government to function effectively. Policy-making requires the expertise and consent of interested parties. There are even occasions when pressure groups operate as agents for government: the Law Society, which is the solicitors' professional body, operates the Government's Legal Aid scheme. Pressure groups gain enhanced status from this interaction with government, in the eyes both of their members and of the public, and from this comes an increased influence. A change in government can, however, alter a pressure group's status. The TUC were the major force in economic policy-making during the Labour Party's period in office between 1974 and 1979, but Mrs Thatcher's antipathy towards the trade unions has caused them to be dropped almost completely from discussions of economic policy.

In the decision-making process of the EEC certain pressure groups are given a formal role in the policy-making process. All proposed EEC regulations must be considered by the Economic and Social Committee, which is made up of representatives of trade unions, employers and consumer groups.

4.5 EFFECTIVENESS OF PRESSURE GROUPS

The chances of success for any pressure group depend on a large number of factors. These include:

1. The determination with which the group pursues its aim.
2. A substantial membership: the actual size of membership is probably less important to a sectional group than the percentage of the potential members who belong to it.
3. Sufficient financial resources.
4. A sound knowledge of the workings of the political system. Many pressure groups employ professional lobbyists whose job it is to establish personal contact with those in power.
5. The ability to gain publicity for campaigns: the ability to gain press and television coverage for campaigns and demonstrations is important for the strategy of many cause groups.
6. Skill in consultation and negotiation.
7. The ability to be able to mobilize public opinion to support a cause.

4.6 PRESSURE GROUPS AND POLITICAL PARTIES

The dividing line between what constitutes a political party and what a pressure group can be very thin. The Labour Party, for example, started its life as the Labour Representation Committee, i.e. as a pressure group, albeit a Parliamentary pressure group for organized labour. It did not take on the title 'party' until six years after its formation in 1900.

A usual definition of the difference between pressure groups and political parties is that political parties seek political power; that is, they wish to become the Government in order to direct policy, whereas pressure groups seek only to influence the direction of policy. This is a useful distinction, although not a sufficient one, as some political parties, such as the nationalist parties, could never aim to gain political power at Westminster.

It is also usually argued that political parties have policies over a wide spectrum covering economic and industrial policy, social affairs and foreign and defence policy, while pressure groups have a much narrower range of concerns. Again, this is broadly true, but there are exceptions: pressure groups such as the Trades Union Congress and the Confederation of British Industry do have a wide range of interests over and above the narrow interests of their members.

Another way of looking at the difference is to say that any group that attempts representation in Parliament is a party and that those groups which do not, even if they sponsor MPs, are regarded as pressure groups. Many pressure groups would themselves accept this distinction. At their conference in November 1980 the Campaign for Nuclear Disarmament debated whether to change their status to that of a political party, which would have involved their putting up candidates in elections. The conference turned down the proposal, preferring to call on members to vote for candidates (from whichever party) who supported nuclear disarmament.

ASSIGNMENTS

A4.1 Imagine that the local authority in whose area you live has published a planning document showing that the street in which you live will eventually be demolished so that a new hypermarket can be built on the site.

(a) What procedures will the local authority have to undertake before the house can be demolished?
(b) Imagine that the local residents decide to form an action committee to fight the authority's plans. How should they set this up and what tactics could they employ at each stage in the planning process?
(c) Write a report for the local newspaper stating the advantages of the scheme from the point of view of the community and the objections to the scheme from the local residents. The article should contain abbreviated material from (a) and (b) above.

A4.2 How does the role of pressure groups differ from that of political parties? Describe the methods by which both pressure groups and political parties seek to achieve their aims.

A4.3 How can a pressure group use the mass media to achieve its aims? What media are available for use by pressure groups? Give example of the ways in which particular pressure groups have used the media.

5
Parliament

Parliament is the legislative branch of Government. It consists of two Houses: the House of Lords and the House of Commons, the latter being the more important chamber. In constitutional terms Parliament is said to be a *sovereign* body, which implies that there are no *legal* limits to its power and that it can legislate on any matter it chooses – even to abolish itself. In practical *political* terms its power is very much constrained, and decision-making power in the United Kingdom is held by the Prime Minister and the Cabinet.

5.1 THE HOUSE OF COMMONS

Composition

The House of Commons consists of 635 Members of Parliament (Table 5.1) who are directly elected to serve a particular constituency. The proceedings of the House are chaired by the Speaker, who enforces the rules of the House for preserving order, decides, subject to convention, who shall speak and interprets the rules of the procedure. The Speaker is an MP elected to office by the House. He or she takes no part in the polical debates and maintains a strict neutrality. The Speaker is assisted by the Deputy Speakers. The Commons is divided

Table 5.1 *The party political composition of the House of Commons in December 1981*

Party	*No. of MPs*
Conservative	334
Labour	241
Social Democrat	26
Liberal	12
Official Unionist	4
Democratic Unionist	3
Scottish National Party	2
Plaid Cymru	2
Ulster Progressive Unionist	1
United Ulster Unionist	1
Independent Socialist	1
Independents	3
The Speaker plus three deputies (who do not vote)	4
Vacancy	1
	635

into Government and Opposition. The party (or parties if it is a coalition) with a majority of seats forms the Government and the other parties form the Opposition. There is no need for the opposition parties to have similar views. In fact all they may have in common is their opposition to the policies and principles of the Government.

Members of Parliament are divided into 'backbenchers' and 'frontbenchers'. This nomenclature refers both to where they sit in the House and to whether they are spokesmen for the official Government or official Opposition view. Backbench or private members therefore have more independence, although rather less opportunity to speak, as most Parliamentary time is taken up with Government business or Opposition criticism of it.

All parties in Parliament have a system of party discipline. This ensures that each party can rely on the support of its MPs. This is particularly important for the Government party, as defeat on a vote of major importance means resignation and the calling of a general election. In order to maintain discipline and to provide party leaders with the views and feelings of the backbenchers, the parties appoint 'whips' – MPs whose job it is to ensure that MPs vote according to party line and to provide a channel of communication to the leadership.

The Opposition

The largest opposition party forms Her Majesty's Loyal Opposition and is led by the Leader of the Opposition, who receives an official salary. This gives criticism of government policy an official standing in British Parliamentary democracy. The Opposition have the right to take up to 29 'supply days' each Parliamentary session to expound their views and to criticize the Government. On these days the matters for debate are chosen by the Opposition. The official Opposition is the alternative government party. It forms a 'shadow cabinet' who 'shadow' Government Ministers. Like the Cabinet, the Opposition 'shadow cabinet' acts on the basis of collective responsibility, which implies that once it has made a decision all members must abide by it. This view was contested by Tony Benn when in June 1981 he put the view that members of the shadow cabinet may take a different line if the view they take is in line with party policy as laid down by the party conference.

In the Labour Party (when in opposition) the 'shadow cabinet' or Parliamentary committee, to give its official title, consists of 12 spokesmen elected by MPs. The leader may co-opt other MPs on to the committee.

5.2 THE WORK OF THE COMMONS

Legislation

Legislation is the most important function of the House of Commons and is the one to which the Commons devotes most of its time. Legislation may arise from a variety of sources:

1. The election manifesto of the Government party.
2. Royal Commission or Departmental Committee Report.
3. Cabinet decision.
4. Pressure from an interest group.
5. From a backbench MP or peer.
6. A decision of the European Community.

If proposed legislation is originated by Government then a *White Paper* will normally be published in advance of the Bill laying out the intentions of the proposed legislation. On occasions a consultative document called a *Green Paper* will be issued in advance of the White Paper. This is done when the Government wishes to find out the views of interest groups on its proposals.

Proposed legislation can be introduced into either the House of Commons or the House of Lords. Usually the most important pieces start their progress in the Commons. A proposed piece of legislation begins its life as a Bill. Bills are of two kinds: public Bills and private Bills.

Public Bills

These deal with some aspect of public policy which has repercussions for the whole community. A public Bill can be introduced by the Government or by private members. (The latter are known as private members' Bills. Private members cannot introduce legislation with financial implications unless they are backed by the Government.) The vast majority of the Bills are Government Bills, as private members have only 10 to 12 Fridays a Parliamentary session allotted to them.

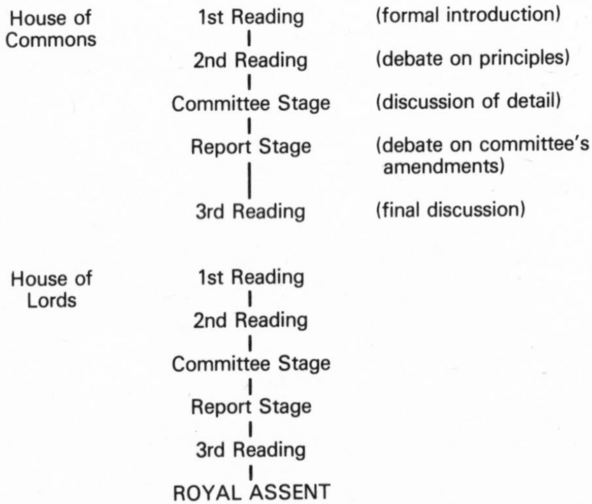

Figure 5.1 *Stages for a public Bill to become law*

A public Bill goes through a number of stages to become law, as Fig. 5.1 shows. The *First Reading* of a Bill is purely formal introduction to

Parliament. At the *Second Reading* a Bill receives a debate on the floor of the House of Commons. (It is possible for the Second Reading to be taken in committee, although this is the case only for non-controversial legislation. Scottish Bills are usually taken in the Scottish Grand Committee.)

Providing the vote on the Second Reading is won, the Bill then goes to *Committee*. (It is possible for this stage to be taken on the floor of the House by a Committee of the whole House.) The committees dealing with Bills are known as *Standing Committees* and consist of between 16 and 50 members. Their composition reflects the party strengths in the Commons. Discussions in committee centre on amendments to the Bill, and the Bill is usually taken clause by clause or certain clauses are selected for discussion. In the 1980–81 session a change in procedure was introduced so that certain Government Bills have open hearings, which allows outside experts to be called to give their views on the proposed legislation to the committee. It is important to note that Standing Committees are occasions when the responsible Minister is defending his or her Bill from amendments by the Opposition. The Whips are on and there are seldom successful major amendments from the Opposition.

Every Bill must have its committee deliberations reported to the House as a whole so that they can be debated. This happens at the *Report Stage*.This is followed by a final *Third Reading* which is a largely formal stage.

If the Bill started life in the House of Commons it must then go to the Lords. The stages are similar, although there are certain differences. The Committee Stage may be dispensed with if there are no amendments or it can be taken on the floor of the House. Amendments are allowed at the Third Reading.

If the second House to receive a bill amends it, the amendments must go back to the first House for their approval. Disagreements are usually solved by compromise but if the Lords should refuse to pass the legislation coming from the Commons the procedure of the *Parliament Acts* can be invoked (see section 5.4). This allows the Bill to go for the Royal Assent despite rejection by the Lords after a year has elapsed, providing that the Bill has been passed by the Commons twice in different sessions. The Royal Assent is a purely formal stage. No monarch has refused to sign a bill since the reign of Queen Anne.

In the 1979–80 session of Parliament 70 Government Bills reached the statute book and 11 private members' Bills became law.

Private Bills

Private Bills are promoted by 'private interests', i.e. individuals, firms, local authorities, public corporations, and are for the limited benefit of those interests. For example, a local authority may require the additional power to operate an airport. The Greater London Council budget is proposed in a private Bill each session.

The procedure is complex and differs considerably from that of a public Bill. As the proposer of the Bill will be granted special powers if the Bill is passed, that proposer must start by petitioning Parliament. The petition must reach Parliament by the end of November each year. The petitioners must advertise their intentions so that potential objectors have the opportunity to present their objections.

The Second Reading of a private Bill differs from a public Bill, as it is not a debate on principles but on whether the facts are correctly stated and whether the intention is unobjectionable from a national point of view. If the Bill receives a second reading it goes to a small committee which operates in a semi-judicial fashion. The proposer and the objectors put their cases and are usually represented by counsel, who may call evidence. If the Bill passes the committee stage it is reported to House. The rest of the stages are similar to those of public Bills. The procedure for a private Bill is lengthy and expensive.

Other functions of the House of Commons

Representing constituents' interests

An important function performed by MPs is to represent their constituents' interests in Parliament and to take up matters on their behalf with the Government. An MP can perform this function in a number of ways:

1. Asking questions of Ministers, either orally during the daily Question Time sessions, or in writing.
2. Putting down motions for the adjournment debates which take place at 10.00 p.m. for half an hour.
3. Promoting private members' legislation.
4. Through debates on matters which may affect constituency interests.
5. Submission of constituents' complaints to the Parliamentary Commissioner for Administration (the Ombudsman) (see Chapter 12).

Debates

Both Houses of Parliament carry on their business in the form of debates. These may be debates on proposed legislation or general debates initiated by Government or Opposition on matters of local, national or international importance. The House of Commons spends about 1500 hours a year debating.

Controlling public expenditure

In order for the Government to spend or raise any money it requires the permission of the House of Commons. The Commons gives this permission in the annual *Finance Act,* which gives effect to the taxation proposals outlined in the Chancellor of the Exchequer's Budget speech. It also provides approval for expenditure by approving the Annual Estimates. However, these permissions do not mean that the House of Commons 'controls' expenditure in any real sense. It cannot, for example, increase expenditure beyond that which the Government asks for, and, since a large proportion of public expenditure is by nationalized industries and local authorities, this is outside its purview. Other expenditure is 'committed', as, once a project such as a motorway scheme has begun, the finance has to be found to complete it.

Initiating expenditure lies with the Executive, but the Commons does have some means, of varying importance, of scrutinizing the ways in which public money is spent. First, there are the 29 Supply Days each annual Parliamentary session. Though by tradition Supply Days are formally for the consideration of the Annual Estimates, these days are used by the Opposition to raise any matter they wish. This means that often the matters for debate are not directly linked to public spending but focus on general aspects of Government policy.

Second, MPs can influence spending during the debates on legislation where changes to taxation or expenditure are introduced. Most of these debates accompany the progress of the annual Finance Bill through the House.

Third, the Commons' *Public Accounts Committee* (PAC) examines the accounts of Government departments to check whether the money has been spent as Parliament intended. The Committee receives copies of the accounts and can call and question witnesses. It is assisted in this work by the *Comptroller and Auditor General* and a staff of 400 auditors. The Comptroller draws the attention of the PAC to any excess of authorized expenditure or any irregular items in the accounts. The new *Treasury and Civil Service Committee* (which replaced the former Expenditure Committee) investigates particular matters of Government policy related to spending decisions.

It is debatable whether the House of Commons has much effect at all in controlling public spending, especially given its dramatic growth in recent years. However, it has improved its procedures recently. For example, in 1978 hearings of the PAC were made public so that the media could report its deliberations. But in the same year the PAC Chairman, Edward DuCann MP, was arguing in the Commons that control over public spending had slipped away from Parliament. If Parliament does have any control over the Executive in the fiscal and monetary field it is through influence rather than through the powers of its committees and procedures.

Governments require majorities to pass financial measures and, as a threatened Conservative backbench revolt in May 1981 over the increase in petrol duty shows, the Executive does have to listen if it is to avoid defeat in the Commons. In this case the Chancellor conceded a 10 pence per gallon reduction in the duty on diesel fuel.

Controlling the Executive

The scrutiny of Government policy is a major function of the Commons. It is carried on in debates, during the daily Question Time sessions and in Select Committee meetings. It is probably true to say that, despite recent reforms such as the new system of Select Committees, the Commons is not as effective as it might be in controlling the Executive.

In periods when a Government has a small majority, as the Labour Government had after 1976, backbenchers may be able to force certain changes on Government. Between 1976 and 1979 the Labour Government lost some significant measures through rebellions by its own backbenchers. For example, on 10 November 1976 it lost key clauses in its Dock Labour Bill because of abstentions by John Mackintosh MP and Brian Walden MP. In January 1978 it was forced to make a crucial amendment to the Devolution Bill for Scotland, making 40 per cent of the electorate voting 'yes' a precondition for the measure to take effect. (This meant that, because of non-voting, 60 per cent of the actual voters were required to pass the measure.) These and other instances show that, in a minority government, MPs can influence Government policy to a significant extent. However, the return of a Conservative Government with a significant majority has reduced the degree of influence available to backbenchers. While all governments will be constrained by the thinking and opinions of their backbenchers, they can usually rely on their own supporters. In the vast majority of situations MPs will vote with their party rather than with their rivals. Frontbenchers have considerable patronage available to them in terms of Government or Shadow Cabinet offices, and loyalty in voting is usually an essential quality for promotion. MPs who constantly vote against their own parties risk losing the 'whip', which involves loss of party membership and with it in all probability their constituency nomination, and hence their seat in the next Parliament. It is therefore true to say that the Executive dominates the Commons and that MPs, rather than controlling the Executive, have to be content with influencing it.

5.3 SELECT COMMITTEES

The function of Select Committees is to discover what the Government is doing and to make individual Government departments publicly accountable for their activities.

Until 1979 the 'system' of Select Committees consisted of certain committees, mainly subject based, which had a permanent existence, such as the Public Accounts Committee and the Expenditure Committee, while others, including Education and Science and Scottish Affairs, had much shorter lives. There was a great deal of discontent with the system as it operated. Some committees had carried out important investigations into areas of policy-making, but in general their reports were ignored by Government and they possessed insufficient power to have any influence on the policy-making process. Many observers unfavourably compared the Commons' Committees with the Congression Committees in the USA. In the latter, committee chairmen are the most important members of the Senate or the House of Representatives. These committees can force Government officials, Cabinet members or even the President to appear before them, and are usually covered by the press and television.

In 1976 the Select Committee on Procedure was set up 'to consider the practice and procedure of the House in relation to public business and to make recommendations for the more effective performance of its functions'. The Committee dealt not only with the Select Committee system, but also with public Bills procedure, delegated legislation,

European Committee legislation, etc. Over half of the reforms proposed by the Committee concerned the structure and powers of the new Select Committees. After a debate in June 1979 the system was reformed much as the Committee recommended.

Table 5.2 *The new Select Committees created in 1979*

Committee	*Government Departments Concerned*	*No. of Members*
Agriculture	Ministry of Agriculture, Fisheries and Food	9
Defence	Ministry of Defence	11
Education, Science and the Arts	Department of Education and Science	9
Employment	Department of Employment	9
Energy	Department of Energy	11
Environment	Department of the Environment	11
Foreign Affairs	Foreign and Commonwealth Office	11
Home Affairs	Home Office	11
Industry and Trade	Department of Industry Department of Trade	11
Scottish Affairs	Scottish Office	13
Social Services	Department of Health and Social Security	9
Transport	Department of Transport	11
Treasury and Civil Service	Treasury Civil Service Department Board of the Inland Revenue Board of Customs and Excise	11
Welsh Affairs	Welsh Office	11

Twelve new committees (Table 5.2) were set up 'to examine the expenditure, administration and policy of the principal Government departments . . . and associated public bodies'. Each Government department is monitored by a Select Committee, although some do have more than one. The Lord Chancellor's Department and the Law Officer's Department are excluded in case the monitoring by a committee would threaten judicial independence. The Scottish and Welsh Departments were originally not included but in the aftermath of the devolution referendum were given their own Select Committees.

Certain existing Select Committees were retained. These are the committees on public accounts, the Parliamentary Commissioner for Administration, European legislation, statutory instruments, privileges, selection, procedure, House of Commons services and sound broadcasting. The following committees disappeared as a result of the changes: Expenditure, Nationalized Industries, Overseas Development, Race Relations and Immigration, and Science and Technology.

Three of the Select Committees have the power to appoint a subcommittee. They are Foreign Affairs, Home Affairs and the Treasury and Civil Service Committees. Those committees which oversee nationalized industries – Energy, Industry and Trade, and Transport – can set up a joint committee to deal with the nationalized industries in general.

The chairmanship of the Select Committees has been divided evenly between the two major parties. Each committee has appointed outside specialist advisers to assist their investigations. The committees have the power 'to send for persons, papers and records', although they do not possess the power to insist that Ministers or senior Civil Servants appear before them. On this last matter they rely on the goodwill of the Government. In the first few years of their operation the new Select Committees have gained a great deal of media attention for their reports. Whether they will be any more effective in controlling the Executive and making Government more publicly accountable will depend largely on the will of Parliament to be less dominated by the Executive and on MPs taking a more independent stance on issues from time to time. Areas of success have included the report by the Home Affairs Committee on the operation of the 'sus' laws (arrest on suspicion of committing an offence). These laws had provoked considerable opposition by the minority black community and, partly as a result of the Committee's report, they were revoked. Obviously Select Committees can deal with controversial topics and make an impact on them. The Treasury Committee produced in 1981 a report attacking the use of monetary policy as practised by the Government, and this found support among the Conservative members of the Committee. But topics which have clear party policies attached to them can make investigation difficult. In 1981 the Environment Committee examined the Government's policy on the sale of council houses. The final report only just managed to pass through the Committee although the voting did not reflect strict party division. The problem is that, when a Committee does not form a consensus view, then the recommendations of its report are likely to receive much less notice from Government.

5.4 THE HOUSE OF LORDS

The second chamber of Parliament was, until the middle of the nineteenth century, the most important of the two Houses of Parliament. Nowadays it plays very much a subordinate role, and there are strong demands in certain quarters, particularly on the left of the Labour Party, to radically reform or even to abolish it completely.

The Lords' membership consists mainly of those members of the aristocracy who have inherited their titles. In its hey-dey the Lords gave direct representation to the great landowners of Britain, and until the Industrial Revolution the ownership of land was the major source of wealth, privilege and power. The rise of the business and industrial community in the eighteenth and nineteenth centuries and the growth of organized labour in the late nineteenth and early twentieth centuries forced on Parliament successive reforms of the franchise of the Commons. As the Commons became more democratic and representative of the adult population, so the Lords declined in power and influence.

Table 5.3 *Membership of the House of Lords (as of 1 January 1981)*

Lords Spiritual		
Archbishops	2	
Bishops	24	26
Lords Temporal		
Hereditary peers:		
Peers of the Royal Blood	3	
Dukes	25	
Marquises	29	
Earls and countesses	157	
Viscounts	105	
Barons	489	808
Life peers under the Appellate Jurisdiction Act 1876 (Law Lords)	18	18
Life peers under the Life Peerages Act 1958	319	319
Total		1171

Membership

The House of Lords is made up of four groups (see Table 5.3): hereditary peers, Law Lords, Lords Spiritual and life peers and peeresses. Of the total of 1171, 86 are without the writ of summons and 170 are on leave of absence from the House.

Hereditary peers

All hereditary peers and peeresses in their own right of the United Kingdom are entitled to sit in the Lords. The hereditary peerage consists of royal dukes, dukes, marquises, earls, viscounts and barons.

Law Lords

The House of Lords is the highest court of appeal in the country. In order to perform this function there has been provision since 1876 for up to 11 Lords of Appeal in Ordinary to be appointed to the House. The Law Lords (by convention non-judicial peers do not take part in the judicial business of the Lords) are serving and retired Lords of Appeal, other peers who have held high judicial office and the Lord Chancellor. The 11 appointed Lords of Appeal receive a salary for their work. They are life peers and they take part in the ordinary work of the Lords.

Lords Spiritual

The Church of England is the established or state church of England (although not of other parts of the United Kingdom). This fact is recognized by the fact that the two archbishops and the 24 most senior bishops of the Church of England are members of the Lords. A bishop loses his seat when he resigns his see.

Life peers and peeresses

These are the most recent additions to the membership of the Lords. They were created by the Life Peerage Act 1958. Life peers have the rank of baron or baroness and have the same rights as hereditary peers except that their titles cannot be inherited by their heirs. Life peers are created by the Crown on the advice of the Prime Minister. People given these titles are usually (retired) politicians, industrialists, civil servants, trade unionists and others prominent in various walks of public life. The result is that the Lords has a wide representation of interests.

Attendance and party allegiances

Although the total membership of the Lords is 1171, in fact only about 250 peers and peeresses regularly take part in the proceedings of the House. The non-attendance of peers can cause problems for the business of the Lords. The *Guardian* reported on 27 December 1980 that the leader of the Labour Party, Michael Foot, was considering requesting the Government to sanction the creation of new Labour peers because of the pressure which was being put on existing Labour peers by the Government's heavy legislative programme. Lords tend to be elderly, particularly on the Labour benches, which consist mainly of life peers appointed after retirement. Only 90 Labour peers regularly take part (out of 140 who take the party's whip), compared with about 200 Tory peers (out of a total of 430 taking the Conservative whip). This situation has caused embarrassment for the Labour Party, whose official policy is the abolition of the Lords and which in recent years has refused to nominate further Labour life peers. Labour ranks have been further weakened by defections to the Social Democratic Party. In 1981 there were 38 peers who declared their allegiance to the Liberal Party, and there was one Communist peer and one SNP peer.

Many peers do not have party political allegiances and can make this clear by sitting neither with the Government nor with the Opposition but on the 'cross-benches'.

Until 1963 members of the House of Lords could not disclaim their titles. As the result of a campaign fought by Tony Benn, who succeeded to the peerage and became Viscount Stangate, the Peerage Act 1963 was passed, allowing those who succeeded to a peerage to disclaim their titles within a month of succession. They are then eligible to stand for election and to take a seat in the House of Commons.

Powers of the Lords

The power within Parliament passed from the Lords to the Commons in the nineteenth century. As a result of the Parliament Acts 1911 and

1949 the Lords' powers have been formally reduced. Until 1911 the Lords' assent had to be gained for a Bill to become law, but as a result of the Lords' rejection of the Finance Bill embodying Lloyd George's 1909 Budget the Lords lost that power. The 1911 Act was passed after a threat that the King would create enough Liberal peers to swamp the Conservative majority in the House and so provide a majority for the Budget measures.

The Lords, as a result of the 1911 Act and the follow-up 1949 Act, cannot veto legislation coming to it from the Commons. The Lords have no powers to effectively delay a money Bill: they have one month to agree a money Bill coming to it. If a Bill is not a money Bill then they can effectively delay its passage by a year. This, of course, can be an effective power at the end of the life of a Government. In order to be passed into law a Bill must be passed twice by the Commons (in different sessions), but on its rejection for a second time by the Lords it may be presented for the Royal Assent. (This does not apply to legislation extending the life of Parliament to more than its normal five years, and it applies only to public Bills.) This procedure is used only infrequently, as the Lords tries to avoid head-on conflicts with the Commons, which could lead to further diminution of its powers.

The work of the Lords

The House of Lords has a number of functions:

1. Its major function is as a revising chamber. The House of Commons, with its crowded timetable, often does not find time for the discussion of details which complex legislation requires. Proposed legislation also requires revision in the light of public discussion. In these situations the House of Lords plays a crucial role. Improvements in the drafting of legislation for the discussion of details, amendments in the light of further discussions, and second thoughts on substantive issues are all part of the Lords' legislative work.
2. The Lords is often used by Governments as the chamber in which to introduce Bills of a non-controversial nature for which there is not enough time in the crowded Commons timetable.
3. The Lords is the chamber in which most of the work on private Bills takes place, as well as private members' Bills from the Commons and private peers' Bills. The less crowded timetable of the Lords makes it an ideal place to deal with non-Governmental legislation.

4. Since Britain's membership of the EEC, the House of Lords has spent a considerable amount of time considering EEC directives.
5. The Judicial Committee of the House of Lords is the highest court of appeal in the land.

The House of Lords may from time to time be able to exert influence over the Government of the day. For example, in 1980 the Lords prevailed over the Government and the Government was forced to abandon plans to make local authorities introduces charges for providing school transport. It also persuaded the Government to encourage more competition between opticians, especially in the area of the sale of spectacles.

The reform of the Lords

There are strong pressures to replace the archaic composition of the Lords. However, there is no consensus on how this should be achieved. On the right of British politics the view is that the chamber, because of its connections with the Crown and its traditional nature, should remain as it is. On the left, the Lords is seen as fundamentally undemocratic and unrepresentative, and the wish is to abolish it completely. The Labour Party is pledged to abolishing the Lords, but it does not have a policy on whether it wishes to replace it and, if it did, what the composition of the new House would be.

The last attempt at reform was by a Labour Government in 1969. The proposal would have ended the right of hereditary peers to a seat (although existing peers would have remained as non-voting members for their lifetime), the 300 or so life members would have remained, and delaying powers would have been reduced to six months. The measure found favour in few quarters and the Government was forced to withdraw it due to an 'unholy alliance' of left-wing Labour MPs led by Michael Foot, who felt that the measure did not go far enough, and right-wing Conservatives, led by Enoch Powell, who wished to retain the Lords as it was.

Much of the problem of Lords reforms centres on the question of the need for a second chamber. A reformed second chamber would undoubtedly compete for power and influence with the Commons and so finds little favour with many MPs or with Governments. A unicameral (single-chamber) Parliament would give the Commons, with its already crowded timetable, a vastly increased workload, and additionally it would leave more power in the hands of the Government, since at least the delaying power of the Lords does allow a period for reflection and second thoughts.

Ideas for a reformed composition have included a new chamber where perhaps two thirds of the members were elected and the other third appointed, and a pressure-group House where the great corporate interests – churches, trade unions, academics, industry, voluntary bodies, etc. – would be represented.

ASSIGNMENTS

A5.1 Imagine that you are a backbench Member of Parliament and that you keep a political diary. Write a week's entry in the diary describing a typical working week while Parliament is in session.

A5.2 Imagine that you are the Leader of the House of Commons and that the Cabinet has requested that you outline to them possible schemes for the reform of the House of Lords.

Write a statement of the possible alternatives and show which particular scheme you favour and why. You should discuss the possible advantages and disadvantages of each particular alternative.

Do you think that your proposals would be different if you were a member of a Labour rather than a Conservative Cabinet?

A5.3 From your readings of the newspapers, select a topic on which you believe that there is an urgent need for Government action. Imagine that you are a backbench MP and draft a question for a Parliamentary answer at Question Time. (State which Minister will be answering it.) In addition, draft a supplementary question.

What answer do you think you might get from:

(a) a Labour Minister; and
(b) a Conservative Minister?

If you did not receive a satisfactory reply from the Minister, how could you pursue the matter further?

6
Prime Minister and Cabinet Government

6.1 THE GOVERNMENT

The Government is the Executive branch of the British political system. In Britain it is formed by the political party which commands a majority in the House of Commons, or by a number of parties in coalition, as happened during both World Wars. The Government has to maintain its hold on the Commons and without its support it must resign. The Government is headed by the Prime Minister, who is chosen by the Monarch to head 'Her Majesty's Government'. By convention the Queen calls upon the leader of the party which can support a majority in the Commons.

Secretary of State
|
Minister of State
|
Under Secretary of State
|
Parliamentary Private Secretary

Figure 6.1 *The ministerial hierarchy*

The Government does not consist of all the members of the majority party but only of those MPs and members of the House of Lords who are given ministerial posts. The Government numbers about 100 Parliamentarians. Administrative support and advice are provided by the Civil Service, and the majority of Ministers have posts which involve their heading a particular Ministry. Ministers are appointed by the Prime Minister and can be sacked or transferred at the PM's will. The ministerial hierarchy is shown in Fig. 6.1.

The functions of Government

The functions of Government are many and various. In order to carry out its activities it is supported by about 700 000 civil servants and an expenditure equal to about half of the Gross National Product. The functions of Government can be divided into three categories:

1. Policy making.
2. Administration and execution of policy.
3. Co-ordination of the operation of policy.

6.2 THE MONARCHY

Constitutionally, the Monarch is the Head of State of the United Kingdom. Her *formal authority* stretches to most activities of government, as laws are passed in her name, taxes are collected by Her Majesty's Inspectors, convicted criminals are sent to Her Majesty's prisons, and she appoints ministers and judges, and confers honours. However, in practical political terms the *actual powers* of the Crown are extremely limited and the role of the Monarch is mainly ceremonial or ambassadorial. The Monarch has an important role to play as a figurehead and a symbol of national unity, and the importance of ceremony on state occasions such as the State Opening of Parliament should not be underestimated. The function is to provide a focus of national loyalty over and above the discord of party politics. The Monarchy in Britain deliberately takes a non-party political stance, and this has helped it both to survive as an institution and to become a national symbol. Despite open criticisms of the Monarchy's wealth and privileges in some quarters, it has in recent years proved popular as an institution, which can be witnessed by the fact that three-quarters of the population are estimated to have watched a Royal

Wedding on television in July 1981.

It is generally said that 'the Queen reigns but does not rule', and this is a fair statement of the role of the Monarchy in British society. But it must be remembered that the Monarch must have a degree of *influence* over the events of the day, although the extent of this influence is impossible to measure. The present Queen has reigned for more than a quarter of a century and during that period has had regular audiences with eight Prime Ministers and has met most of the important figures in Britain and across the world. Such contacts must give influence. Additionally, the Monarch does have what can be called constitutional 'reserve powers'; that is, though most of the acts of the Sovereign are in fact based on the decisions of Government, in times of emergency the Monarch might be able to exercise certain powers on her own behalf. On two occasions this century the Monarch has had a political role to play during periods of political difficulty. The first was in the period before the passing of the Parliament Act 1911, which restricted the power of the House of Lords. After the second chamber's rejection of the Liberals' Budget of 1909, the King, George V, agreed after an election to create enough Liberal peers to pass the measure if the Conservative-dominated Lords did not agree to the Budget proposals. The other instance was in 1931, when the National Government was formed at a time of great economic difficulties. The Monarch had a hand in the negotiations to form the Government and a real choice of Prime Minister.

The Monarch could have a role to play in a 'hung Parliament' where it was not clear which party had a majority. But this could happen only if the two-party system broke down, so that the choice of Prime Minister was no longer clear.

In the 1860s Walter Bagehot argued in his book *The English Constitution* that the Monarch has three rights – 'the right to be consulted, the right to encourage, the right to warn'. This is probably just as true today as it was then, but they are rights generally exercised in private to avoid any suspicion of partisanship.

6.3 THE PRIME MINISTER

The Prime Minister is the Head of Government in the United Kingdom and is the leader of the party which can command a majority in the House of Commons. Table 6.1 lists twentieth-century Prime Ministers and their parties. The powers of the Prime Minister are not embodied in statute but instead are established by convention. The

Table 6.1 *Governments and Prime Ministers in the twentieth century*

	Party in Government	*Prime Minister*
1895–1902	Conservative	Marquis of Salisbury
1902–1905	Conservative	A.J. Balfour
1905–1908	Liberal	Sir Henry Campbell-Bannerman
1908–1915	Liberal	Herbert Asquith
1915–1916	Coalition	Herbert Asquith
1916–1922	Coalition	David Lloyd George
1922–1923	Conservative	Andrew Bonar Law
1923–1924	Conservative	Stanley Baldwin
1924	Labour	Ramsay Macdonald
1924–1929	Conservative	Stanley Baldwin
1929–1931	Labour	Ramsay Macdonald
1931–1935	National	Ramsay Macdonald
1935–1937	National	Stanley Baldwin
1937–1939	National	Neville Chamberlain
1939–1940	Coalition	Neville Chamberlain
1940–1945	Coalition	Winston Churchill
1945	Conservative	Winston Churchill
1945–1951	Labour	Clement Attlee
1951–1955	Conservative	Winston Churchill
1955–1957	Conservative	Sir Anthony Eden
1957–1963	Conservative	Harold Macmillan
1963–1964	Conservative	Sir Alex Douglas-Home
1964–1970	Labour	Harold Wilson
1970–1974	Conservative	Edward Heath
1974–1976	Labour	Harold Wilson
1976–1979	Labour	James Callaghan
1979–	Conservative	Margaret Thatcher

principal powers of the Prime Minister are:

1. The appointment of members of the Cabinet and other holders of Government office. Though in theory the PM can pick and choose among MPs and peers of his or her own party for ministerial office, in practice this power is tempered by the need for the Prime Minister to maintain party support. This necessitates choosing leading members of the various factions within his or her party. Hence Labour Cabinets always contain a balance of left-wing members, right-wing members and centrists, and Mrs Thatcher's Cabinet, appointed in 1979, contained many 'wets' despite the right-wing monetarist views to which the Prime Minister was committed. However, many of the 'wets' were dropped from the Cabinet after a shuffle in September 1981.
2. The Prime Minister can dismiss or transfer Ministers. This is a very important power but it is not absolute and is tempered, as is

the power to appoint Ministers, by the dictates of practical politics. The most famous use of the power in recent political history was Harold Macmillan's 'night of the long knives' in 1962, when he simultaneously dismissed seven Cabinet Ministers. This incident is, however, an exception. Prime Ministers like their Cabinet to appear united and usually try to avoid too many dismissals or transfers. Prime Ministers do use this power selectively to show their authority and to bring particular party factions into line. In January 1981 the Prime Minister, Margaret Thatcher, removed from her Cabinet one leading 'wet', the Chancellor of the Duchy of Lancaster, Norman St John Stevas, who was known to be opposed to the Prime Minister's hard-line monetarist economic policy. The speculation in the media was that Mr Stevas had been removed as a warning to other 'wets' in the Cabinet to fall into line. The Defence Secretary, Francis Pym, who was thought to be on the verge of resigning over proposed cuts in the defence budget, was transferred to Mr Stevas's former post.

3. The Prime Minister determines the membership of Cabinet committees, which are dealt with in more detail later in the chapter. They are seldom commented on in the media but they are the places where most Cabinet business is transacted. Their composition is therefore crucial to the outcome of decisions.
4. The Prime Minister draws up the Cabinet agenda. This is a particularly important power, as anyone who has ever sat on a committee knows. The agenda determines what are and what are not proper subjects for discussion.
5. The Prime Minister summons Cabinet meetings.
6. The Prime Minister chairs Cabinet meetings.
7. The Prime Minister dispenses a huge amount of patronage in both posts and honours. Besides Cabinet and other ministerial posts, there are the chairmanships of nationalized industries and a whole range of Government committees and boards, as well as honours and titles. This power and its use have come in for particular criticism, especially after Sir Harold Wilson's resignation Honours List of 1977, when some observers felt that the recipients of certain honours were not worthy of them. Potential candidates for honours are now scrutinized by a Commons committee. The Prime Minister still has a free hand in the much more important area of Government appointments.
8. The Prime Minister decides on the date of the general election. Unlike many other political systems, the British system has no fixed date for general elections providing they are held within the

five-year term. The decision 'to go to the country' rests with the Prime Minister. It is an important power, as it allows the Prime Minister to consult public opinion polls and to choose the best time for his or her party to be returned to office. However, in recent elections it seems to be an overrated power, since in five out of the last seven elections the incumbent Prime Minister has lost the election.

9. The Prime Minister is the Minister responsible for the Civil Service, and this puts the whole of the Government machine directly under the Prime Minister's control.
10. In foreign affairs the Prime Minister has a particularly important role in negotiations and consultations with other governments and heads of state.

6.4 THE CABINET

The executive function of policy-making and co-ordination in British Government is fulfilled by the Cabinet. This committee of 20 or so senior Ministers is chaired by the Prime Minister. Its members are either MPs or members of the House of Lords. (Non-parliamentarians may temporarily hold Cabinet office while they are attempting to win a seat at a by-election. For example, Patrick Gordon-Walker was Foreign Secretary for four months from October 1964 to January 1965 after losing his seat at the general election, but resigned after losing a by-election.) The work of the Cabinet consists of deciding the policies and priorities of the Government and co-ordinating the work of the machinery of Government.

Table 6.2 lists the posts represented in the Conservative Cabinet in January 1981.

Cabinet committees

So great is the volume of government business that not all decisions can be made in Cabinet. To facilitate the discussions of government business the Cabinet has a system of committees. These committees are secret, and lists of them and their membership are not published. Ministers themselves know only the details of the discussions of the committees on which they sit, and appointment to a committee is the prerogative of the Prime Minister.

Table 6.2 *Posts represented in the Conservative Cabinet (as at 7 January 1981)*

Prime Minister and First Lord of the Treasury[a]
Secretary of State for Home Affairs[b]
Lord Chancellor[c]
Secretary of State for Foreign and Commonwealth Affairs
Chancellor of the Exchequer[d]
Secretary of State for Industry
Chancellor of the Duchy of Lancaster and Paymaster General[e]
Lord President of the Council[f]
Secretary of State for Employment
Lord Privy Seal[g]
Secretary of State for Agriculture, Fisheries and Food
Secretary of State for the Environment
Secretary of State for Scottish Affairs
Secretary of State for Welsh Affairs
Secretary of State for Northern Ireland
Secretary of State for Social Services
Secretary of State for Defence
Secretary of State for Trade
Secretary of State for Energy
Secretary of State for Education and Science
Secretary of State for Transport
Chief Secretary to the Treasury[h]

[a] The office of First Lord of the Treasury is always combined with that of the Prime Minister.

[b] In Mrs Thatcher's Cabinet formed in 1979 the Home Secretary, William Whitelaw, also held the post of Deputy Prime Minister.

[c] The Lord Chancellor is the head of the legal system. In other countries he would have a title such as Minister of Justice. Besides being a politician he can act as a judge in the judicial committee of the House of Lords. He appoints judges. The Lord Chancellor acts as Speaker of the House of Lords.

[d] The Chancellor of the Exchequer is the chief Economic Minister. In other countries he would have a title such as Minister for Economic Affairs.

[e] The Chancellor of the Duchy of Lancaster and the Paymaster General are posts which may be combined or held separately. From May 1979 to January 1981 in Mrs Thatcher's Cabinet, they were held as separate posts. The Chancellor of the Duchy of Lancaster (then Mr Norman St John Stevas) was leader of the House of Commons while the Paymaster General (then Mr Angus Maude) co-ordinated Government information. The combining of the posts in January 1981 involved the combining of these two functions. These two offices, together with Lord Privy Seal, Lord President of the Council, and Minister without Portfolio, have been used for a wide variety of functions. As chairmen of Cabinet Committees they are independent and have no departmental axe to grind as the 'spending ministers' have. A previous Conservative Chancellor of the Duchy of Lancaster, Geoffrey Rippon, negotiated Britain's entry into the EEC in 1972.

[f] The Lord President of the Council in Mrs Thatcher's Cabinet (until September 1981), Lord Soames, was appointed Minister in charge of the Civil Service, although the Civil Service is directly under the Prime Minister's control. Lord Soames also

acted as the last Governor of Rhodesia during the period of transition to the State of Zimbabwe in 1980. The previous office-holder, Michael Foot (Labour), held the office while being Leader of the House of Commons and Deputy Prime Minister.

g The Lord Privy Seal can exercise a variety of functions. In Mrs Thatcher's Cabinet, Sir Ian Gilmour was appointed Deputy Foreign Secretary and was foreign affairs spokesman (until 1981) in the Commons, as the Foreign Secretary, Lord Carrington, sat as a member of the House of Lords.

h The holder of the post of Chief Secretary to the Treasury is deputy to the Chancellor of the Exchequer. This is a post which is not always included in the Cabinet.

In 1978 Mr Bruce Page published an article in the *New Statesman* (21 July 1978) which revealed that the then Labour Cabinet had about 25 standing Cabinet committees and something of the order of 130 *ad hoc* ones. The main standing committees included Defence and Foreign Affairs, Home and Social Policy, and Overseas Aid. *Ad hoc* committees included such areas as Inner Cities, Southern Africa and the Press.

Collective responsibility

The most important convention governing the operation of the Cabinet is that of collective responsibility. This means that the members of the Cabinet are collectively responsible for the exercise of executive authority. The convention requires that all Ministers show a united front and do not publicly disagree with Government decisions and policies. If they do actively disagree with Government policies, then Cabinet Ministers must at least either refrain from public criticism of them or resign. The doctrine of collective responsibility has grown up so that the Government is not publicly seen to be divided on issues. The existence of the doctrine does not imply that all Cabinet Ministers agree on all issues. Biographies of former Cabinet Ministers, such as the late Richard Crossman's *Diary of a Cabinet Minister,* and frequent newspaper leaks make it clear that Cabinet disagreements, sometimes almost to the point of resignation, are a usual occurrence. The Conservative Cabinet of Mrs Thatcher has been known publicly, in the press, to be divided over issues of public expenditure cuts and the control of the economy. In that Cabinet a division between so-called 'wets', who wish to see a moderate line taken, and 'monetarists', supporting Mrs Thatcher's stringent economic policy, has been well reported in the media. On matters of great constitutional significance, where political parties themselves are divided, the doctrine may be breached. In 1975 there was 'an agreement to differ' between Cabinet members on the issue of Britain's continuing membership of the European Community during the period of public debate leading up to the referendum in that year. Ministers from the then Labour Government publicly campaigned on both sides. The Prime Minister, Harold Wilson, was firm that this was the only issue on which Ministers could publicly disagree.

The Cabinet Office

The Cabinet Office is headed by the Secretary to the Cabinet, who is responsible to the Prime Minister for its direction. It comprises:

1. Cabinet Secretariat.
2. Office of Personnel Management.
3. Central Policy Review Staff.
4. Central Statistical Office.
5. Historical Section.

The Cabinet Secretariat serves the Cabinet in the conduct of its business and is a body which helps with the co-ordination of policy. It is concerned with the preparation of agenda and minutes, the circulation of memoranda, following the progress of decisions and providing for the security of documents.

In November 1981 the Cabinet Office took over some of the personnel functions from the disbanded Civil Service Department. These functions, which include recruitment and training, are directed by the new Office of Personnel Management. The Head of the Cabinet Office is now the head of the Civil Service.

6.5 THE CENTRAL POLICY REVIEW STAFF (CPRS)

The CPRS or the 'Think Tank', as it is popularly known, was set up by Edward Heath's Conservative Government in 1971. The idea was for the Cabinet and the Prime Minister to have a source of ideas, as an alternative to Civil Service thinking, from independent experts. The original objectives of the CPRS were to:

1. Analyse the policy options before the Cabinet and assist in establishing the priorities among them.
2. Relate individual proposals and ideas to the Government's overall strategy.

3. Bring fresh thinking to the policy-making process, as about half of the members were to be drawn from outside the Civil Service.

The CPRS works partly by holding strategy meetings with the Cabinet in order to help it to make collective decisions on policy options. It briefs Ministers and provides advice to the Cabinet. It also acts as a research body and during its life has produced reports on Energy, Race Relations, the Motor Car Industry, Joint Approach to Social Policy, British Embassies Abroad and the Steel Industry.

When it was set up it was thought that opposition to its activities might come from the Civil Service, but this seems not to have been the case. The success of the Think Tank depends on the notice that Prime Ministers take of it and its work. Each Prime Minister has used it in a different way and it is known that Harold Wilson at one time had decided to abolish it when he came to office in 1974. Mrs Thatcher has changed its orientation so that it now concentrates less on social problems and more on industrial strategy. Its strength lies in the quality of the advice which it brings to Cabinet decision-making.

6.6 PRIME MINISTERIAL OR CABINET GOVERNMENT?

There has been a continuing debate among academics about whether Britain has Cabinet or Prime Ministerial Government. The argument is over whether it is the Cabinet which *collectively* takes major policy decisions, or whether the Prime Minister is the dominant force in the policy process.

The argument for Prime Ministerial Government was put forcefully by the late Richard Crossman, a leading Cabinet Minister in the Labour Government 1964–70. He held that Britain now had a '*presidential*'-style executive with the Prime Minister as the dominant person in the decision-making process. The Prime Minister's power to appoint, dismiss or move Ministers, and the overview of policy which he or she can exercise, enable the Prime Minister to allocate values within the Cabinet. This enables the Prime Minister to change or confirm an individual Minister's policy and to determine the general strategy which the Government will follow. In this view the Prime Minister is seen to be much more than *primus inter pares* (first among equals) with his or her Cabinet colleagues. The Prime Minister is effectively the *manager* of the Cabinet.

Obviously, the actual style of government will vary with the personality of the Prime Minister, the strength and standing of Cabinet Ministers and the issues of policy involved, but where there is a strong and experienced team of Ministers it is reasonable to suppose that decisions will tend to be made collectively by the Cabinet. Such was the case with the Labour Cabinet 1974–76 under Harold Wilson's premiership. The Cabinet contained such experienced Ministers as Denis Healey, Jim Callaghan, Anthony Crosland, Roy Jenkins and Barbara Castle. The Cabinet of 1976–1979 under Callaghan had a rather less experienced team. Callaghan himself had great political experience (he was the only Prime Minister to have held all three great offices of State — Chancellor of the Exchequer, Foreign Secretary and Home Secretary), and he is generally agreed to have had a more predominant role than his predecessor. Margaret Thatcher has exercised a strong managerial control over her Cabinet colleagues. Before the 1979 election she is quoted as saying 'As Prime Minister I could not waste time in having any internal arguments (in Cabinet)'. She has made a habit of making policy announcements in public speeches, occasionally even before announcing them to her colleagues.

Regardless of which party has been in power, there have been occasions where the Cabinet has not been consulted by the Prime Minister and decisions have been made by the Prime Minister alone or with a small inner circle of Ministers. This seems to suggest that Britain has Prime Ministerial government rather than a system where important decisions are made solely in Cabinet meetings. Bernard Donoughue, former Senior Policy Adviser to Harold Wilson and James Callaghan 1974–1979, claimed on BBC1's *Platform One* programme on 1 April 1980 that, under James Callaghan, important decisions on monetary policy were not always made by the Cabinet. Economic decisions were made by what he described as a 'seminar' consisting of the Prime Minister, the Chancellor of the Exchequer, the Chancellor of the Duchy of Lancaster, the Governor of the Bank of England, and the Permanent Secretary to the Treasury. Monetary and fiscal policy decisions were made without reference to the Ministers concerned.

Similar examples can be given from other periods in the history of British government. Clement Attlee committed Britain to being a nuclear power after consulting only his closest associates in the late 1940s. Britain's decision to spend £5 billion on the Trident defence system which replaces the Polaris submarines, which was publicly announced in March 1981, was reported not to have been made by the full Cabinet but in secret by a Cabinet committee in the summer of 1980.

ASSIGNMENTS

A6.1 Imagine that you are the Minister in charge of the Civil Service in the present Government. The Cabinet has instructed you to reduce the strength of the Service by 50 000 within the next five years.

(a) Outline the case for the policy and draft notes for a speech to Parliament justifying the policy and giving details of how it is going to be implemented.
(b) What will the likely response be from the Civil Service unions to the policy and why should they hold these particular views?

A6.2 What powers does a modern Prime Minister possess? What are the sources of the Prime Minister's authority and what are the practical and constitutional limits to the Prime Minister's powers?

A6.3 Choose an area of government policy (examples could include defence, health, education, the social services, and the economy) and draw up a list of the institutions, pressure groups and individuals who will be involved in policy changes in your area of study.
In your opinion, how much freedom of manoeuvre does a Government have in policy-making if the major pressure groups in a particular policy are are all opposed to its policy? Give examples from your own study of current affairs.

7
Policy Implementation and Government Administration

7.1 THE CIVIL SERVICE

The Civil Service exists to administer legislation passed by Parliament and to advise on and carry out the policy of the Government of the day. In constitutional theory, civil servants are, as their name implies, the 'servants' of the elected Government. In reality it is difficult to draw such a clear distinction between policy-making (carried out by elected politicians) and its administration (carried out by civil servants). Senior civil servants do play a crucial role in the policy formulation process, but not all are involved with the heights of policy-making and the giving of advice to Ministers. In fact this is the province of the minority. The vast majority of the 690 000 or so men and women who make up the service are involved in a wide range of posts which serve the community, for example weather forecasters, social security officers, prison officers, officers in the National Savings banks, map makers working for the ordnance survey, and those employed in job centres.

The structure of the Civil Service has undergone considerable criticism and change in the past 20 years. It has been the subject of two major critical reports, the Fulton Report of the late 1960s and the English Committee report in the 1970s, both of which will be investigated in this chapter.

Successive governments concerned with Britain's poor economic performance and their own management of the economy have attempted various reorganizations within their own bureaucracy in order to improve both its efficiency and its ability to deal with the nation's problems. In 1961 an important system of public expenditure control, the Public Expenditure Survey Committees (PESC) (see Chapter 11), was introduced so that Government expenditure planning could be rolled forwards over a five-year period. PESC was designed to bring Government departments together so that policy could be better co-ordinated. In the late 1960s there were moves to create larger departments to bring related policy areas under one roof and to prevent the parochialism which is often endemic in small units. The new Conservative Government published in October 1970 a White Paper entitled *The Reorganisation of Central Government,* in which the new administration intended to give form to its election pledges to create 'a new style of government'.

The White Paper claimed that there were weaknesses in the apparatus of policy formulation and to improve the situation it proposed a reorganization of departments. They were to be grouped so that each would cover a wide span of policy and would be multi-functional. This, it was argued, would allow greater co-ordination among related policy areas. It would also allow all major Civil Service departments to be included in the Cabinet without an increase in its size. Within each department, areas of work would be delegated to accountable units of management, which would lessen the load on the top departmental management. Examples of these new groupings were the creation of the Department of the Environment from the former Ministries of Housing and Local Government, Public Buildings and Works, and Transport. The Department of Trade and Industry was created out of the Board of Trade, the Ministry of Technology and part of the Department of Employment. And as a result of the Fulton Committee's recommendations, a new Civil Service Department was set up to provide specialist personnel services. The Central Policy Review Staff – the 'Think Tank' – was created both to provide an additional source of advice and to assist the co-ordination of policy advice.

The enthusiasm for the new macro-ministries has waned with successive governments. When Labour came to power in 1974 the DTI was broken down into Trade, Industry, and Energy, and Transport was separated from the Department of the Environment.

The Conservative Government of 1979 has concentrated its Civil Service reforms on slimming down the Service both by reducing the numbers employed in it and by reducing the cost of the central bureaucracy.

7.2 GOVERNMENT DEPARTMENTS

The Home Office

The Home Office is responsible for internal matters in England and Wales which are not the responsibility of other departments. The Home Secretary is concerned with the supervision of the police (the actual forces are organized by local authorities outside London, while in London the Metropolitan Police Force is the direct responsibility of the Home Secretary), the fire service, civil defence, immigration and nationality, community relations, probation and broadcasting. The Home Office was formerly responsible for the Prison Service, but from 1980 this responsibility has been transferred to a semi-autonomous Prison Board.

The Foreign and Commonwealth Office

This department is responsible for communications with foreign and commonwealth governments and international organizations such as the EEC and NATO, and for the maintenance of diplomatic missions abroad. It is also responsible for the administration of dependent colonies and territories.

Department of Industry

The Department of Industry is concerned with policies to improve industrial performance and with giving assistance to the regions in which unemployment is above the national average. It also has responsibility for a number of nationalized industries – British Aerospace, British Steel, the Post Office, British Telecom, British Shipbuilders, BL, and Rolls Royce Ltd. The Department supervises the work of the National Enterprise Board.

Ministry of Defence

The Ministry of Defence is responsible for the formulation and co-ordination of defence policy and has responsibility for the Army, the Navy and the Air Force. It also supervises the Royal Ordnance factories.

The Treasury

This is the economic ministry and is concerned with the implementation and formulation of monetary and fiscal policy. It has sections concerned with balance of payments policies, public expenditure, fiscal and monetary policies and country-inflationary policies. The Chief Economic Adviser is responsible for the preparation of short-term and medium-term forecasts and for providing economic policy advice. The Boards of the Inland Revenue and the Customs and Excise come under Treasury supervision. In November 1981 the Treasury took over responsibility for certain Civil Service personnel matters from the former Civil Service Department.

Ministry of Agriculture, Fisheries and Food

This department is concerned with agricultural and fishing policy for England and Wales in the context of the EEC's Common Agricultural Policy. It is also concerned with research into plant and animal disease, safety, quality and labelling of foodstuffs and public health standards in the production of foodstuffs. It has overall responsibility for the maintenance of an adequate food supply.

Department of the Environment

The Department of the Environment is responsible for the overall supervision of local government and its expenditure in England, including the setting of the Rate Support Grant. It is also responsible for housing policy, inner city renewal, control of pollution, development of sport and recreation, and countryside affairs. The Property Services Agency is concerned with the maintenance of public and historical buildings and public works.

The Scottish Office

This is a multi-functional department and, because of the separate judicial system of Scotland, the Office has a degree of autonomy. In Scotland the Secretary of State for Scotland exercises control over a range of services which in England and Wales are controlled by the Department of Education and Science, the Department of Employment, the Department of Health and Social Security, the Home Office, and the Ministry of Agriculture, Food and Fisheries. The Scottish Office is based in Edinburgh and it has a major role in the planning of the Scottish economy. It has responsibility for the Scottish Manpower Services Commission and for certain public corporations – the North of Scotland Hydro-Electricity Board, the South of Scotland Electricity Board, and the Scottish Transport Group.

The Secretary of State is responsible for legal services in Scotland and the functions of the Scottish law officers – the Lord Advocate and the Solicitor General for Scotland.

The Welsh Office

The Welsh Office has responsibility for a wide range of services for Wales, including primary and secondary education, health, local government, tourism, new towns, water and, in conjunction with the Ministry of Agriculture, Food and Fisheries, agriculture. The Welsh Development Agency has important industrial and economic planning functions.

The Northern Ireland Office

This is the responsibility of the Secretary of State for Northern Ireland and is accountable to Parliament for activities in the areas of agriculture, commerce, education, economic development and the security of the province. Some of its functions are those exercised by local authorities in the rest of the United Kingdom. The Office is divided into the following departments:

1. Department of the Civil Service.
2. Department of Education.
3. Department of Agriculture.
4. Department of Commerce.
5. Department of Finance.
6. Department of Health and Social Security.
7. Department of the Environment.
8. Department of Manpower Services.

The Department of Health and Social Security

This department is responsible for the administration of the National Health Service, the supervision of local authority social services, and social security payments.

The Department of Trade

The Department of Trade is responsible for the promotion of internal and external trade. It promotes British goods and services overseas. It is responsible for commercial legislation, patents, tourism, shipping and the control and supervision of British Airways, the British Airports Authority and the Civil Aviation Authority. *The Export Credits Guarantee Department* is a separate department under the Secretary of State for Trade which offers facilities to British exporters including loans, insurance and export finance.

Department of Energy

The Department of Energy is responsible for energy policy and the control and supervision of the public corporation in the energy field – the Electricity Council, the Central Electricity Generating Board, the National Coal Board, the British Gas Corporation, the United Kingdom Atomic Energy Authority, and the British National Oil Corporation.

The Department of Education and Science

This department is responsible for national policy and standards in education and supervises the public education service provided by the local authorities in England.

The Civil Service Department

This department was responsible for the management, organization, recruitment and training of the Civil Service. The political head was the Prime Minister but day-to-day control lay with the Lord President of the Council. The Department was abolished in November 1981 and its functions have been dispersed to the Treasury and the Cabinet Office.

Department of Transport

The Department of Transport is concerned with most aspects of transport and the control of the nationalized industries in the area – British Rail, British Transport Docks Board, the National Bus Company, and the National Freight Corporation.

Law Officers Department

This department provides legal advice to the Government. It is headed by the Attorney-General and the Solicitor General.

Lord Chancellor's Department

This department is responsible for the administration of justice, the courts, legal aid and the appointment of judges and magistrates.

7.3 CASE STUDY: MANPOWER POLICY – THE DEPARTMENT OF EMPLOYMENT GROUP

The Department of Employment (DE) is a large department employing approximately 23 000 people both in London and in local and regional offices. In common with other Civil Service departments, it is accountable to Parliament via the Secretary of State for Employment, who is a Cabinet member. He or she is assisted by a Minister of State and two Parliamentary Under Secretaries. In addition to having responsibility for the DE the Secretary of State co-ordinates the work of three semi-autonomous bodies of QUANGOs which, together with the DE, are known as the Department of Employment Group. The semi-autonomous bodies are the Manpower Services Commission (MSC), the Health and Safety Commission (HSC) and the Advisory, Conciliation and Arbitration Service (ACAS).

The responsibilities of the DE

The DE has a wide range of functions and provides a number of services, including the following.

The unemployment benefit service

Over 20 000 civil servants are employed in 1000 local offices with the responsibility for the payment of unemployment benefits and supplementary benefits. This involves the DE in liaison with the DHSS on the policy objectives of benefits to the unemployed. Such policy decisions involve recent measures such as the Social Security (No. 2) Act 1980, which abolished the earnings-related supplement to unemployment benefits, and the Government's policy of taxing social security benefits paid to the unemployed and to strikers from April 1982.

Industrial relations

The Secretary of State is responsible for the Government's policy on and for any proposed legislation affecting industrial relations. The DE is often involved in negotiations in major industrial disputes and strikes.

The careers service

Local authorities provide the careers service for young people and it is the DE's function to provide them with guidance under the Employment and Training Act 1973.

Race relations and employment

The DE is responsible for the promotion of good race relations in the employment field – an area where racial discrimination can easily be a problem.

Manpower policy

The department produces statistics and research as an aid to the planning of manpower requirements in relation to the needs of the economy.

Wages councils

Certain trades and occupations have their wage levels laid down by wages councils. The DE is responsible for their administration under the Wages Councils Act 1959.

During periods when Governments have operated incomes policies to control wage levels in the economy, the DE has had the task of implementing these policies in both the public and the private sectors.

'Hived-off boards'

The DE has overall control of manpower policies, but some special aspects of manpower have been grouped under three semi-autonomous boards. The three boards – the Manpower Services Commission (MSC), the Health and Safety Commission (HSC) and the Advisory, Conciliation and Arbitration Service (ACAS) – were set up in 1974–75 in order to provide what are known as *accountable units*. The Fulton Report had drawn attention to the sometimes vague accountability of parts of the Civil Service. These boards have clear, definite areas of responsibility and an independent management. They were set up as a means of providing clear public accountability. The Secretary of State is still answerable to Parliament for their operation, although each board is technically separate from Government. This degree of separateness gives each board a considerable degree of autonomy in organizing its tasks.

The Manpower Services Commission

The statutory basis for the MSC's activities is the Employment and Training Act 1973. This Act set up a Commission of ten members – a chairman, three members appointed by the employers' organization the CBI, three from the trade unions represented by the TUC, two from local authority associations, and one from educational interests.

Initially the executive arms of the MSC consisted of two corporate bodies – the Employment Services Agency (ESA) and the Training Services Agency (TSA). The MSC was originally a small body whose function was to take a strategic view of the labour market. The rising unemployment of the recession which began in the late 1970s required a far more co-ordinated approach to manpower problems. In 1977–78 agency status was removed from the ESA and the TSA and they became divisions of the MSC. This allowed the MSC to take a corporate approach to the planning of manpower services. At present there are three divisions of the MSC (see Fig. 7.1):

1. The Employment Services Division.
2. The Training Services Division.
3. The Special Programmes Division.

The manpower of these divisions is given in Table 7.1.

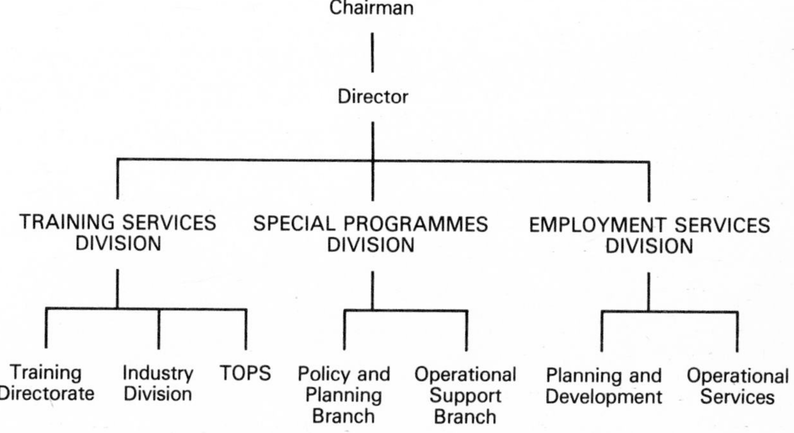

Figure 7.1 *The organization of the MSC. From A Guide to the DE Group, Department of Employment, July 1978. Reproduced with the permission of the Department of Employment.*

Table 7.1 *MSC Manpower (March 1980)*

Employment Services	14 772
Training Services	8 425
Special Programmes	1 250
Central and Regional Management	1 421
Total staff	25 868

From the Manpower Services Commission Annual Report 1979–80. Reproduced with the permission of the Department of Employment.

Employment Services Division. This division is responsible for helping the unemployed to find work, and for helping people who wish to change jobs. In order to do this it has been modernizing its services with the establishment of 'self-service' High Street Job Centres. The Centres provide details of jobs in open display and self-service systems; the service has generally proved to be a popular method of finding work. Occupational guidance is available for those who require it. In setting up the Job Centres a division was made between the finding of work and the payment of unemployment benefit.

The division also provides assistance for disabled people seeking work and Sheltered Workshops for the same group.

Training Services Division. The aim of the TSD is to promote the development of an efficient national training scheme to meet the needs of the economy and of working people. In 1979–80 it had a budget of £329.2 million. The aim is fulfilled through three Directorates:

1. *The Industry Directorate.* Most training in Britain is carried out by employers, and the TSD works to improve its quality. The directorate works with the Industrial Training Boards (ITBs) which in turn are responsible for the training needs in specific industries. (At the time of writing, 1981, the Secretary of State for Employment is seeking powers to abolish certain ITBs and to hand control of training back to firms in certain industries. Most ITBs were abolished in November 1981.)
2. *Training Opportunities Scheme Directorate (TOPS).* The TSD also does its own training at its own skill centres and at colleges of further education under the TOPS scheme (see Tables 7.2 and 7.3).

Table 7.2 *Retraining under TOPS*

Completions		*Cost by Financial Year (£m)*
1974–75	45 416	58.2
1975–76	60 724	118.6
1976–77	86 651	183.5
1977–78	98 964	197.1
1978–79	91 310	202.6
1979–80	74 489	226.2

From the Manpower Services Commission Annual Report 1979–80. Reproduced with the permission of the Department of Employment.

Table 7.3 *Analysis of skills taught under TOPS 1979–80*

Clerical and commercial	25 917	(34.79%)
Engineering and automotive	17 011	(22.84%)
Construction	6 315	(8.48%)
Heavy goods vehicle	3 404	(4.58%)
Others	21 842	(29.32%)
Total	74 489	

From the Manpower Services Commission Annual Report 1979–80. Reproduced with the permission of the Department of Employment.

3. *Directorate of Training.* This directorate aims to improve the efficiency of training through an advisory service, development work, research and surveys.

Special Programmes Division. This division was launched in 1978 to meet the needs of two special groups of unemployed. They are:

1. Unemployed young people, who are catered for by the Youth Opportunities Programmes (YOPS), which provide training and work experience for unemployed young people. Some 216 400 were catered for in 1979–80. The YOPS scheme has gained in prominence as part of MSC work, especially due to the large numbers of 16 to 18-year-olds who are without jobs as a result of the recession of the early 1980s. In 1981 it was estimated that nearly 50 per cent of the labour force under 18 were unemployed – some 600 000 individuals. In July 1981 the Prime Minister introduced a financial package costing between £400 and £500 million a year to create, among other things, an extra 110 000 Youth Opportunity places in 1981–82.
2. The long-term adult unemployed, who are catered for by the Special Temporary Employment Programme (STEP), which aims to provide temporary work for this group. STEP was severely reduced in 1979 when the programme was restricted to certain designated areas of high unemployment.

The Health and Safety Commission

The Commission was appointed in 1974 under the provisions of the Health and Safety at Work Act 1974. It is responsible to the Secretary of State for Employment for taking appropriate steps to secure the health, safety and welfare of people at work and to protect the public generally from risks to health or safety at work.

Like the MSC, the Health and Safety Commission is made up of a forum of interest groups from management, the trade unions and local authorities. The Commission works through an executive arm, the Health and Safety Executive, which is responsible for:

1. Reviewing legislation and codes of practice relating to health and safety at work.
2. The enforcement of employers' duties under the Act. This is carried out by the Executive's inspectors.
3. Encouraging safety awareness among employers and employees.
4. Promoting safety training.
5. Promoting two-way communication, via National Industry Groups, between management, unions, suppliers and professional associations on the health and safety problems in particular industries.
6. Providing information and an advisory service to industry.

The Advisory, Conciliation and Arbitration Service

ACAS came into being in 1974 and became an independent statutory body in 1976 under the terms of the Employment Protection Act 1975. The service is run by a council appointed by the Secretary of State for Employment. The main functions of ACAS are to provide:

1. Advice on industrial relations to parties involved in a trade dispute.
2. Conciliation between the parties involved in a trade dispute.
3. Arbitration and mediation services.
4. Help in improving industrial relations.

ACAS is often called into industrial disputes when employers and employees cannot reach agreement through the normal process of collective bargaining. ACAS can offer conciliation when it feels it may be helpful. It is seen to be fair and impartial by both sides in disputes, and this is an important aspect of a body which is, nominally at least, a governmental or neo-governmental body. ACAS's impartial stance shows how far a QUANGO can develop autonomy and distance itself from central government.

7.4 ORGANIZATION OF THE CIVIL SERVICE

The foundations of the modern Civil Service can be dated to the middle of the nineteenth century with the publication of the Northcote–Trevelyan Report of 1854. Before the acceptance of the Report's recommendations, Civil Service posts were filled through nepotism and patronage, with the consequence that the service was inefficient. The reforms in the Report were designed to produce an efficient service in which promotion was based on merit and entry was by competitive examination. In addition, a hierarchy of posts was established which, by the 1920s, was known as the 'class system'. General administrators were divided into three classes:

1. The Administrative class, which consisted of senior managers and policy advisers.
2. The Executive class, which comprised the middle management grades.
3. The Clerical class, consisting of people who performed routine tasks.

In addition to the general administrators, more and more specialists – scientists, engineers, lawyers, etc. – were recruited into the service as the responsibilities of government developed in the twentieth century. Each group of specialists had its own hierarchy and grading system. By the 1960s the service was divided into 47 general classes and 1400 departmental classes.

The Northcote–Trevelyan reforms were designed to produce an efficient service for nineteenth-century governments who responsibilities, by modern standards, were small. The development of the welfare state and the recognition by governments of their key role in managing the economy led to a huge growth in the central bureaucracy in the twentieth century. By the early 1960s there was, despite certain reforms since the turn of the century, serious concern over the efficiency and organization of the service.

7.5 THE FULTON REPORT

The Committee on the Civil Service, under the Chairmanship of Lord Fulton, was set up in 1966 to report on the reforms required to bring the Civil Service into line with the needs of modern government. The Committee reported in 1968 and listed six main areas in which it felt that change was required:

1. It argued that the service was based on the philosophy of the 'generalist', the amateur and the 'all-rounder'. By this the Committee meant that senior civil servants did not specialize in particular areas of work, and that it was accepted in the service that an administrator could move from department to department without special training.
2. Specialists in the service – engineers, lawyers, accountants, etc. – were not given sufficient responsibilities, and had too little opportunity to become senior managers. This is linked with the first criticism that the service had a generalist bias. Specialists were seen as being 'on tap but not on top'.
3. The class system was too complex and there were too many grades. The grading system hindered mobility within the service.
4. Too few civil servants were specialist managers. The generalist administrators were given insufficient training in management skills. Senior civil servants did not give sufficient importance to the task of management, and management was not seen by them as their most important task. They saw their job as providing policy advice to the Government.
5. There was too little contact and interchange of personnel between the Civil Service and the outside world, particularly industry.
6. Too little attention was paid to personnel matters in the Civil Service. Personnel and manpower planning were dealt with by the Treasury, but their functions were seen as a sideline activity by senior Treasury administrators.

The Fulton Committee looked at the service from the point of view of management efficiency, and its recommendations to improve the service must be looked at in this light. The most important of the Report's recommendations were:

1. The setting up of a new Civil Service Department, under the Prime Minister, to be responsible for the service as a whole. This new department would take over from the Treasury its responsibilities for personnel matters, recruitment and training.
2. The development of a greater professionalism in management among civil servants.
3. The introduction of a new grading system which would be introduced to create an Administration Group. This would involve the abolition of the 'class system'.

4. A greater emphasis should be given to training. The Report recommended the establishment of a Civil Service College to provide training in administration for specialists, post-entry training for graduates and post-experience courses for managers.
5. There should be more interchange of personnel between the service and industry. (This has been slow to happen: in 1976 there were only 15 direct appointments from industry and commerce to the rank of Principal.) The Civil Service unions are generally opposed to the idea.
6. Specialists should be allowed more responsibility and should be allowed to reach the top.
7. Principles of accountable management should be applied to the service. Managers should be held responsible for their performance, which should be measured as objectively as possible. Each department should have a management services unit capable of carrying out efficiency audits of the department's work.
8. Departments should have planning and research units with responsibility for long-term planning. These units would be headed by a Senior Policy Adviser who would have unrestricted access to the Minister.
9. The Government should take steps to remove unnecessary secrecy in formulating policy.

7.6 THE POST-FULTON CIVIL SERVICE

Certain aspects of the Fulton Report were rapidly introduced. In 1968 the Civil Service Department was set up, and its new Permanent Secretary, who also became Head of the Home Civil Service, Sir William Armstrong, made a commitment to implementing the reforms. The Civil Service College opened in 1969, the Administrative, Executive and Clerical classes were merged in 1971 into the Administration Group, and other specialist grades and classes were reorganized and simplified. However, despite these changes, many aspects of the service remained unreformed. The Labour Prime Minister, Harold Wilson, rejected in 1968 the Committee's recommendation that relevance in applicants' degree courses should be looked for, and similarly the notion of special policy advisers with access to Ministers was also rejected. The Conservative Government elected in 1970, though in favour of modernizing the service, did not push hard in the direction of merging specialist and generalist grades. This left the specialists in their own hierarchies and effectively left the generalists in the advising positions to Ministers at the top of the service.

The Fulton Report was, in the main, concerned with the top 2000 or so senior civil servants. Its view was that a change to a service based on business lines, with specialized and accountable managers, would promote greater efficiency within the service as a whole. Though many of its recommendations have been accepted, the 'philosophy of the generalist' is still dominant in the service. In 1977 a House of Commons Select Committee under the chairmanship of Mr Michael English MP reported on the workings of the Civil Service and had an opportunity to monitor and report on post-Fulton developments. This had been the first Parliamentary investigation of the service since 1875 and it was concerned with such issues as the outlook, efficiency and accountability of the service, but it also looked at the political dimension, which was outside Fulton's brief, of the relationship between Ministers and civil servants. While the English Committee made many important recommendations, some of its more important were as follows.

First, with regard to the Civil Service Department, the Committee was critical of its role and wished to see internal auditing, manpower planning and cash limits being returned to the Treasury, although they did believe that the CSD should retain its responsibility for personnel matters, appointments, recruitment and training. The Committee saw the main problem as being the divorce between the Treasury's responsibility for expenditure planning and the CSD's for expenditure planning and efficiency audits, a divorce which has been partly responsible for the growth in the number of civil servants during recent periods of tight public expenditure control. The rationale for the separate existence of the CSD was put in a letter to *The Times* in July 1980 by the late Lord Armstrong, who as Sir William Armstrong was the first head of the CSD. He argued from his experience in the pre-Fulton Treasury that final decisions on personnel had to be made by the political boss, the Chancellor of the Exchequer, who, because of the economic pressures of his post, found the internal organization of the Civil Service very much a secondary concern. Lord Armstrong argued that the Prime Minister was the appropriate CSD 'boss', as some of the CSD's functions – such as the appointment and promotion of senior civil servants, changes in the machinery of government, and the recommendation to the Queen for the award of honours – were properly the responsibility of the Prime Minister.

Second, the English Committee made recommendations on the

relationship between senior civil servants and Ministers. The Committee believed that civil servants had gained too much power and often used their power to block organizational changes or altered the policies of Ministers when they were contrary to a departmental view. This view will be discussed in detail later in this section, but the Committee recommended that senior civil sevants should revert to the role they hold in constitutional theory – that of advising and taking instructions from Ministers.

Third, the Committee argued that the control which Parliament exercised over the Civil Service, Ministers and public spending was weak and argued for a new system of specialist select committees of MPs. Each committee would monitor an individual department. A similar system was introduced in 1979 into the Commons.

On training, the Committee was not impressed by the record of the Civil Service College and called for it to be wound up, although this has not happened. They found that, though the Fulton Committee had seen the College as being the dynamic force behind the new 'managerialism', it had in fact carried out only 10 per cent of the total Civil Service training. Neither had it promoted dialogue between the service and outside industry.

7.7 POLITICS AND ADMINISTRATION

The usual view of the relationship between politics and administration is that elected politicians *make policy* and salaried career administrators *implement policy*. The administrator's job in this view is 'politically neutral' and 'value free'. Policy is implemented regardless of which political party is in power and administrators are not concerned with questions of value, such as 'Is this the best policy for our society?', but rather with questions of fact and procedure, such as 'How can this policy be most effectively implemented?'. Constitutionally, this is the view of the relationship in Britain. It is the elected politicians who are accountable to the electorate for the decisions which are made. Administrators are accountable to politicians for the quality and efficiency of their work, but they do not carry *public accountability* in their role.

This view has been challenged on two fronts. First, it is argued that in fact senior administrators do make policy decisions. And second, it is claimed that the process of policy implementation is inherently political, albeit not party political.

In practical terms, an absolute distinction cannot be made between politics and administration. Senior civil servants do have an important role in decision-making. In reality, in all government departments there is a power balance. Ministers have manifesto pledges to implement, but senior civil servants do have their own views on policy (although they do not publicly express them) and they have a lifetime's experience in the public service on which to base those views. In evidence before the House of Commons Select Committee on the Treasury and the Civil Service in July 1980, Sir Douglas Wass, Permanent Secretary at the Treasury, is reported to have said that the role, influence and power of civil servants depend on the attitude of Ministers (see the *Guardian*, 3 July 1980). Presumably, strong Ministers with definite views get their way while weak Ministers are overwhelmed by Civil Service views. Sir Douglas is reported to have argued that where Ministers have only very broad objectives rather than definite plans, officials play a much larger role in the policy formulation process. Many examples of strong roles in policy formulation by civil servants can be cited. For example, during Edward Heath's premiership in the early 1970s, the Head of the Home Civil Service, Sir William (later Lord) Armstrong was publicly seen to be backing Government policy on income restraint. He was dubbed 'Deputy Prime Minister' by Mr Vic Feather, the then General Secretary of the TUC (see the *Observer*, 13 July 1980).

Through networks of contacts and committees, senior civil servants can control the framework within which policy is discussed, even if they do not make the final decisions themselves. Ministers may be guided towards policies which the Civil Service prefer and Ministers can be presented with information which backs up the Civil Service view.

The second argument put forward to counter the concept of politically neutral administration is concerned with the inherently *political* nature of the process of policy implementation. This is an argument which has been given less prominence than the role of senior civil servants in the policy formulation process. Attention has centred on policy-making because this is where Ministers are intimately involved. But Ministers are far less concerned with how policy is carried out, unless of course it goes wrong. Michael Hill, among other writers, in his book *The State, Administration and the Individual* (1976), has pointed out that to the ordinary citizen the way in which policies are implemented and services delivered is crucial. It is important to the way democracy works because the quality and efficiency of service provision affects the public's attitudes to public services and hence to government.

Administrators are allowed some *discretion* in the way they work, and the manner in which that discretion is exercised will affect the way in which services are delivered and who receives them. This is the *political* dimension in policy implementation. The ordinary citizen's contacts with bureaucracy are usually at the level of minor officials, receptionists and others, and the manner in which they are treated by these 'gatekeepers' will often depend on the administrator's own values. Officials may, consciously or unconsciously, exercise biases in operating their discretion, discriminating in favour of or against certain groups according to their own concept of who is or is not deserving of assistance. If this view is accepted then administration has a real political dimension and it reinforces the demands for more 'open government', so that administrative procedures can be more thoroughly scrutinized.

7.8 THE MONITORING AND EVALUATION OF POLICY

Introduction

At election time political parties (if they have been in Government) talk of 'standing on their record' or, if they have been in opposition, attack the record of the outgoing Government and put forward alternative policies. It is surprising, therefore, to find that in British Government there are few formal mechanisms for the detailed review and analysis of policy – means of measuring how successful policies have been. The Government spends huge sums of public money but there are few means of checking that it has been *effectively* spent, as opposed to checking that it has been *properly* spent. This lack of monitoring of policy has often been criticized but, except for a short period of time (discussed below), there have been few attempts to measure whether strategies to achieve objectives have been successful and have fulfilled the original aspirations of Parliament and the Government.

Output budgeting

In Britain, Governmental budgets have traditionally been 'input budgets', i.e. they have concentrated on the allocation of resources to spending programmes and activities (inputs). This is traditional accounting practice, but it is not a helpful means of measuring the *results* of the programmes on which money has been spent. In order to measure the outputs of policy a system known as *Programme Planning and Budgeting* was developed by the US Federal Government in the early 1960s. PPBS or 'output budgeting' is a planning system which relates the outcomes of policy decisions to the original policy objectives so that estimates of the effectiveness of those policies can be made. The Ministry of Defence first used an output budgeting system in the mid-1960s and PPBS was later adopted by other departments.

Linked to this development was the call in the Fulton Committee Report for more long-term planning in government. This would involve the establishment of policy units in individual departments so that medium-term and long-term objectives could be identified and resources planned to meet them. The intention was that resources would be allocated to areas of greatest need. In order to complete the planning process, evaluation and review procedures had to be introduced. This happened when in 1970 the new Conservative Government set up the Central Policy Review Staff – the 'Think Tank' – and introduced Programme Analysis and Review (PAR) as a means of evaluating individual programmes.

Programme Analysis and Review

PAR had a brief life in the Civil Service. Set up by the Heath Government in 1971, it was abolished by Mrs Thatcher's Government in 1979. It is generally thought to have been fully effective only in its first two or three years of operation. The PAR exercises provided a monitoring procedure for governmental programmes. The initial concept was that departmental PAR exercises should be fed into the annual PESC exercise. This would enable public expenditure to be planned in such a way that the alternative use of resources could be considered.

The problems which PAR quickly ran into were partly the result of the exercise's political nature. The original idea from the CPRS was that there would be about a dozen PAR exercises a year (although in fact the average was about half this number). The selection of the programmes for review was itself a political act and so there was internal controversy over what was going to be investigated and who was going to undertake the review. This led to delays in the exercises, which became more and more *ad hoc* and so did not always dovetail into the Budget cycle.

The other problem with the PAR exercise was that for many of the programmes investigated the original programme objectives were not sufficiently clear: what *exactly* did the Government want to achieve with the Urban Aid Programme? Politicians did not always want to be confronted with this type of question, which could show their objectives to be imprecise or their policies to be ineffective. For this reason PAR reports were kept secret. The Treasury were concerned that PAR might lead to demands for additional expenditure if it was shown that programmes were not working effectively for want of resources.

The enthusiasm for the exercise came to an end in 1973, when the Conservative Government faced the problems of the miners' strike and the oil crisis. The thinking of the Government turned from long-term planning to the solution of immediate problems. When the Labour Government came to power in 1974 it showed little enthusiasm for PAR exercises. With the abolition of PAR there are now no regular procedures for monitoring policy decisions in central government.

Efficiency and effectiveness

When PAR was abolished in 1979 the Conservatives did introduce exercises, under Sir Derek Rayner of Marks and Spencer Ltd, to look at the efficiency of various areas of Civil Service activity. Sir Derek had previously been employed by the 1970 Conservative Government. His task was to cut out waste and duplication and to reduce the number of QUANGOs. The Rayner exercises were not replacements for PAR, as the purpose was *not* to look systematically and analytically at policy options in a search for *effectiveness,* but rather they were concerned with the different issue of the search for *efficiency*. Difficult questions which have to be asked in effectiveness audits, such as 'What is poverty?' or 'What constitutes good health?' or 'How can programmes in this area be considered a success?', need not be considered in Rayner-style exercises. The efficiency exercises consider cost minimization to be all important, whereas in effectiveness audits consideration is given to the success of the outputs from programmes.

7.9 CIVIL SERVICE MANPOWER

In October 1980 there were 697 100 civil servants, of whom 153 900 were industrial civil servants (employed in such places as Royal Ordnance factories, naval dockyards, etc.), while the other 543 200 were involved in non-industrial occupations (Table 7.4). Non-industrial

Table 7.4 *Civil Service numbers*

	Numbers employed at October 1980 (full-time equivalent, '000s)
Agriculture, Fisheries and Food	14.0
Chancellor of the Duchy of Lancaster's Departments	1.1
Chancellor of the Exchequer's Departments (includes Treasury, Inland Revenue & Customs and Excise, National Surveys)	117.3
Education and Science	2.6
Employment	50.9
Energy	1.2
Environment	49.4
Foreign and Commonwealth	11.6
Home	34.9
Industry	9.1
Scotland	13.6
Social Services	100.6
Trade	9.5
Transport	13.3
Wales	30.3
Total civil departments	461.8
Royal Ordnance Factories	21.8
Defence	213.4
Total all departments	697.1
Of which:	
Non-industrial	543.2
Industrial	153.9

Source: Central Statistical Office, Monthly Digest of Statistics No. 427 July 1981. Reproduced with the permission of the Controller of Her Majesty's Stationery Office.

civil servants account for a little over 2 per cent of the total working population. The number has fallen from its high point in 1977, when a total of 745 600 were employed. The Conservative Government elected in 1979 came into office with a platform which included reducing the numbers employed in the public sector. This measure involved a temporary halt to recruitment and the imposition of strict cash limits on Civil Service salary bills. The cash limit for 1980–81 was 14 per cent, although this was exceeded by a pay settlement of 20 per cent. The idea of cash limits is that pay settlements above the limit are to be financed by manpower reductions.

In 1981 the Government's imposition of a 6 per cent pay limit for public sector workers led to industrial action by a number of key civil servants. The Government policy on borrowing was disrupted by the non-collection of certain taxes by the Inland Revenue. The Conservative Government target is to reduce the number of civil servants by 14 per cent during the lifetime of the Government, to produced a planned figure of 630 000 civil servants in 1984.

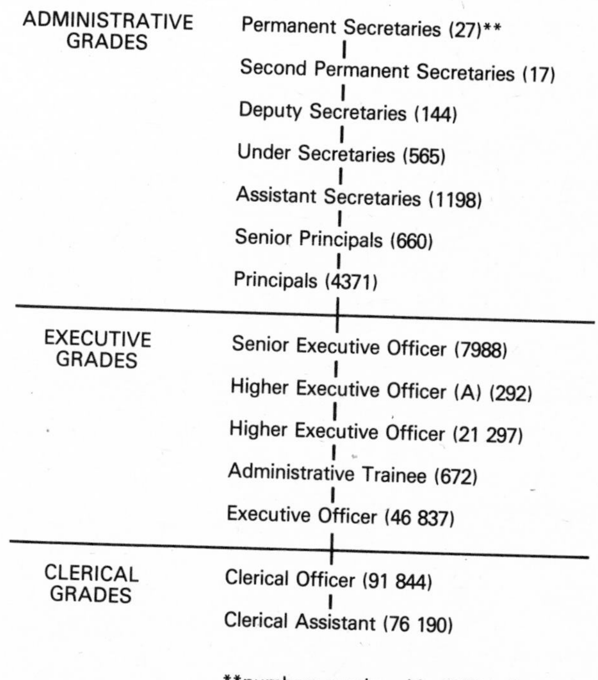

Figure 7.2 *The grading system of the Civil Service Administration Group*

Administration Group

The Administration Group within the Civil Service comprises the pre-Fulton Clerical, Executive and Administrative classes. The grading system is as shown in Fig. 7.2.

The Administrative Grades, which make up 3 per cent of the Civil Service's manpower (Principal and above), are concerned with policy-implementation ministerial advice and senior management. The Executive Grades (30 per cent of the service's manpower at Executive Officer and above) are concerned with middle management functions. Routine tasks are carried out by the Clerical Grades (67 per cent of the manpower).

7.10 THE BACKGROUND OF SENIOR CIVIL SERVANTS

The Fulton Report was particularly critical of the domination of the higher echelons of the Civil Service (Principal and above) by graduates from Oxford and Cambridge Universities with degrees in the Humanities. According to the Report this created an administrative élite who were ill equipped to deal with the management, planning and accounting tasks of modern government, and who did not have the background and expertise to make judgements on technical issues. In addition, it enhanced the overall 'philosophy of the generalist' which prevailed in the service.

Entrants to the Civil Service Administration Grades have socially exclusive backgrounds. The majority are from middle-class homes and were educated at public schools and the Universities of Oxford and Cambridge. For example, 85 per cent of those who joined the Civil Service in the years 1961 to 1965 and who will now be holding relatively senior positions came from middle-class homes. Of the same entrants, 63 per cent had been to public schools and 73 per cent had been to either Oxford or Cambridge. Of these entrants, 71 per cent had Arts degrees, mainly in History or Classics.

Entry into the Administration Grades is via the Administrative Trainee scheme which was introduced as a result of the Fulton Report. There is very strong competition for the 200 to 300 administrative trainee places offered annually. In 1974, for example, there were 1400 applications, of which only 200 were finally accepted. The selection test is rigorous, consisting of an examination, three days' testing and interviewing at the Civil Service Selection Board and a final interview. Between 1971 and 1975, between 123 and 211 applicants a year came from outside the Civil Service, usually straight from university, and another 19 to 53 were already employed in the Civil Service.

The best of the entrants are placed in the so-called fast stream for promotion. Over 85 per cent of external entrants and 65 per cent of internal administrative trainees were placed in the fast stream between 1971 and 1975.

Despite Fulton's call for a greater openness of the upper echelons of the service in its recruitment, the pattern has changed little in recent years. There are many explanations for this, including a bias in the Civil Service Commission responsible for recruitment in favour of a certain type of graduate, and the fact that certain types of school and Oxbridge have a tradition of public service and encourage their graduates to look to the Civil Service when planning a career. Certain ideas of Fulton's, for example encouraging late entrants to the Civil Service, more engineers and scientists applying for management positions, and a greater degree of transferability with industry and commerce, have not happened to any great extent. In years to come the Civil Service will continue to be dominated by people from a narrow social and educational background. The administrative problem is not that it is unfair in various respects, although this might be a valid point, but whether there is a sufficient breadth and range of expertise to deal with contemporary problems. At a time when local authorities are being more closely controlled by central government, when there is a desperate need for urban renewal, when industrial and economic policy is in a state of dilemma, it is necessary for the senior administrators in the Civil Service to be intimately acquainted with these and other pressing problems. The Fulton Report believed at the time that it reported that they were not, and since then recruitment patterns have not altered significantly.

7.11 COLLECTIVE BARGAINING IN THE CIVIL SERVICE

The Civil Service has for many years had a very high degree of unionization. Since the end of the First World War there has been a formal system of collective bargaining which originated in an arrangement arising out of the Whitley Committee Report of 1918–19. Since that date it has been official policy to encourage union membership in the

Civil Service. This has been seen as a means of promoting good staff relations and aiding negotiations over pay and conditions of service. Some 80 per cent of non-industrial civil servants are members of a trade union, and membership extends to the very top of the hierarchy. This figure of 80 per cent unionization compares with only 12 per cent union membership among white-collar workers in the manufacturing industries.

Civil Service unions

The unions, with a total membership of over 500 000, operating in the Civil Service are as follows.

The Civil and Public Services Association (CPSA)

(Membership 226 495, of whom some 40 000 are employed in the Post Office.) This is the recognized union for clerical, typing and machine-operating grades in the Civil Service. Some 70 per cent of its members are women.

Institution of Professional Civil Servants (IPCS)

(The second largest union in the Civil Service, with a membership of 99 000.) Its membership is among professional, scientific and technical grades and it embraces a wide range of professions including architects, engineers, photographers, catering officers, patents officers, etc.

Society of Civil and Public Servants (SCPS)

(Membership 105 000, including some 10 000 members in the Post Office and the United Kingdom Atomic Energy Authority.) The membership is in executive and directing grades.

Inland Revenue Staffs Federation (IRSF)

(Membership 67 000.) The federation has some 96 per cent of its potential membership and recruits many from clerical and tax officer grades. There is little recruitment among tax inspectors, who have their own association.

Civil Service Union (CSU)

(Membership 46 000.) It represents civil servants in basic and unskilled grades.

Prison Officers Association (POA)

(Membership 21 000.) Is is the recognized union for prison officers and staff in special hospitals.

Association of Government Supervisors and Radio Officers (AGSRO)

(Membership 12 000.) AGSRO represents non-manual staff primarily in technical supervision, electronic and radio operating staff. It also has members in the Civil Aviation Authority.

Association of First Division Civil Servants (FDA)

(Membership 8000.) The FDA represents senior grades within the Administrative Class and has 90 per cent of the total possible membership, ranging from administrative trainees to permanent secretaries.

Association of Her Majesty's Inspectors of Taxes

(Membership 2500.) It represents tax inspectors employed in the Inland Revenue.

7.12 PAY POLICY IN THE CIVIL SERVICE

Unlike in the private sector, the payment of employees in the public sector cannot be determined easily by their output or by the demand for or the supply of their labour. Yet within the Civil Service many people perform tasks very similar to those in the private sector, e.g. scientists, engineers, accountants, office managers, clerical assistants, etc. In order to establish an orderly system of pay the Royal Commission on Civil Service Pay 1956 (the Priestly Commission) recommended the establishment of a system which provided for a comparison of civil servants' work with that of outside industry and commerce. The aim was to take Civil Service pay out of the political arena and to avoid industrial action taking place within the service. The Priestly Commission did, however, reject the idea that the Civil Service should take a lead in setting payment rates in its various employment fields. Rather it believed the service should act as a 'good employer', setting rates above the average for particular jobs or professions.

In order that comparisons could be made the Civil Service Pay Research Unit was set up. This was an independent fact-finding and research body which produced reports on comparability which were then used as the basis of subsequent negotiations over pay and conditions. The difficulty with this comparability exercise was that successive governments saw the Unit's reports as potentially inflationary and they often proved embarrassing, especially in periods when the Government of the day wished to use the Civil Service as a leader in wage restraint.

In October 1980 the Conservative Government suspended the entire pay comparability exercise and refused to allow the Pay Research Unit to publish two outstanding reports. In its place the Government substituted cash limits to pay and introduced a 6 per cent limit for public sector pay claims. Additionally, the index-linked pensions for civil servants came in for considerable scrutiny. The idea of cash limits is that pay rises negotiated above the limit are to be paid for by a loss of jobs. The suspension of the comparability exercise has led to Civil Service pay being brought back into the political arena. In 1981 selective industrial action was taken by civil servants. Private consultants employed by the unions estimated that comparability awards of about 19 per cent would have been needed to keep Civil Service pay in line with similar work in the private sector at the time when the 6 per cent limit was introduced. In June 1981 the Government announced the abolition of the Pay Research Unit because, as they argued, it no longer 'commanded public confidence'. In its place the Government promised to establish an independent inquiry into Civil Service pay and pensions.

7.13 REGIONAL GOVERNMENT AND DEVOLUTION

Unitary and federal government

The United Kingdom has, as its name suggests, a *unitary* system of government; that is, there is one supreme law-making body for the state as a whole. (This has to an extent been altered as a result of Britain's membership of the European Community, but the description is still largely true.)

Many other states, including Canada, Australia, the United States of America and the German Federal Republic, have *federal* systems of government. In federal systems, state, regional or provincial governments have areas of sovereignty and the power to legislate on certain specified matters. The federal government in such states usually possesses legislative and executive powers only in matters which affect the national interest, such as defence or economic policy-making. The degree of power exercised by the federal government varies from state to state. In *confederations,* formed by the alliance of sovereign states, central power is weak, but even in federal states with strong central government the powers of constituent regional governments are usually protected in a constitution.

In federal systems there are obvious variations between regions, especially in the type and provision of public services, and it often happens that conflicts may arise between regional and federal governments. Examples of such conflict can be seen in Canada over the issue of the degree of autonomy which French-speaking Quebec province should enjoy from the rest of English-speaking Canada, and the control of revenue from oil finds in certain western provinces. The Liberal Party in Britain favours a federal government for the United Kingdom. Since 1894 they have been committed to home rule for England, Ireland, Scotland and Wales. In recent years they have been in favour of a system of regional government in which each region would have its own assembly or parliament and thus could reflect regional and local feelings, and which would minimize the control of the country from London.

Regional government in the United Kingdom

England does *not* have any regional government despite the arguments put forward by, among others, the Redcliffe-Maud Commission for a system of provincial councils to form an intermediate tier between central and local government. There is, however, a large area of *regional administration,* and in Scotland and Wales this is of considerable importance.

In England many central government departments, such as the Department of the Environment, the Department of Health and Social Security and the Department of Employment, organize many of their services on a regional basis; and many *ad hoc* authorities, including the Gas and Electricity Boards, Water Authorities and the National Health Service, are either organized regionally or substantial powers are given to regional tiers of administration. Regional administration in England is carried out by:

1. Regional Health Authorities.
2. Regional Water Authorities.
3. Regional offices of various central government departments.
4. Regional Economic Planning Boards.
5. Regional Economic Planning Councils.

In 1965 a system of regional economic planning was set up. The UK was divided into ten Economic Planning Regions: Scotland, Northern Ireland, Yorkshire and Humberside, the North West, Wales, the West Midlands, the East Midlands, the South West, the South East and East Anglia. In each region an *Economic Planning Council* was set up, consisting of representatives of government, trade unions, industry and commerce, and they were supported by civil servants who formed the *Economic Planning Boards.* The function of the boards and councils is to develop long-term strategies for the development of their region. Originally they were seen to be part of the indicative planning process associated with the 1965 National Plan, but they remained after the Plan's demise. They are now advisers to the Department of the Environment, which can accept or reject their recommendations.

Scotland and Wales have a much more devolved system of regional administration than England does. The respective Secretaries of State and their departments exercise the powers and responsibilities over matters such as education, housing, health, transport, water, etc. which in England are the responsibility of separate departments or *ad hoc* bodies.

Devolution

The separate nature of Scotland and Wales has led to repeated calls for a greater degree of governmental autonomy for both countries to reflect the national aspirations of a large proportion of their populations.

Both countries were at one time separate sovereign nations. Wales formed a union with England in 1536, and Scotland joined England in an Act of Union in 1707, although the two countries had had a joint monarchy since 1603. Both countries are distinctive in a number of ways. Scotland has its own legal system based on Roman rather than English common law (and for this reason separate legislation always has to be passed for Scotland). Its religion is different, with the established Church being Presbyterian. The other main difference in cultural terms is Scotland's education system, which differs in many respects from that of England. The main national feature of Wales is its language. Though only 30 per cent of the Welsh speak Welsh, its existence is a focal point for the nationalist movement. In terms of the separateness of Scotland and Wales, the major factor is that of identity; that is, many people of those countries see themselves as Scots and Welsh.

Both countries have nationalist movements whose history can be traced back to the last century. In both countries the movements, with their policy of eventual independence from England, took off in terms of mass support in the late 1960s. In 1966 and 1967 Plaid Cymru and the Scottish National Party won by-elections, and by 1968 they appeared to mount a serious challenge to the Labour Party in those countries. This was a serious threat to Labour, as Scotland and Wales are traditional strongholds. In order to attempt to placate the rising nationalist tide the Labour Government appointed a Royal Commission on the Constitution to inquire into possible forms of devolved government. Neither party fared particularly well in the 1970 general election, and only one seat was gained in Scotland. The Welsh Nationalists gained 13.9 per cent of the vote and the Scottish Nationalists 12.2 per cent in their respective countries. Nevertheless, the pressure for some form of greater autonomy or devolution of power continued to build up. The higher-than-average levels of unemployment in both countries, general industrial decline, lower-than-average living standards, and a feeling of neglect by politicians and civil servants in London were all relevant factors. In Scotland an important issue was that of the discovery of North Sea oil. The Scottish National Party argued that the oil revenues should stay in Scotland and be used exclusively for Scotland's benefit rather than be seen as a United Kingdom resource.

In the two elections of 1974 the Nationalists performed well. In

February 1974 the Scottish Nationalists gained seven seats and Plaid Cymru two, and in October 1974 this was increased to eleven and three respectively. In October 1974 this represented 30.4 per cent of the Scottish vote and 10 per cent of the Welsh vote. For the latter part of the 1974–79 Labour Government's life the two parties had a substantial influence because the Government was a minority one.

In 1975 the Royal Commission on the Constitution reported. The Kilbrandon Report, as it was known, was divided into two reports. In the first, eight out of eleven members of the Commission supported a scheme for legislative devolution for Scotland. This would have involved transferring most legislative powers and the functions of the Scottish Office to an assembly elected by the single transferable vote. Scotland would have had its own executive and the post of Secretary of State for Scotland would have disappeared. Six of the eleven members wanted a similar scheme for Wales. A scheme for English devolution gained no support, but there was a majority in favour of a tier of regional local government.

In the second report – the minority report – a system of seven assemblies, elected by STV, was proposed – one each for Scotland and Wales and the other five for English regions. The assemblies were to have had substantial powers.

Table 7.5 *Referenda results*

	Actual Voters			*Registered Voters*		
	Yes (%)	*No (%)*	*Turnout (%)*	*Yes (%)*	*No (%)*	*Did not vote (%)*
Scotland	52	48	63	33	30	37
Wales	20	80	58	12	46	42

Note: figures have been rounded.

In 1978 two Acts were passed giving Scotland and Wales devolved government. The Scotland Act 1978 provided for a devolved assembly in Edinburgh with extensive legislative powers. The Wales Act 1978 provided for a similar assembly in Cardiff, but the Welsh Assembly was not to be given legislative power, although it would have had control over substantial areas of administration. Both Acts provided for devolution subject to the holding of a referendum. There was a requirement that 40 per cent of the *registered voters* (not just those who voted) should be in favour. In the event, in referenda held in March 1979, 32.9 per cent of the Scottish registered voters voted 'Yes', as did 11.9 per cent of the Welsh (see Table 7.5). As a result the measures were not implemented.

Northern Ireland

The exception to the unitary state of the United Kingdom was the province of Northern Ireland, which from 1922 to 1972 had its own Parliament and Government at Stormont. The Northern Ireland Parliament was set up by the Government of Ireland Act 1920, which also gave independence to the Irish Free State (later Eire). Under the Act Northern Ireland continued to send representatives to Westminster, but all internal matters were subject to the jurisdiction of the Irish Parliament and Government. Westminster was still responsible for defence, economic policy, taxation and trade. Northern Ireland had its own executive, with a Prime Minister and Cabinet. The Parliament at Stormont was bicameral. There was a Senate with 26 seats (24 elected by the Northern Ireland House of Commons plus the Lord Mayors of Belfast and Londonderry). The House of Commons had 52 members.

Because of the sectarian nature of Northern Irish society, the politics has reflected the division of the community into Protestants and Catholics. The Protestants make up two-thirds of the population. Because of their numerical advantage, the Unionist Party (Protestant) won every election since 1921 and so the Catholics were excluded from power. Additionally, Catholics were discriminated against. Housing and employment (where these were controlled by local government) went predominantly to Protestants, and electoral boundaries were gerrymandered to reduce Catholic representation even further. Civil rights were the main issue which in the late 1960s led to the beginning of the present troubles. The violence of the years between 1969 and 1972 led the British Government to pass the Northern Ireland (Temporary Provisions) Act 1972. Executive powers were transferred to the Secretary of State for Northern Ireland and to the Northern Ireland Office. The Stormont Parliament was prorogued.

In 1973, as a result of the Sunningdale Agreement, an attempt was made to reintroduce representative government into the province. A power-sharing Executive and Assembly were set up by the Northern Ireland Constitution Act 1973. The new Assembly of 78 members was elected by proportional representation, and the Executive was chosen by the Northern Ireland Secretary. Brian Faulkner, a former Unionist Prime Minister, became Chief Executive and his deputy was Gerry Fitt (formerly of the Catholic Social Democratic Labour Party). The Executive was brought down shortly afterwards by the Protestant workers' strike which was called to object to the notion of a Council of Ireland contained in the Sunningdale Agreement. As a result direct rule was re-imposed.

In July 1981 the then Northern Ireland Secretary, Humphrey Atkins, proposed the setting up of a Northern Ireland Council. The proposal was for 50 already elected representatives – MPs, Members of the European Parliament, and certain district councillors – to form an all-party council. This would have only an advisory function and would be consulted by the Secretary of State in his administration of the province's affairs.

7.14 ADMINISTRATION AND ENFORCEMENT OF THE LAW

English law is divided into two main branches, civil and criminal (see Figs 7.3 and 7.4). The court structure broadly follows this categoriz-

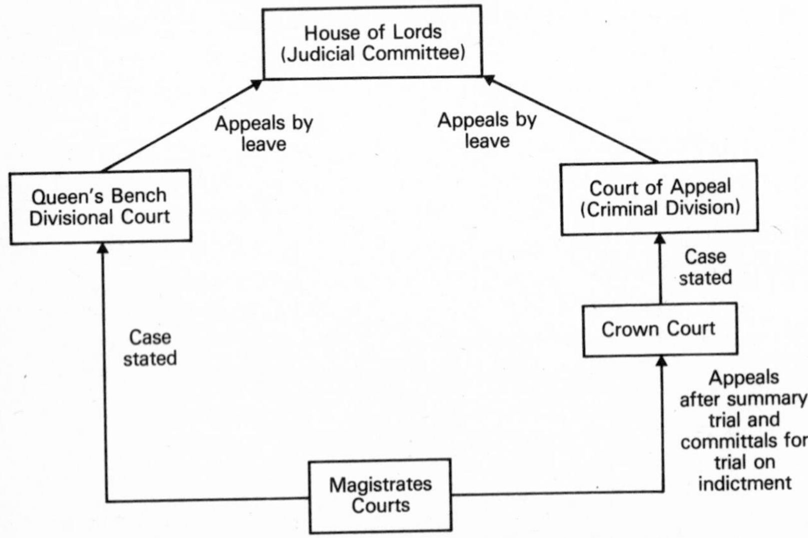

Figure 7.3 *Courts of law (criminal) in England and Wales*

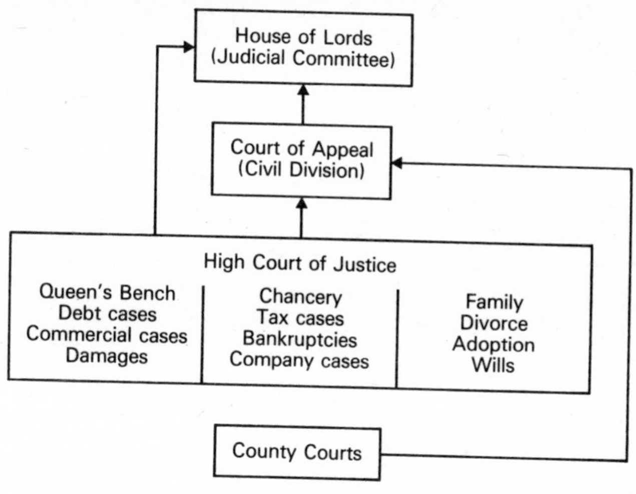

Figure 7.4 *Courts of law (civil) in England and Wales*

ation, although many courts have jurisdiction in both areas. Briefly, criminal law is that area of law where the state punishes an act of disobedience. Criminal acts are seen as being harmful to the community as a whole and not only to the individuals or group who have been wronged. Criminal acts include theft, rape, murder, assault, etc. The punishment for crimes committed ranges from fines for minor offences to life imprisonment.

Civil law is concerned in the main with rights and duties of individuals towards each other. Breaches of the civil law affect the rights of particular individuals and do not damage the community as a whole. Whereas in criminal law it is the state which enforces the law, in civil matters it is the citizens or groups of citizens who bring actions to establish their rights against other citizens. There is no concept of punishment in civil law, although damages may have to be paid if a citizen infringes the rights of others. The civil law covers the following areas:

1. *Law of contract.* This concerns the area of law dealing with legally enforceable promises.
2. *Law of torts.* Briefly, these can be defined as civil wrongs, and include negligence, nuisance, trespass and defamation.
3. *Family law.* This is the area of law concerned with the rights and duties of members of families and with divorce, adoption, etc.

4. *Property law*. This concerns the rights which citizens have over property – rights to ownership, leaseholds, etc.

Magistrates Courts

Less serious criminal offences are tried summarily, i.e. without a jury. Cases are heard by lay (legally unqualified) Justices of the Peace or by legally qualified Stipendiary magistrates. Magistrates Courts deal with 97 per cent of all criminal cases. Magistrates can pass sentences of only up to six months' imprisonment, but they can send a convicted person to the Crown Court for sentence if their powers are too limited. For more serious crimes, Magistrates Courts conduct committal proceedings to determine whether the person charged has a case to answer before the Crown Court. Appeals are to the Crown Court, where the appeal takes the form of a re-hearing of the case. There is also appeal to the Divisional Court of the Queen's Bench of the High Court. This happens if it is alleged that magistrates have exceeded their powers or jurisdiction. Magistrates Courts have certain civil functions in matrimonial and family matters, and Magistrates also form the Juvenile Courts.

Crown Courts

The Crown Courts were set up in 1971 by the Courts Act and replaced the Courts of Assize and Quarter Sessions. The Crown Courts have jurisdiction over serious criminal offences (trials on indictments). They are staffed by High Court judges, circuit judges and recorders (part-time judges). Appeals lie with the Court of Appeal (Criminal Division), which draws its membership from the Lord Chief Justice, the Lords Justices of Appeal and High Court judges. Judges sit with juries of twelve. Appeals may be made to the House of Lords.

County Courts

County Courts were set up in 1846 to deal quickly and cheaply with relatively minor civil matters including breaches of contract, uncontested divorce cases, mortgages, sales of land, etc. The majority of cases are dealt with by these local courts. They are staffed by circuit judges.

The High Court

The High Court is divided into three divisions:

1. *The Family Division,* which exercises jurisdiction over matrimonial matters, adoption and wardship.
2. *The Chancery Division,* which hears cases relating to property, mortgages, dissolution of companies and partnerships, income tax and trusts.
3. *The Queen's Bench Division,* which deals with all other matters not covered by the other two divisions. It exercises supervision over criminal matters and over the jurisdiction of tribunals and other public bodies. The division hears cases of a commercial nature. The Court of Appeal (Civil Division) hears appeals on matters of fact and matters of law from the High Court and on questions of law from County Courts.

House of Lords

This is the highest court in the land, except on matters of European Community law, which are within the jurisdiction of the European Court (see Chapter 9). The House of Lords hears appeals from courts in Scotland and Northern Ireland as well as from courts in England and Wales. In practice the judicial function of the House of Lords is exercised by its Appellate Committee. This is made up of nine Law Lords, the Lord Chancellor and any members of the House of Lords who have held high judicial office. The Court is usually made up of five members. Appeals to the Lords may be on civil or criminal matters, but they can be taken only on matters which are thought to be of public importance. Occasionally, in civil matters, the Court of Appeal may be 'leapfrogged' and appeals can be taken directly from the High Court.

The Judicial Committee of the Privy Council

The Privy Council is the Monarch's advisory council. At one time, when the Monarch held all executive power, it had an important function. Today, however, the Council has few functions except that Orders in Council are still a principal means of giving effect to delegated legislation. Membership of the Privy Council, denoted by the title 'Right Honourable', is nowadays a titular honour.

The Council has a Judicial Committee which is the final court of appeal for a number of Commonwealth countries, colonies and dependencies.

Court structure in Scotland

Scottish law is entirely different from English law, as it is based on Roman and not English common law. Because of this, the administration of justice in Scotland is entirely separate from that in England and Wales, both in the structure of its courts and in the legal personnel. In brief, the structure of the courts is as follows.

Civil

The Sheriff Courts are similar to the English County Courts but have a wider jurisdiction and are the lower civil courts. The *Court of Session* is the superior civil court and has jurisdiction over the whole country. Appeal from it is to the House of Lords.

Criminal

Minor cases are dealt with by *District Courts,* which were set up through the District Courts (Scotland) Act 1975. They are a system of lay summary courts and are based on the districts and island areas of local government. The judges are Justices of the Peace. The bulk of criminal work is carried out by the *Sheriff Courts,* which have sole jurisdiction over serious crimes. Scotland is divided into sheriffdoms, which are then further subdivided into sheriff court districts. The Sheriff sits with a jury of 15 but has limited powers of sentence. The *High Court of Justiciary* is Scotland's supreme criminal court. It is both a trial and an appeal court, dealing with all appeals against conviction or sentences, or both. There are no further appeals to the House of Lords.

7.15 THE POLICE

Law enforcement in Britain is the responsibility of the police forces, of which there are 52 (43 in England and Wales, eight in Scotland and one in Northern Ireland), employing approximately 125 000 policemen and policewomen. The county councils in England and Wales and the regional authorities in Scotland are the police authorities. The City of London has its own force, the Metropolitan Police Force, which is administered by the Home Secretary, and in Northern Ireland the Royal Ulster Constabulary is the responsibility of the Secretary of State for Northern Ireland. The 1962 Royal Commission on the Police rejected the idea of a national and unified force and argued that the police forces were best administered by local government.

Outside London the police forces under their chief constables are maintained by local authorities through their police committees. These are made up of two-thirds elected councillors and one-third magistrates. The committees are responsible for providing an efficient force and supervising its use. Fifty per cent of the finance for the police comes from an Exchequer grant which is conditional on the Home Secretary being satisfied that an area is being properly policed. Inspectors are used for this purpose. The Home Secretary also has other controls, including those in areas of administration, grading, pay, appointments and manpower. The Police Act 1964 gives the Home Secretary the duty of promoting police efficiency.

The question of public accountability arises with the organization of the police forces. The local authority is not in control of the police: the control of a police force rests with the chief constable. An authority can dismiss a chief constable for inefficiency, but only with the approval of the Home Secretary. The issue of accountability of forces to elected councillors has been raised in the wake of the urban riots in 1981. A number of commentators have suggested that methods of policing have aggravated tensions in certain inner-city areas, particularly where there are large minority communities. In August 1981 there was public disagreement in Liverpool between the Chairman of the Merseyside Police Committee and the Chief Constable in the aftermath of the riots in the Toxteth area of the city. The Police Committee had called for greater control over the police so that they could direct policing methods, an area which the Chief Constable regarded as his responsibility. The intention behind the strict division of responsibilities was to leave policing methods free from political influence, but this does mean that the police are not accountable to elected representatives for the way in which a community is policed. A similar argument was put forward in London after the Labour Party won the GLC elections in May 1981. As a result of criticism of police action during the Brixton riots the Council called for the transfer of the

Metropolitan Police from the Home Secretary. The GLC set up a police committee, although it has no powers in this area.

The other issue which has caused a great deal of public concern is the system of dealing with complaints against the police. Until the 1964 Police Act a chief constable investigated complaints about his own force. Since 1964 it has been possible to request a chief constable of another force to conduct the investigation. Reports of all investigations are sent to the Director of Public Prosecutions if it is suspected that a criminal offence has been committed. However, this procedure was seen by many to be unsatisfactory. It was argued that it did not conform to the rules of natural justice, as it left the police as judges in their own cause. The Police Act 1976 established a Police Complaints Board to deal with complaints from members of the public against the police. Under this system the chief constable is assisted by lay commoners when dealing with complaints.

As a result of the publication, in November 1981, of the report by Lord Scarman on the Brixton riots of 1981, the Home Secretary, William Whitelaw, promised to set up a review of police complaints procedure.

Lord Scarman called for more consultation between the police and the local communities they serve, and recommended that police authorities and chief police officers should have powers to set up local liaison committees. This report also recommended that an independent element be introduced into police complaints procedures.

ASSIGNMENTS

A7.1 Write short notes on the functions and work of the following Civil Service departments:

(a) the Treasury;
(b) the Civil Service Department;
(c) the Department of the Environment;
(d) the Department of Education and Science;
(e) another Civil Service department of your choice.

A7.2 The Fulton Committee's report of 1968 marked a landmark in the history of the British Civil Service. Comment on:

(a) the Report's main conclusions;
(b) the moves that have been made since 1968 to implement the proposals contained in the Report.

In answering (b) you should refer to the House of Commons' Expenditure Committee Report on the Civil Service of 1977 (the English Committee Report).

A7.3 Civil Service unions have become more militant in recent years. Give reasons for this change in attitude and discuss any constitutional problems that you can see arising from industrial actions by civil servants.

A7.4 It is argued in many quarters that the present system of police accountability to elected representatives is inadequate. State why this view has arisen and whether you agree with it.
Outline a proposal for a new system of police accountability and state how your proposal would affect the freedom of action of chief constables.

8
Public Enterprises and Public Bodies

8.1 PUBLIC ENTERPRISES

The Government of the United Kingdom has an important stake in industry. State-owned enterprises produce some 12 per cent of the country's total output, account for 17 per cent of gross investment and employ just over 2 million people (or 8 per cent of the labour force). In 1979 they produced goods and services to the value of £18 200 million and earned nearly £3000 million for Britain overseas. Their economic health and success are therefore of major importance to the rest of the economy.

The term 'public enterprise' refers to those industries which produce goods and services for sale and which are owned by the Government (see Table 8.1). Firms which are not *owned* and controlled by the Government are said to be private enterprise. There is often some confusion over the use of the term 'public'. For example, most public-sector organizations have a legal incorporation as *public corporations*, and should *not* be confused with *public limited companies*, which are private enterprise. The 'public' in public corporation refers to the Government's ownership on behalf of the general public, whereas in public limited companies the term 'public' implies that shares in them are available for purchase by the general public. Unfortunately, even this distinction is becoming less clear. Certain Government-owned industries, like Rolls Royce and BL, are public limited companies.

Table 8.1 *Examples of public enterprises*

Energy/Resources	*Transport*	*Manufacturing*[a]	*Communications*	*Finance*
National Coal Board	British Rail	British Aerospace[c, d]	British Broadcasting Corporation	Bank of England
Atomic Energy Authority	British Transport Docks Board	British Steel Corporation	Independent Broadcasting Authority	
British National Oil Corporation	British Waterways Board	British Shipbuilders	Post Office Corporation	
Electricity Council	National Bus Company	British Leyland[b]	British Tele-communications	
Central Electricity Generating Board and 12 area boards	National Freight Corporation[c]	Rolls Royce[b]		
North of Scotland Hydro-Electricity Board	Scottish Transport Group			
South of Scotland Electricity Board	British Airways Board[c]			
British Gas Corporation				
National Water Council and regional water authorities				

[a] This is not a complete list, as it does not include subsidiaries and holdings of the National Enterprise Board.
[b] These are wholly Government-owned limited companies and for statistical reasons are not included in the public sector. Former NEB subsidiaries, they are now directly accountable to the Secretary of State for Industry.
[c] These are no longer public corporations but Companies Act companies. In the case of the National Freight Corporation it was the Government's to sell the corporation to its workers.
[d] The Government now owns only a 48 per cent stake.

From 1981 British Airways, British Aerospace and the National Freight Corporation became Companies Act companies (i.e. public limited companies) and shares in them are available for purchase by the public, although the Government will remain a major shareholder. The reason behind the creation of these *mixed enterprises* is to provide additional sources of finance as well as to engender a greater thrust for efficiency and profits. These industries will be accountable to private shareholders, who will be able to withdraw their capital if they are dissatisfied with the industry's performance.

The term 'nationalized industry' is often used to describe the public ownership of industry. Strictly speaking it applies only to those industries which the Government has taken over, or nationalized, by the compulsory purchase of their shares. Certain Government-owned industries, like the Post Office and the Atomic Energy Authority, were started by Government and hence were never nationalized, but it is common to refer to all Government-owned industries as nationalized industries.

Municipalization refers to the ownership of industries by local as opposed to central government. Examples are the Greater London Council's ownership of London Transport and the ownership of provincial airports and bus services by local authorities.

What is a public corporation?

The main characteristics of public corporations, which is the legal status of most Government-owned industries, are as follows:

1. They have corporate status. They can enter into contracts on their own behalf. They can sue and be sued.
2. They can supply goods and services to the public and industry and charge the customer for them.
3. They aim to be self-financing. By law they are supposed to charge economic prices which will at least cover costs. This aim is not always achieved and in practice nationalized industries are heavily dependent on Government financing. This is because many of the first public corporations were not commercially viable, yet the Government believed that their continued existence was needed by the nation.
4. Their employees are not civil servants, but are the employees of the individual corporations.
5. Each industry is managed by a board, the members of which are appointed by the appropriate Minister. Ministers have the power

to dismiss board members and their chairmen.

8.2 THE POLITICS OF PUBLIC OWNERSHIP

Britain's nationalized industries have passed into the hands of the Government for a variety of reasons. The period of the Labour Government 1945–51 saw the major acts of nationalization. During these years coal, iron and steel, the railways and the canals were nationalized, civil aviation was re-organized, the Bank of England was taken into public ownership, and electricity and gas, which had been partially nationalized, were fully nationalized. These acts of nationalization were carried out partly for reasons of socialist dogma – that 'the commanding heights of the economy' should be controlled by the state for the public benefit – but also out of necessity. Many industries, such as the railways and the mines, had been seriously depleted of capital investment as a result of the Second World War and only Government had the finance necessary to re-equip and re-organize them.

Much political controversy surrounds public ownership. It is an area of major difference between the main political parties. The Labour Party has had the paramount role in establishing and supporting public ownership, since it has seen public ownership as a means of ending private monopoly power, making industries more accountable to the community, and achieving the planning of the economy. Additional measures of nationalization are usual features of Labour Party election manifestoes.

The Conservative Party believes that the public sector of industry is largely inefficient and lacks the cutting edge of competition which private enterprises have. It believes that governments should not own industry. Conservative Governments have carried out acts of denationalization, e.g. of the iron and steel industry in 1953, and the 'hiving off' of certain nationalized concerns such as Thomas Cook (the travel agents) and the Carlisle state brewery in 1973. The Conservative Government elected in 1979 came into office with the intention of selling shares in British Petroleum, British Aerospace, British Airways and the British National Oil Corporation. In 1981 it decided to dispose of the shares in Cable and Wireless Ltd and to denationalize some of British Rail's subsidiaries, such as Sealink Ferries, and its hotels. The state bus monopoly has been broken by the 1980 Transport Act. Private equity capital has been introduced into the British National Oil Corporation.

Conservative attitudes to nationalized industries have been dogmatic as well as pragmatic. They were pragmatic when in 1971 Rolls Royce Ltd went bankrupt and, to save the company, a Conservative Government nationalized it. But they have been doctrinaire when it comes to such areas as capital funding. Most nationalized industries have to obtain funds for capital investment from the state. They cannot go to the capital market like private enterprises. The amount of money they can obtain from Government was laid down by the 1979 Conservative Government in EFLs (external financing limits) which represent the maximum sum which any public-sector industry can call on in any year, any excess being deducted the next year. The Conservatives believe that funds going to public enterprises 'crowd out' funds available to private enterprise and have, therefore, used the EFLs to limit nationalized industry investment programmes.

Public enterprise can be seen as an area between the major political parties in which differences over the ownership and control of the economy come into sharp focus. But political differences have caused major difficulties for the industries themselves. They have been used as a means of controlling inflation, as an extension of the social services (for example British Rail has a statutory obligation to run socially necessary, financially non-viable services as a result of its 'public service obligation'), as a means of reflating the economy and at other times of deflating it. Nationalized industries are expected to follow often contradictory policies and ones which change as Governments change. In the 1970s they were expected both to be profitable and to hold down prices. In 1980 the Post Office had to return some of its profits to the customers of its telephone service because it had made too much profit.

8.3 INVESTMENT IN NATIONALIZED INDUSTRIES

As the nationalized industries undertake some 17 per cent of the nation's investment, it is important that a suitable rate of return from it is achieved. The aim of White Papers on nationalized industries in 1961, 1967 and 1978 has been to ensure that the rate is comparable with that achieved by the private sector.

The latest White Paper, *The Nationalised Industries* (Cmnd 7131) (1978), introduced the idea of the *required rate of return* (RRR). The RRR makes use of the concept of 'opportunity cost' of capital, i.e.

resources are looked at in terms of what other uses could be made of them. This is set as a return which industries are required to make on new investment. The RRR is set at 5 per cent in real terms (that is, after allowance has been made for inflation). This figure was arrived at after consideration of the returns being earned by firms in the private sector. As a Treasury *Economic Progress Report* of July 1981 has shown, this means that the real rate of return has to be more than the cost of borrowing. The opportunity cost that resources could yield if invested elsewhere is greater than the nominal (actual) cost of capital borrowing.

However, the measurement of the efficiency of capital investment by nationalized industries is a very difficult matter. Much investment is undertaken as much for social reasons as for economic ones. Arguments about the electrification of the railways in the early 1980s were as much about the effect of this on helping the economy out of the recession as they were about the value for money of the investment. Nationalized industries can borrow only from the Government. In recent years the amounts that a particular industry can borrow have been limited by a form of cash limit known as the external financing limits (EFLs). In June 1981 the National Economic Development Council set up a task force to consider the desirability of nationalized industries being able to borrow directly from the market like private-sector organizations. The argument is that a proper market relationship would be introduced into borrowing. The lenders would require an agreed rate of return which would force nationalized industries to look at the efficiency of their operations. On the other side, it is argued that the lending to nationalized industries could 'crowd out' funds currently available to the private sector, and that nationalized industries would find the cost of borrowing in the money markets higher than the cost of borrowing from the Government.

8.4 THE CONTROL OF PUBLIC CORPORATIONS

Managerial control

Public corporations are given powers under Acts of Parliament to manage their own particular areas of concern. For example, under the Coal Industry Nationalization Act 1946 the National Coal Board was established and was charged to secure the efficient development of the coal mining industry and to make supplies available as seems best in the national interest.

Each corporation has a chairman who, together with the board, is responsible for the industry's management. The chairman and the board members, some of whom may be part-time, are appointed by the appropriate Minister. The board of each industry is accountable to the Minister for the efficient running of that industry. Their responsibility is for the day-to-day operation of the industry and the achievement of its objectives.

Ministerial control and public accountability

In order to ensure public accountability for the operation of nationalized industries Ministers have statutory power over the operation of the corporations. These powers include the power to appoint and dismiss board members (this power is frequently used and tenure is often for a limited period) and the power of veto over a large number of activities, particularly capital spending programmes. Ministers have the power to override the decisions of a corporation's board if they feel that their action is in the national interest.

Ministerial control over nationalized industries is an area which has caused a great deal of difficulty and the resignation of a number of chairmen. The problem lies with the dividing line between public accountability and managerial control. Ministers have the power to give directions of a general character and can take major policy decisions, and these powers may be seen by a board as direct intervention in its responsibilities for day-to-day operations. Conflicts between particular industries and Ministers are most likely to occur if Ministerial intervention is seen to be for reasons of political expediency rather than as part of a long-term plan. British Governments have rarely had a corporate approach to the public sector in the way that Continental countries like France have to their state-owned industries. This lack of clear, long-term objectives has led to frequent public disagreements. The chairmen of public corporations often see themselves as public figures and are prepared to publicize their disagreements with Ministers. For example, in June 1980 Sir Charles Villiers resigned as Chairman of British Steel after a 13-week steel strike. He and his Minister, Sir Keith Joseph, had an acrimonious public exchange in the press about each other's actions during the strike. Sir Keith blamed British Steel's management for failing to keep him adequately informed, while the Chairman of British Steel complained of unwarranted interference.

Because public corporations often see themselves as political footballs, their chairmen have founded a pressure group, the Nationalized Industries Chairmen's Group, to push for Government to provide them with clear and long-term objectives. In the early 1980s the group has called for an end to denationalization and the abandonment of external financing limits on capital spending.

The accountability of public corporations

Attempts have been made to clarify the relationship between Ministerial and managerial control (Fig. 8.1). The National Economic

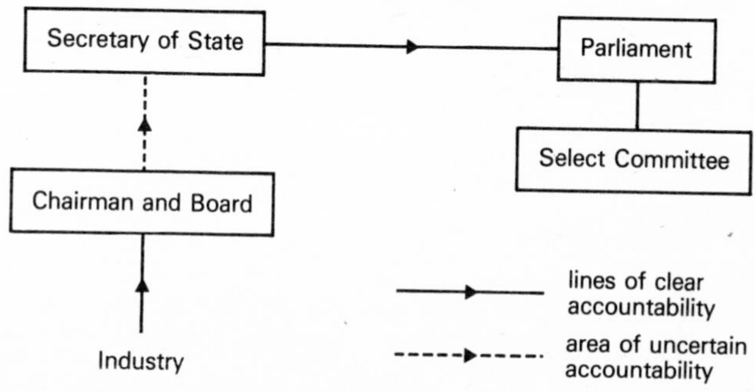

Figure 8.1 *The accountability of public corporations*

Development Office undertook a wide-ranging study in 1975–76. Its report, *A Study of United Kingdom Nationalised Industries* (the McIntosh Report), was published in 1976. The report's solution to the problem of control and political interference was to segregate politics and management. This was to be done by the creation of a two-board system. A policy council would act as an intermediary between the Minister and the management board. It would lay down corporate aims and the strategies required to achieve them, and would monitor results. It would also decide on criteria for judging success or failure. The policy council would be made up of senior civil servants, trade unionists, some independents and senior managers.

The McIntosh system was not accepted in the 1976 *White Paper on Nationalised Industries*. The NEDO Policy Council idea was rejected because it was seen as providing yet another tier of administration without clearing up the problem of accountability. As a result of the White Paper, civil servants were drafted on to the boards of corporations in order to draw Whitehall and the industries closer together.

Other ideas have been suggested to overcome the problem, including a national forum of nationalized industry chairmen and Ministers to thrash out problems. Other ideas have seen the problem as being endemic in the current organization of the industries, and the argument has been put forward that all nationalized industries should be made Companies Act companies with the shares being held by semi-autonomous holding companies along the lines of the National Enterprise Board. These holding companies would act rather like the McIntosh Report's policy councils and provide a forum for setting long-term objectives for each industry. As companies the industries would be able to borrow in the market without Treasury control.

Parliamentary control

The ultimate accountability of nationalized industries is to Parliament. MPs can ask questions of the appropriate Minister providing they come into the area of the Minister's responsibility. The questions have to be of a general character or in the national interest. Before the reorganization of the Select Committee system in 1979, there was a Select Committee on Nationalized Industries. It played a leading role in highlighting many of the problems associated with the operations of nationalized industries. With the new system of Select Committees the appropriate departmental committee is responsible for investigating individual industries' affairs. The main committees concerned are Energy, Trade and Industry. They can set up sub-committees to investigate particular industries' operations, or they can set up a joint committee to consider nationalized industries as a whole.

8.5 THE NATIONAL ENTERPRISE BOARD

The National Enterprise Board (NEB) was set up by the Industry Act 1975. It was the creation of the then Labour Government and its original function was to act as a state holding company which would own shares in and provide capital to joint stock companies. The NEB was originally provided with funds to make investments in firms and to purchase equities. Its original aim was 'to develop or assist the economy, promote industrial efficiency and international competitiveness and provide, maintain or safeguard productive employment in any part of the UK'. The Labour Government saw the NEB as a means of channelling funds to British industry and at the same time retaining accountability for the money which the Government had invested. Conservative opponents saw the NEB's shareholdings in private enterprise as a means of 'backdoor nationalization'.

Towards the end of 1979 the NEB had investments in more than 30 companies, including Fairey Engineering Holdings Ltd, ICL, Twinlock Ltd and Ferranti Ltd. The NEB was additionally given the responsibility to act as an umbrella organization for 'lame duck' industries, i.e. those industries which had gone bankrupt but which the Government wished to put on a new commercial footing rather than see them go into liquidation. Included among these were Rolls Royce Ltd, British Leyland and the toolmakers Alfred Herbert Ltd.

The NEB was set up as an organization which would perform a function not currently being carried out in Britain – that of channelling large sums of public money into British industry where there was obvious social need (e.g. 'lame ducks') or where the investments were too risky for ordinary investors to take risks (e.g. in high-technology industries). The NEB has, for example, set up Inmos, an NEB subsidiary, to provide Britain with a manufacturer of advanced microcircuits.

The role of the NEB was drastically curtailed by the Conservative Government after it came into power in May 1979, which resulted in all the directors of the NEB handing in their resignations. In 1980 another spate of resignations, including those of the new Chairman and the Chief Executive, was brought about by the Secretary of State for Industry, Sir Keith Joseph's, further reduction of the Board's powers. This included the sale of the NEB holdings in Fairey, Ferranti and ICL, bringing in profits of £2 million, £54 million and £13 million respectively.

After 1979 the Secretary of State for Industry took over direct control of British Leyland and Rolls Royce Ltd from the NEB, allowing them to report directly to him as other nationalized industries do.

At the same time the NEB lost its investment independence under the 1980 Industry Act. The NEB must now submit its financial programmes annually to the Secretary of State for his approval. Its investment role is severely limited, as it can now invest in an industry only if other sources of finance have been tried and have failed. The NEB must also show that its investments have the prospect of 'an adequate rate of return within a reasonable period', and they have to be made with the maximum of private-sector financial participation. What this means in practice is that the NEB would be limited to investing in companies involved in high technology, where the risks are too high for private capital, and to providing aid in assisted areas with higher-than-average rates of unemployment.

The NEB must now run down its equity holdings in private companies. The effect of this will be to leave it as a body to harbour 'lame ducks' where there is no private demand for their equity.

To sum up, the NEB operates in the following areas:

1. It is a provider of high-risk capital for high-technology industries, e.g. small and medium-sized firms' ventures into computers and micro-electronic technology.
2. It is a regional development agency for England. (The Welsh, Scottish and Northern Ireland Development Agencies play a similar role for those countries.)
3. It is a vehicle for the regeneration of 'lame duck' industries.

The original intention of the NEB as a means of promoting public ownership, industrial reorganization and industrial democracy has been dramatically altered. Its aim is now that of 'promoting the private ownership of interests in industrial undertakings by the disposal of securities and other properties held by the NEB or any of its subsidiaries'. However, the argument continues about its role and about whether the NEB should become a state merchant banker providing risk funds to industry.

8.6 THE NATIONAL HEALTH SERVICE

Background

The Second World War provides the background to the creation of a national and largely free public health service. During the war an Emergency Medical Service was set up which took over local authority and voluntary hospital and medical services. The first proposal for a National Health Service came in 1941 from the wartime Minister of Health, Ernest Brown, with his announcement of an intention to form a national hospital service after the war. In 1944 a new Minister, Henry Willnick, produced a White Paper laying out plans for a free health service which would be administered by joint committees of local authorities. The British Medical Association (BMA) disliked the concept of local authority control, as they saw this as meaning that decisions on health would ultimately be taken by politicians, and they disliked any suggestion that doctors should be salaried employees of the new service. For this reason the 1944 plan left the general practitioner services working independently on contract to the health service. In 1946 the new Labour Health Minister, Aneurin Bevan, published his National Health Service Bill. The Bill had a great deal of opposition from the BMA and the structure created reflects a compromise between the Government and the BMA. The National Health Service (NHS) came into existence in 1948 with the objective of providing a free and comprehensive system of health care to the community. However, as a result of a succession of legislation beginning in 1949, charges were introduced for certain parts of the scheme (prescriptions, dental treatment, glasses, etc.).

The tripartite structure of health care 1948–1974

The 1946 Act did not provide for a unified structure. The tripartite structure which was introduced reflected the three sets of services which were in operation before the Act was passed. The new structure, which lasted until 1974, was as follows:

1. *The regional hospital boards* controlled most of the hospitals and were ultimately accountable to the Minister of Health.
2. *The local authorities* retained some health functions, being responsible for the ambulance service, environmental and public health, the school health service, and health centres.
3. *Family practitioner services* were undertaken by GPs, dentists, etc. They were not NHS employees but worked under contract. They were organized locally by executive councils.

The system was criticized for being too fragmented, as there was insufficient co-ordination between the different parts of the structure. Health care did not fall neatly into three categories. There was also too little public accountability under the system for hospital and GP services. The tripartite system brought about a wasteful duplication of services and administrative structures.

The reorganized system

The NHS was reorganized in 1974 along with other local services – local government and the water authorities. The new system brought about a more unified system by bringing together the three parts of the service.The GP services are still to some extent separate, although there is now better co-ordination between services. Local authorities lost most of their health functions except for a limited number concerned with environmental health.

The structure of the reformed service was based on the management principle 'maximum delegation downwards matched by maximum accountability upwards'. An elaborate structure of management was created to achieve this (see Fig. 8.2). This structure has come in for a great deal of criticism for being 'too bureaucratic', and the Conservative Government elected in 1979 was committed to simplifying it. Their principal reform was to be the abolition of the area health authorities.

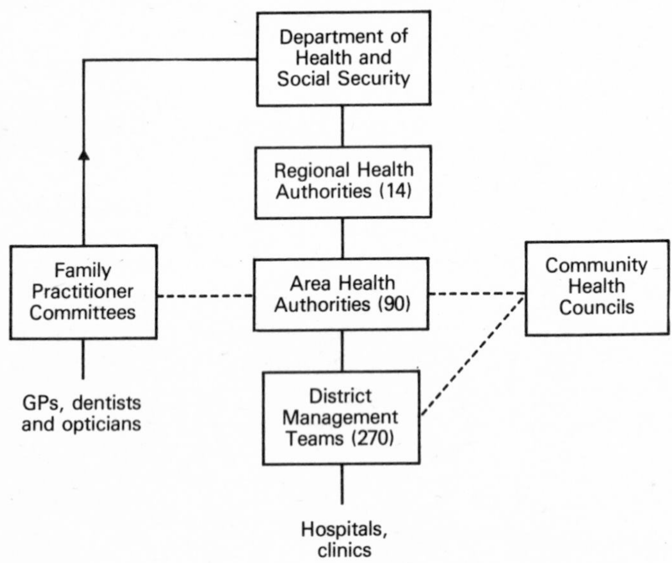

Figure 8.2 *Structure of the reformed NHS (1974)*

In 1981–82 the NHS cost over £13 000 million to run, which is an outlay of £240 per head of the population. The NHS now absorbs 6 per cent of the gross national product and has about 1 million employees.

Department of Health and Social Security

The Department of Health and Social Security is responsible for the allocation of funds and overall policy development in the NHS. It is involved with strategy planning and monitors the performance of the service. The Secretary of State is accountable to Parliament for the NHS. In Scotland and Wales these functions are exercised by the Scottish and Welsh Offices respectively.

Regional health authorities

The RHAs consist of about 20 unpaid, part-time representatives of the health professions, employees' unions, local authorities and universities, appointed by the Secretary of State. They have the function of deciding regional priorities, allocating resources to the area health authorities, monitoring performance in their regions and making provision for major capital projects. RHAs do not exist in Scotland or Wales.

Area health authorities

The area health authorities consist of about 20 part-time, unpaid appointed representatives engaged by the Secretary of State. Their areas are conterminous with the areas of county and metropolitan district authorities, except in London, where area health authority boundaries are not identical with London borough boundaries. They assess health needs in their areas and plan the provision of appropriate services, liaising closely with local authorities. The area health authorities are divided into *district management teams* which are organized around a district general hospital. These teams consist of six members and have to take a 'consensus' or corporate approach to management. No decision can be made unless all members are in agreement.

Family practitioner committees

These are area health authority committees, but they also retain a great deal of independence and are ultimately accountable to the DHSS, which provides the funding. They pay the fees and allowances of the GPs and dentists.

Community health councils

The community health councils were set up to represent the interests of the local community in health service matters. They have up to 30 members appointed by local authorities, voluntary organizations, political parties, and others concerned with health matters, and meet about four times a year. Although they are financed by the area health authorities they are independent of them. Their function is to act as a 'consumer watch-dog'. The community health councils have to be consulted on health service plans, e.g. hospital closures, and there are formal meetings between the area health authorities and the community health councils.

The Royal Commission on the NHS 1979

The Royal Commission, under the chairmanship of Sir Alexander Merrison, reported in 1979. It was set up to consider the management and financing of the NHS and was a response to criticisms which had been voiced concerning the structure and administration of the service. The most important criticisms were that the new structure was too bureaucratic, and that there were too many tiers of management and too many administrators, which meant that decisions took too long to make.

The report stressed that the NHS should remain largely free and should remain a national service, but one that must be responsible and responsive to local needs. Among other recommendations, the Commission wished to slim down the administrative apparatus and merge the family practitioner committees with the area health authorities, and to scale down the latter's scale of operations.

The 1980 Green Paper

In response to the report of the Royal Commission, the Government published in 1980 a consultative document entitled *The National Health Service in England and Wales – Patients First.* The Green Paper concentrated on structural changes, arguing for more decisions to be made locally at the community and hospital level. It also proposed the abolition of the area health authorities and the establishment of district health authorities, which would be followed by a greater delegation of decision-making powers to hospitals. The new district health authorities would be directly accountable to the regional health authorities. Some fear has been expressed that, instead of more decisions being made locally, this will provide greater central and regional control, as the district health authorities will be too small to wield much political muscle.

8.7 QUANGOS

There are many bodies and organizations in the United Kingdom which have a large degree of autonomy and which perform public functions on behalf of central and occasionally local government. They are in a sense midway between the public and the private sectors, and often have only the most limited form of public accountability. They have been called 'fringe bodies', but in recent years the acronym 'QUANGO' has been used to cover them; this stands for quasi-autonomous non-governmental organizations.

It is difficult to talk about QUANGOs as a species, since they perform a large variety of functions, take on a wide range of forms and have various legal statuses. Before discussing them in detail it may be useful to give some examples. The exact number of QUANGOs that exist depends on the definition of a QUANGO, but most authorities estimate the number of such bodies in hundreds. Some examples are: Aeronautical Research Council, Basildon Development Corporation, British Board of Film Censors, Central Midwives Board for Scotland, Charity Commission, Dental Estimates Board, Design Council, Eggs Authority, Fire Services Examination Board, Great Britain – China Centre, Horse Race Totalisator Board, Imperial War Museum, Joint Board for Clinical Nursing Studies, Land Authority for Wales, Law Commission, Metrication Board, National Dock Labour Board, Office of Population Censuses and Surveys, Parole Board, Red Deer Commission, Scottish Arts Council, Trustee Savings Banks Inspection Committee, United Kingdom Seeds Executive, White Fish Authority.

The Business Education Council is a QUANGO. It was set up by the Department of Education and Science to plan and organize business education below degree level, but it is not part of the DES. Its legal status is as a company limited by guarantee. It is financially independent of Government. Its income comes from student registration fees.

QUANGOs have been established at various times for a variety of functions and reasons. They are an interface between the Government and the outside world, and the areas of public life covered by them are guaranteed a degree of freedom from party political interference. They have proved to be a useful means (although not always without criticism) of administering funds to independent and professional organizations which are dependent on Government subsidy. Examples include: the Arts Council, which administers funds to the arts, writers, artists and others; the University Grants Committee, which administers funds to the universities; and the Social Science Research Council, which provides grants for research in the social services.

It is claimed for QUANGOs that, besides political and Governmental independence, they have the advantage of usually being small and flexible organizations which do not suffer from the bureaucratic diseconomies of scale which could occur if their functions were directly administered by a Government department. They have considerable expertise in often highly specialized and technical fields, and they can and do employ specialists to carry out work which in the Civil Service would have to be done by 'generalist' administrators. Additionally, a large number of outside experts participate in the work of QUANGOs. In recent years the growth of these autonomous bodies has caused much public concern. The Conservative Government elected in May 1979 came to office committed to reducing their number as part of its general policy of reducing the size and cost of the public sector. In September 1979 Michael Heseltine, Secretary of State for the Environment, axed 57 bodies which were connected with his department. These included the Clean Air Council, the Detergent and Allied Products Voluntary Notification Scheme and Scrutiny Group, the Transportation Research Advisory Council, and the Location of Offices Bureau.

Although it is clear that QUANGOs play an essential part in many aspects of public administration, there have been many criticisms levelled at them, the main ones being:

1. They are not accountable in the way in which other public bodies are. Different QUANGOs have different forms of accountability: some can be investigated by the Ombudsman, others present annual reports and/or accounts to Parliament, and others have their finances and expenditure scrutinized by the Comptroller and Auditor General. However, despite these forms of accountability, they are not in the main accountable to Parliament.
2. Many of these bodies have their memberships appointed by Ministers. It is often felt that this kind of patronage should be reformed and that more bodies should have their membership

filled through open competition.

3. QUANGOs spend large sums of public money without sufficient control and without their activities being properly scrutinized by Parliament or in the media.
4. Many QUANGOs have been created by Ministers 'hiving off' parts of their departments into autonomous agencies. For instance, this has been true in the case of the Office of Fair Trading, the Manpower Services Commission, and the Health and Safety Commission. Though there may be very good reasons for 'hiving off', there has been some suspicion that it has been used as a means by which Ministers can give the illusion of reducing public service staff without actually removing staff or their functions.

ASSIGNMENTS

A8.1 Choose two nationalized industries for study, and:

(a) state in which areas those industries operate;
(b) state what the financial objectives of those industries are;
(c) outline the main features of their organizational structure;
(d) draw a diagram showing the accountability of the industries.

A8.2 Make up a scrapbook from newspaper articles on an industrial relations problem in one nationalized industry. Write a report from the material, showing:

(a) the nature of the dispute;
(b) the main unions involved;
(c) the reasons for and the background to the dispute;
(d) the attitudes of the employers, the trade unions and the Government;
(e) the formula by which the dispute was settled;
(f) the effect of the dispute on the public and on the national economy.

A8.3 Outline the financial policies of one nationalized industry. What relevance do these policies have for the workers in the industry, for consumers, and for the national economy?

A8.4 What is the current role played by the National Enterprise Board? Show how this role has changed since its original conception in the 1975 Industry Act.

A8.5 Outline the arguments for and against introducing charges for treatment in the National Health Service. Show what could be the practical effect of such a measure on different groups within society.

9 Public Administration and International Organizations

9.1 BRITAIN'S INTERNATIONAL ROLE

International relationships have always been crucial to Britain's well-being, formerly because of its overseas Empire and its dominance in world affairs, and today because of the importance of international trade and finance to the economy. Britain is a member of a large number of international organizations and maintains diplomatic links with some 150 countries. In international terms Britain's most important role is as a member of the western alliance, which is for defence purposes and is carried out through the North Atlantic Treaty Organization (NATO).

In economic terms Britain's membership of the European Economic Community is of particular importance. The Commonwealth, of which the Queen is the Head, contains most members of the former Empire and provides a useful forum for dialogue between developed and developing countries. Britain is a permanent member of the Security Council of the United Nations.

Britain's overseas relationships are administered in the main by the Foreign and Commonwealth Office. The staff of this department, known as the Diplomatic Service, advise the Secretary of State for Foreign and Commonwealth Affairs and provide the staff for Britain's 200 or so embassies and missions abroad, both to foreign countries and to international organizations. Various other departments, principally the Department of Trade and the Ministry of Defence, are concerned with various aspects of international relations. The major international organizations of which Britain is a member are listed below.

Political

United Nations (UN)
Commonwealth
European Community
Western European Union
Council of Europe

Economic

International Monetary Fund (IMF)
International Bank for Reconstruction and Development (World Bank)
General Agreement on Tariffs and Trade (GATT)
International Labour Organization (ILO)
European Economic Community (EEC)
Organization for Economic Co-operation and Development (OECD)
International Finance Corporation (IFC)
European Coal and Steel Community (ECSC)

Legal

International Court of Justice
European Commission on Human Rights

Military/defence

North Atlantic Treaty Organization (NATO)

Scientific/technical/educational

United Nations Educational, Scientific and Cultural Organization (UNESCO)
World Health Organization (WHO)
World Meteorological Union

International Atomic Energy Authority
European Atomic Energy Community (Euratom)
European Space Agency (ESA)

Post/telecommunications

International Telecommunications Union
Universal Postal Union

9.2 THE UNITED NATIONS

The United Nations came into existence in 1945 after the Second World War, with the objective of securing international peace and security. It has a membership of 147 states. The UN cannot intervene in the domestic affairs of any member state, but it acts to try to prevent disputes which threaten international peace and stability. In addition to the issues of war and peace, the UN acts as an international forum for discussion on such issues as the world environment, energy, the use of world resources, world poverty, arms control and disaster relief. The headquarters of the UN are in New York, and it operates through a number of bodies, the major ones being as follows.

The General Assembly

The General Assembly consists of all UN members, and each national delegation has one vote. The Assembly can discuss any matter within the scope of the UN charter, which effectively allows it to debate any matters concerned with international relations. Much of its work is carried on in specialist committees concerned with political security, legal matters, economic and financial matters, social and humanitarian and cultural matters, and trust and non self-governing territories.

The Security Council

This consists of 15 members: five permanent members – China, France, United Kingdom, USA, USSR – and ten non-permanent members elected for a two-year term. The Security Council has the prime responsibility for the maintenance of peace and security in the world. A Council decision can be blocked if a permanent member uses its veto.

The Economic and Social Council

This council is responsible for health, educational, economic and social matters.

International Court of Justice

The International Court of Justice consists of 15 independent judges appointed by member nations. The Court adjudicates in disputes between member states over such matters as international treaties and conventions and matters of international law.

9.3 NORTH ATLANTIC TREATY ORGANIZATION

Britain's defence policy is based around NATO. The members are Belgium, Canada, Denmark, France, Greece, Iceland, Italy, Luxemburg, the Netherlands, Norway, Portugal, Turkey, the USA and West Germany. (Neither France nor Greece participates fully in NATO's integrated military structure.)

The military strategy of NATO is based on the concept of *forward defence*. This concept embraces both defence and *détente* and is based on the notion that stability and peace can best be secured if a potential aggressor is convinced that it will lose far more than it could gain in an attack. Under Article 5 of the North Atlantic Treaty, which was signed in 1949, the members of NATO affirmed their commitment to collective defence: 'the Parties agree that an armed attack on one or more of them in Europe or North America shall be considered an attack against them all.'

Britain's armed forces make a major contribution to NATO, including both conventional and nuclear forces. The Royal Navy is the largest NATO navy in Western Europe. Almost all the RAF's combat aircraft are assigned to NATO, as well as a substantial proportion of the British army.

9.4 THE EUROPEAN COMMUNITY

The European Community consists of ten states: the original six signatories of the Second Treaty of Rome 1957 – Belgium, France, Italy, Luxemburg, the Netherlands and West Germany; three states which joined in 1973 – Denmark, Eire and the United Kingdom; and Greece, which joined in 1981. Spain and Portugal will probably join the Community at least by the end of the 1980s.

The European Community consists of three communities which were set up by separate treaties, but which all share the same institutions. The three communities are:

1. *The European Coal and Steel Community (ECSC).* The ECSC was set up by the Treaty of Paris in 1951, and as an organization it paved the way for the establishment of a 'common market' as an approach to European economic integration. The ECSC is based on a community approach to the supply of coal and steel to member countries. It is concerned with such matters as the rationalization of steel production, the resettlement of workers where the exhaustion of coal seams or the need to restructure steel plants has led to a loss of jobs, and the creation of new jobs for such people, and assistance to redundant workers.
2. *The European Atomic Energy Community (Euratom).* Euratom was set up by the first Treaty of Rome in 1957. Its purpose is to provide a co-ordinated approach to the development of members' atomic energy industries and to promote the peaceful use of atomic energy.
3. *The European Economic Community (EEC).* The EEC was set up by the second Treaty of Rome in 1957 and came into existence in 1958. Its purpose is to promote economic growth and well-being in member states by establishing a common market for goods and services and creating free movement of labour and capital. The EEC is a *customs union*, and not just a free trade area, as member states have common customs duties and barriers against non-member states. The EEC has a common policy on agriculture (the Common Agricultural Policy) and has attempted to devise other common policies in such areas as fisheries and energy, but with only limited success. The ultimate aim is to establish economic and

monetary union, and a European Monetary System (of which Britain is not a member) already operates to link the exchange rates of member countries within broad bands.

Aims of the Community

The aims of the Community can be listed as follows:

1. To prevent further wars between Western European nations.
2. To promote prosperity in Western Europe based on the free movement of labour and capital.
3. To produce standardization in many areas of economic life to facilitate trade.
4. To attempt to integrate the fiscal and monetary systems of member countries.
5. To produce common policies in various important areas of economic life, such as agriculture, coal, steel, fisheries, energy, etc.
6. To act as a first step towards the creation of a federal European state. (This last aim is not shared by all supporters of the Community.)

Community institutions

There are four main Community institutions: the Council of Ministers, the Commission, the European Parliament and the Court of Justice.

The Council of Ministers

Power within the Community rests with the Council of Ministers. It is the principal decision-making body and carries out both the executive and the legislative functions of the Community. Member states are represented, usually by their foreign ministers, and each state takes it in turn to hold the presidency for a period of six months. The Council of Ministers makes decisions on proposals put to it by the Commission after consultation with the Parliament. As decisions made by the Council are binding on all member states, they are usually made only if all states agree, although the Treaty of Rome does allow for majority voting.

The Commission

This is the administrative and policy-planning branch of the Community. It is responsible for formulating detailed policy proposals for submission to the Council of Ministers. Its powers are much wider than would be usual for a national bureaucracy, and it acts as:

1. *A policy-planning body,* initiating Community policies.
2. *A mediator* between governments, steering policy through the Council and adjusting policy proposals in the light of discussion.
3. *An executant,* in that power has been delegated to it to make many detailed administrative decisions, mainly in agriculture.
4. *A 'watchdog'*, which in the last resort can take member governments or firms to the Court for breaches of Community law.
5. *An administrative body* responsible for carrying out the decisions made by the Council of Ministers.

The Commission is composed of 14 commissioners nominated by member governments. France, Germany, Italy and the United Kingdom nominate two commissioners each, while the others nominate one each. They are appointed for a four-year renewable term. One commissioner becomes the President, who is appointed for a two-year renewable term, and his or her function is the general administration of the Commission's work. Once appointed, the commissioners are *not* national representatives but Community statesmen, and only the Parliament can remove them. The reason for this is that the Commission is pledged by the Treaty of Rome to act independently of national interests and to formulate policy in the interests of the Community as a whole.

The Parliament

Originally the Parliament was a consultative body, but it is now a part of the legislative process. It cannot, however, be called *the* legislative body of the Community, as this function is performed by the Council of Ministers.

Until 1979 the Parliament had 198 members, all of whom were nominated by the parliaments of member states. In 1979 the first direct elections were held. This was the first ever example of an international election. The number of representatives was increased to 410 (81 seats each for West Germany, the United Kingdom, Italy and France, 25 seats for the Netherlands, 24 seats for Belgium, 16 seats for Denmark,

15 seats for Eire, and 6 seats for Luxemburg). The present powers of the Parliament are limited, although direct election has swung a certain power towards it. It has been argued that it is very much up to the Parliament to demonstrate the need for legislation to be made by directly elected representatives. Its present powers consist of:

1. The right to dismiss the Commission as a whole by a two-thirds majority.
2. The right to reject the Commission's draft budget as a whole. This the Parliament did in 1980. It can also increase the budget in certain areas. (This is a unique power not normally held by national parliaments.)
3. The right to investigate Community accounts.
4. The right to be consulted on all proposals put to the Council by the Commission. If the Parliament and the Council are in conflict over a proposal there is a formal conciliation procedure which has to be used in order to settle the disagreement. If this fails the Council has the right to make the final decision.

The Parliament works through specialist committees (like English local government). Its work is often concerned with highly technical matters. Proposals from the Commission go to an appropriate committee which makes a report for the plenary session of the Commission, which then debates and votes on the proposal.

The Parliament works through political groups which are organized on the basis of political philosophy rather than on a national basis. Fourteen members are necessary to form a political group. The political groups are as follows (1980):

1. Socialist Group: 112 members (including the British Labour Party).
2. European Peoples Party: 99 members (formerly the Christian Democrats).
3. European Democrats: 63 members (including the British Conservative Party).
4. Liberal and Democrat Group: 47 members.
5. Communist Group: 44 members.
6. European Progressive Democrats: 22 members.
7. Independents: 21 members. (Some of the independent members have formed a group for technical co-operation.)

The Parliament has a President and 12 Vice-presidents.

European Court of Justice

The Court of Justice interprets and adjudicates on the meaning of treaties and community law. It deals with disputes between member states and between the Community, firms and individuals. It is the final adjudicator on all legal questions under Community law and, as such, its rulings are binding on all member states. The Court consists of ten judges jointly appointed by all member states.

Advisory committees

One interesting and important aspect of the workings of the European Community is the formal integration of pressure groups into the policy-making process. There are more than 70 consultative committees which aid the Community's work. These include an Economic Policy Committee, a Scientific and Technical Committee, a Committee for the Social Security of Migrant Workers and a Monetary Committee.

The most important of these consultative committees is the 156-member *Economic and Social Committee.* This committee is made up of a cross-section of economic interests – employers, trade unions and consumer groups from member states – and is consulted by the Council of Ministers and the Commission during the policy-making process. This Committee follows the French concept of making pressure groups a formal part of the legislative process. In Britain this is usually *de facto* the case, but in the Community they have a *de jure* role. Since the inclusion of the British Trades Union Congress following Britain's membership, the ESC has played a stronger role. It has no real power and its advisory capabilities depend on the strength and commitment of its members.

The legislative process of the European Community

The legislative process of the European Community is summarized in Fig. 9.1. Community law is of four types:

1. Regulations. These are binding on and directly applicable to all member states.
2. Directions. These are binding as to the results to be achieved, but each state can choose the means of implementation.
3. Decisions. These are binding on those to whom they are addressed.
4. Recommendations. These have no binding force.

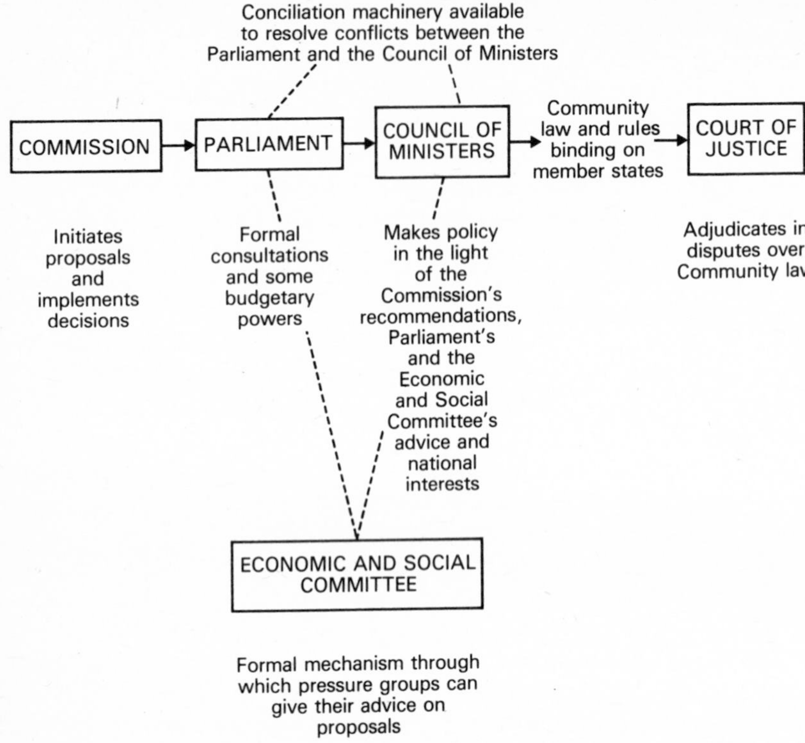

Figure 9.1 *The legislative process of the European Community*

Community policies

The Common Agricultural Policy

The most important and most controversial Community policy is the Common Agricultural Policy (CAP). This works to provide adequate food supplies, a guaranteed income to farmers and a self-reliant agricultural sector. It involves the Community intervening on the 'supply side' and purchasing surplus stocks to prevent price falls for certain commodities. Though farmers are guaranteed a particular price for their products it does lead to the infamous 'butter mountains' and 'wine lakes', which is the popular image of the CAP. It is argued that the policy does little to encourage efficiency in farming or to prevent farmers from overproducing. Farmers are shielded from the effect of market conditions and this means that consumers pay higher prices for community produce than they would if food from the rest of the world could enter the Community freely. These disadvantages have to be weighed against the fact that, as a result of the CAP, Europe does have a prosperous farming sector. The importance of the rural vote in West Germany, France and Italy has meant that their governments have resisted attempts by Britain to reform the CAP. Britain, with a far more efficient agricultural sector, is a net contributor and subsidizes the generally less efficient farmers of these countries.

Other Community policies and institutions

The European Social Fund finances training schemes for young people at work, migrant workers and workers subject to redundancy because of technological and market changes.

The *European Regional Fund* provides grants to less prosperous regions in order to finance new development projects, particularly in areas of high unemployment.

The European Monetary Fund, which was established in 1979, is the first step towards achieving one of the Community's main objectives, which is a European monetary union. The EMF involves a system of linked exchange rates. Britain is the only Community country which does not participate in this arrangement.

The Community has established close ties with a large number of developing countries through the two *Lomé Conventions*. Sixty-one developing countries have agreements giving their products entry to European markets on favourable terms. In addition, the *European Investment Bank* provides aid and lends money for agricultural and industrial development aid to help to stabilize earnings from exports from these countries through STABEXE (the Stabilization of Export Earnings).

Additionally, the Community provides a forum for views on world matters for the leaders of the ten Community countries. This has led to common Community policies on such issues as the Soviet invasion of Afghanistan, and the establishment of a common view on events in the Middle East.

The Community and sovereignty

In 1975 a referendum was held on the issue of Britain's continuing membership of the Community. Of those who voted, 64.5 per cent said 'Yes' to continued membership. Yet, despite the referendum, Britain's membership of the EEC remains an important political issue. In general terms, a majority of Conservative, Liberal and Social Democratic opinion favours continued membership and a majority of Labour opinion favours withdrawal. At the 1980 Labour Party conference, withdrawal from the Community became party policy.

The ambivalence to the Community felt in Britain (witness the low turnout figures for the first direct elections in 1979, when only 32.7 per cent of the electorate voted) stems from two main sources. First, it was hoped that Community membership would bring increased living standards. This has not happened and the Community, like other western countries, has been affected by the recession following the oil crisis in the mid-1970s. Second, it is argued that Britain's membership has reduced the country's sovereignty and hence its independence.

Community policies are implemented by regulations which are legally binding on and applicable to all member states. Community regulations override domestic legislation. Membership of a supranational Community obviously involves the loss of a country's freedom of action in certain spheres and reduces the sovereignty which its Parliament traditionally enjoyed over the making of law. The Community is, however, involved in only a limited area of social and economic life: national legislatures and governments retain their sovereignty over most activities. In answer to those who suggest that membership reduces sovereignty it is argued that withdrawal would not make Britain independent of Community policies, since Britain's trade and economic links are too close. Rather the Government would cease to have a direct say in how the Community makes policy.

9.5 THE COMMONWEALTH

The Commonwealth is a voluntary association of 44 independent states, of which Britain is one. They have a combined population of over 1 billion people, and all member countries were a part of Britain's former Empire.

The Commonwealth began with the granting of self-government to the older colonies – Canada, Australia, New Zealand and South Africa (which left the Commonwealth in 1961) – in the nineteenth century and the early part of the twentieth century. The expansion of the association took place in the period after the Second World War, when most of Britain's colonies gained their independence, although not all chose to join. The Queen is the Head of the Commonwealth; for some countries, like Australia, Canada and New Zealand, she is also head of state, while other members choose their own parliaments.

The Commonwealth provides a forum for discussion on matters of mutual interest and is particularly important in bringing together developed and developing nations.

9.6 BRITAIN'S COLONIES AND DEPENDENCIES

Britain still has 12 colonies: Bermuda, British Antarctic Territory, British Indian Ocean Territory, British Virgin Islands, Cayman Islands, Falkland Islands, Gibraltar, Hong Kong, Montserrat, Pitcairn Island, St Helena, and the Turks and Caicos Islands.

Most of the dependencies are so small that self-government is not a practicable proposition or, in the cases of Gibraltar and the Falkland Islands, they are territories where another country also claims sovereignty.

ASSIGNMENTS

A9.1 Write a brief account of the functions of the following:

(a) the European Parliament;
(b) the European Commission;
(c) the Council of Ministers;
(d) the European Court of Justice.

Discuss the way in which law is made in the European Community and the relationships between the various Community institutions in the law-making process.

A9.2 Why has the operation of the European Economic Community's Common Agricultural Policy caused so much controversy? Suggest ways in which the policy could be reformed, bearing in mind the effects on both the consumer and the farming community.

A9.3 Choose one international organization of which Britain is a member and write an account of its role and functions.

10

Public Administration and Local Government

10.1 WHAT IS LOCAL GOVERNMENT?

Local government in Great Britain is the responsibility of democratically elected local authorities, which provide a wide range of services in their local areas under powers conferred on them by Parliament.

There has been a tradition of local self-government in Britain stretching back to before the Norman Conquest, but it is only since the end of the nineteenth century that the democratic principle has been established. For mainly historical reasons the structure of local government in Scotland and Northern Ireland differs from that in England and Wales, so the structure of Scottish and Northern Irish local government will be dealt with separately in this chapter. A good definition of the purpose of local government was provided by the Herbert Commission, which reported on the structure of London government in 1960. The Commission defined its purpose as doing '. . . for people what a group of persons, elected according to the law by a majority of citizens but on election becoming representatives of them all, conceive to be good within the limits of their legal powers.'

Local government and local administration

A distinction has to be made between democratic local government and the administration of local services provided by central government and other public bodies. The Water Authorities, the Gas and Electricity Boards, the Post Office, Health Authorities, the Department of Health and Social Security, the Manpower Services Commission, the Inland Revenue, and the Department of Employment, among others, all provide locally administered services. Some of the services provided by certain of these organizations were once the province of local government, including parts of the health service, gas and water.

Local government has no inherent right to be responsible for a particular service. It is Parliament which decides who provides what service. It is important to make the distinction between local government and local administration. Local government is directly accountable to the consumers of its services through the system of the election of councillors, whereas the accountability for other services is ultimately Parliament's.

The main features of local government

Local democratic control

Local government is controlled by elected councillors. Councillors and their councils are not law-makers (although they do have powers to make by-laws), but they do, as corporate bodies, have the power and duties to make decisions about the operation of the services they administer. Though councils have only those powers which the law allows them, they do have a certain amount of *discretion*, which enables them to tailor services to local needs. This means that local conditions and political views can be reflected in the way in which services are administered.

Local self-government

A basic principle of local government is that certain services are best provided by local people who understand the needs of their community. This principle provides for:

1. Efficiency in service provision, as the quality and cost of the services are provided, monitored and controlled by representatives of the local community.

2. Participation by local people in the government of their community.
3. Liberty for the individual citizen, as the existence of elected local government provides a buffer against the direct control of local services by central government.

Local self-finance

An important element in local self-government is the existence of an independent source of revenue. Local authorities have their own tax – the local rates – as well as income from other sources, such as bus fares and council house rents. However, these sources of income provide only a third of local revenue. The rest is provided by central government. The effect this has on local authorities' freedom of action is discussed later in this chapter.

Local service provision

The services provided by local government can be categorized as follows (see Table 10.1):

1. *Social and welfare services,* including education, personal social services, children's homes, and homes for the elderly and mentally handicapped.
2. *Planning and environmental services,* including town and country planning, housing, traffic control, refuse collection, slum clearance, and road building and maintenance.
3. *Protection services,* including the police service (outside London), the fire service, consumer protection and public health service.
4. *Amenities and recreation,* including parks, swimming pools, sports facilities, libraries and museums.
5. *Trading activities,* including public transport and markets.
6. *Housing.* Some 30 per cent of all the housing stock in Britain is owned by local authorities.

Table 10.1 *Provision of local government services in England and Wales*

Service	*GLC*	*London boroughs*	*Metropolitan counties*	*Metropolitan districts*	*County councils*	*District councils*
Education	√ ILEA Inner London	√ Outer London		√	√	
Social services		√		√	√	
Police	Central	Government	√		√	
Fire	√		√		√	
Refuse disposal	√		√		√	
Refuse collection		√		√		√
Housing		√		√		√
Libraries		√		√	√	
Main roads and traffic control	√		√		√	
Minor roads		√		√		√
Strategic planning	√		√		√	
Transport	√		√		√	
Main sewers	√		√		√	
Local sewers		√		√		√
Parks	√	√	√	√	√	√
Consumer protection		√	√		√	
Cemeteries and Crematoria		√		√		√
Local planning		√		√		√
Recreation facilities		√		√		√
Environmental health		√		√		√
Collection of rates		√		√		√
Allotments and smallholdings		√		√		√

10.2 THE STRUCTURE OF LOCAL GOVERNMENT

The modern system of local government was established by three nineteenth-century Acts of Parliament, the Local Government Acts 1888, 1894 and 1899.

Local Government Acts 1888 and 1894

These Acts laid the foundations of the system, outside London, which lasted until 1974. They established an essentially two-tier system of government (Fig. 10.1), the first tier being county councils, based on ancient county boundaries, with district councils operating as the second tier. In rural areas a third tier of parish councils and parish meetings was established. Large urban areas were designated county boroughs (a single tier of government) outside the control of the counties.

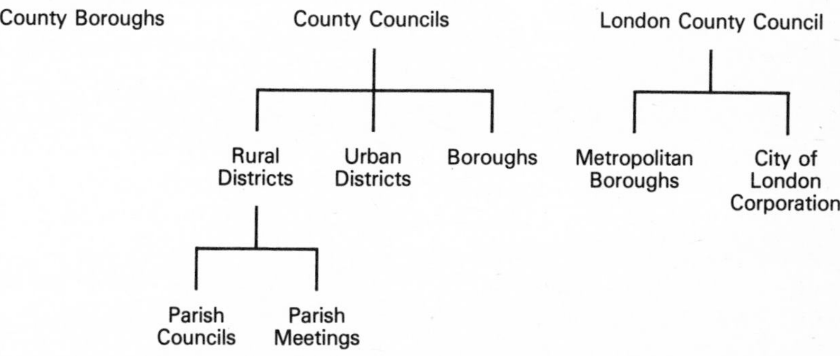

Figure 10.1 *The unreformed structure of local government in England*

The system was founded on two main principles:

1. All local authorities should be elected bodies.
2. The towns should be governed separately from the rural areas to take into account their different problems.

Local Government Act 1899

This Act created the Government of London by forming the London County Council. Twenty-eight Metropolitan Boroughs were formed as a second tier. The City of London, with its ancient constitution, retained its individuality, exercising its own powers and those of a Metropolitan Borough.

10.3 THE REFORM OF LOCAL GOVERNMENT

The structure of local government was reformed in London in 1965, and in the rest of England in 1974. The reasons for reform were as follows. First, though the structure of local government had remained essentially unaltered for more than 70 years, there had been a remarkable increase in the range and scope of local government services. When they were first incorporated, local authority functions were centred on public health, highways, the police and regulatory duties. Since then they have become responsible for education, housing, personal social services, traffic administration, town and country planning, libraries, fire services and many other functions. Many of the old authorities were too small to provide effectively such a wide range of services. Before the reorganization in 1974 there were 1191 county districts, and only 496 had populations greater than 20 000.

Second, the rise of the motor-car, the change in work patterns, and growth of the suburbs broke down the nineteenth-century distinction between urban and rural areas.

The re-examination of the local government system in England, which took place between 1958 and 1972, was largely the work of two independent Royal Commissions:

1. *The Royal Commission on Local Government in London* (the Herbert Commission) 1957–1960.
2. *The Royal Commission on Local Government in England* (the Redcliffe-Maud Commission) 1966–1969.

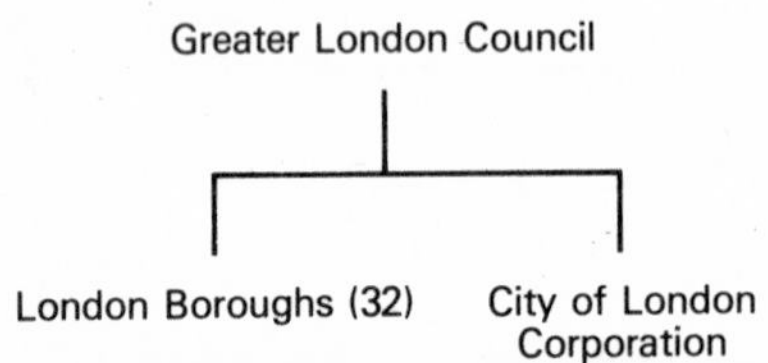

Figure 10.2 *The structure of London government*

The reform of London government

The Herbert Commission recommended an enlargement of London as an administrative unit, and this formed the central feature of the

London Government Act 1963. The major features of the Act were as follows.

Greater London Council

A Greater London Council (Fig. 10.2) was set up, covering the 8 million inhabitants of the built-up area of greater London. Under the Act, parts of Surrey, Kent and Hertfordshire, and the whole of the County of Middlesex, were merged with the London County Council to form the GLC. (Table 10.2 shows the services provided by the GLC.)

Table 10.2 *The division of local government services in London*

Greater London Council	*London boroughs*
Fire	Libraries
Refuse disposal	Refuse collection
Drainage and flood prevention	Consumer protection
Smallholdings	Environmental health
Housing (Inner London and overspill housing[a])	Cemeteries and crematoria
Main roads and traffic	Social services
Regulation	Collection of the rates
Education (ILEA in Inner London)	Minor roads
Strategic planning	Housing
Main sewers	Sewers
London Transport	Local planning and development
Parks (Inner London)	Education (Outer London)
	Swimming baths

[a] These functions have been transferred to the London boroughs. Eventually the only housing functions which the GLC will have will be in the areas of strategic planning and the granting of mortgages for home ownership.

London boroughs

As a second tier of government, 32 London boroughs (Fig. 10.3) were created, with populations of between 150 000 and 350 000, to provide local services. The City of London Corporation remained unreformed. (See Table 10.2 for the services provided by the boroughs.)

Figure 10.3 *Greater London and the London boroughs. From Local Government in Britain, HMSO 1975. Reproduced with the permission of the Controller of Her Majesty's Stationery Office.*

Inner London Education Authority

The former LCC education provision remained intact, with the creation of the Inner London Education Authority. This body, unique in local government, is a virtually autonomous committee of the Greater London Council. It is composed of one representative from each of the 16 inner London boroughs (the old LCC area), together with the GLC councillors for the area. It was created as a result of strong pressure from the London Teachers Association, the Labour Party, who had traditionally controlled the LCC, and other pressure groups which did not wish to see the inner London education service being split among the inner boroughs. The outer London boroughs are their own education authorities.

There has been considerable controversy over the form and even the existence of the ILEA, especially since the Conservatives were returned to power nationally in 1979. The Conservative-controlled GLC of the time wished to dismantle the ILEA's permanent Labour majority, and two inner London boroughs – Wandsworth and Westminster (both Conservative controlled) – campaigned to become their own education authorities. A committee under the chairmanship of Lady Young, the then Minister of State at the Department of Education and Science, examined the organization and success of the ILEA in 1980. The committee reported in 1981 and were in favour of its continued existence, but recommended that in future it should contain only representatives from the inner London boroughs – an idea rejected by the Cabinet. Much of the controversy surrounding the ILEA stems from its high spending. In 1981–82 it had a planned expenditure of £694 million, and this gives it a higher expenditure per pupil than any other education authority. Though the ILEA sets its own rate demands for the inner London boroughs, its members are only indirectly elected, and have no fear of rejection by the electorate if rate demands are seen as excessive.

The reform of local government in the rest of England

The Royal Commission on Local Government in England, chaired by Lord Redcliffe-Maud, was appointed in 1966 to examine the structure of local government in England (outside London). The dilemma which faced the Royal Commission in reforming the system was the choice between democracy and efficiency. Efficiency implies large units able to yield economies of scale, while democracy at the local level is usually best served by small units with which local people can easily identify. The Royal Commission found four basic faults in the existing system:

1. The existing system did not fit the pattern of life and work of the people of England.
2. The division between town and country made the proper planning of development and transport impossible.
3. The division of responsibilities between county councils, district councils and county boroughs meant that services which should have been in the hands of one authority were divided among

several. This meant that the work of meeting the different needs of families and individuals was greatly complicated.

4. Many local authorities were too small in size and in revenue to employ the necessary specialized staff and technical equipment to fulfil their functions effectively.

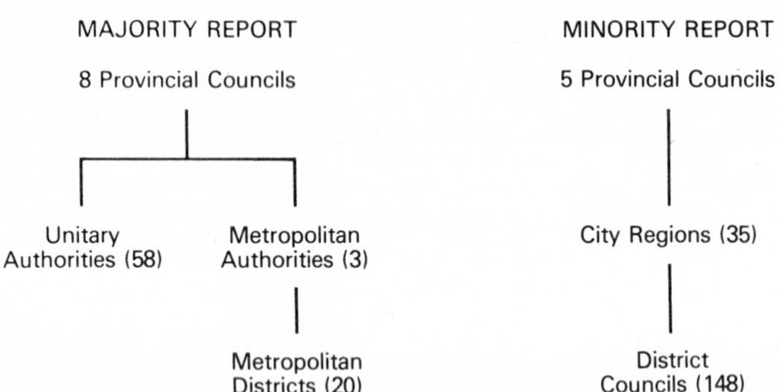

Figure 10.4 *The structure of local government proposed by the Redcliffe-Maude Commission*

The Commission, which reported in 1969, proposed a system by which England would be divided into 58 unitary (single-tier) authorities (Fig. 10.4) which would be responsible for providing all local government services and would unite town and country. This reversed the conventional idea that rural areas in particular needed two-tier authorities because of their large size and scattered populations. These unitary authorities were to be grouped under eight indirectly elected provincial councils which would be responsible for strategic planning in their regions.

The argument put forward by the Commission for a single tier of government was that it would avoid the division of functions which ought to be planned as a whole.

In the three largest conurbations, the areas around Liverpool, Manchester and Birmingham, a two-tier system was proposed. One member of the Commission, Mr Derek Senior, disagreed with the Majority Report. In his Minority Report he argued for the creation of regions grouped around major cities.

The Local Government Act 1972

This Act created a new structure of local government for England and Wales which came into existence in April 1974. The Conservative Government of the time rejected the Maud proposal for unitary authorities, although it had been accepted by the previous Labour Government, and instead retained a two-tier system (Fig. 10.5).

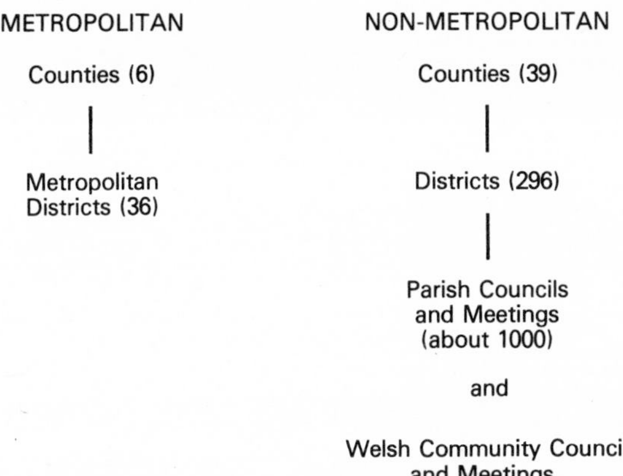

Figure 10.5 *Present structure of local government in England and Wales (outside London)*

Superficially, the new structure looks very similar to the old, but the 1972 Act did bring about some important changes:

1. All-purpose county boroughs were abolished.
2. The number of administrative units was substantially reduced. Under the previous system there had been 79 county boroughs, 48 counties and 1191 county districts. Under the reorganized system the number of counties was reduced to 45 (six metropolitan and 39 non-metropolitan), while the number of second-tier authorities fell to 332.
3. The rural/urban divide was eliminated by the amalgamation of districts, and the Local Government Boundary Commission has the task of keeping the boundaries up to date.
4. Two types of counties were created under the Act (Fig. 10.6):

   (a) Non-metropolitan counties, which cover the country except for the major conurbations.
   (b) Metropolitan counties, based on six major conurbations. The

Figure 10.6 *Counties in England and Wales. From Local Authorities in Britain, HMSO 1975. Reproduced with the permission of the Controller of Her Majesty's Stationery Office.*

six metropolitan counties are Merseyside, Tyne and Wear, Greater Manchester, West Midlands, West Yorkshire and South Yorkshire.

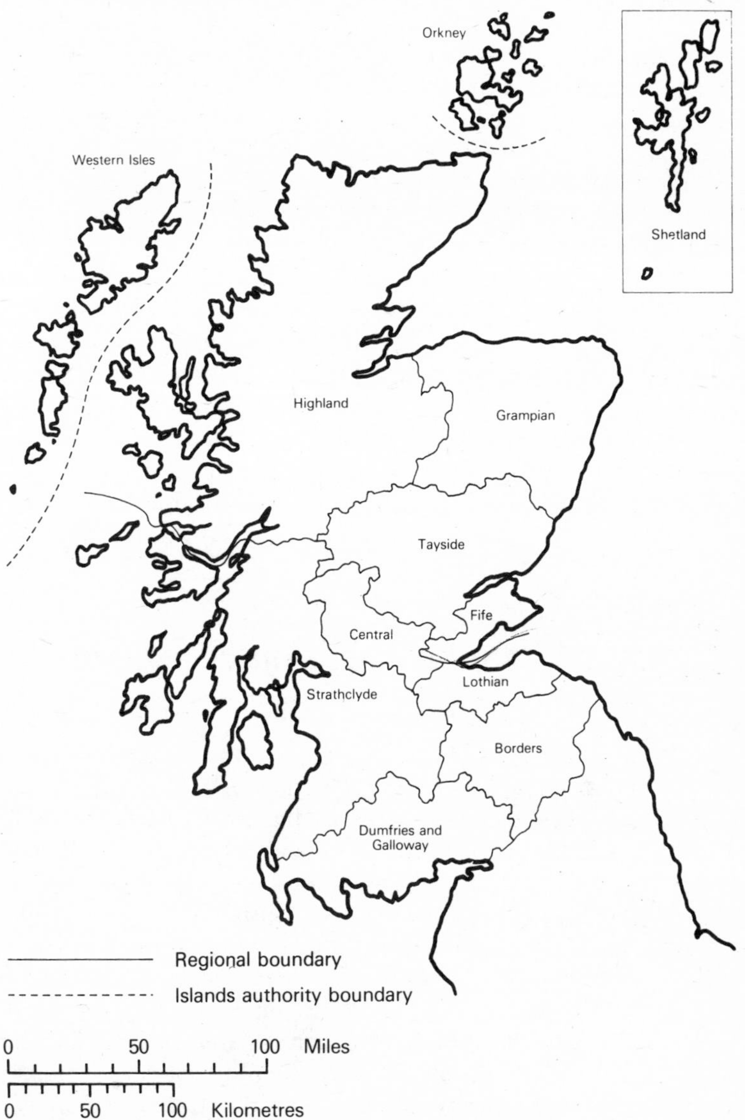

Figure 10.7 *Islands and regional authorities in Scotland. From Local Authorities in Britain, HMSO 1975. Reproduced with the permission of the Controller of Her Majesty's Stationery Office.*

10.4 LOCAL GOVERNMENT IN SCOTLAND

Reform of local government in Scotland broadly parallels that in England and Wales. Because of Scotland's separate historical development Scottish reform proceeded separately. The Local Government (Scotland) Act 1973 broadly echoed the findings of the 1969 Royal Commission on Local Government in Scotland.

The main features of the Act were the creation of nine regional authorities (Fig. 10.7) and 53 district authorities, which exercise broadly similar functions to the county and district authorities in England. The only exceptions are in Orkney, Shetland and the Western Isles, which, because they are so isolated, have single all-purpose authorities. The areas of the district authorities are worked out to try to ensure that they meet the needs of local communities and that they have the necessary resources to meet their range of functions. Because of the nature of the population distribution of Scotland the Glasgow district contains nearly 1 million people, while at the other extreme the Highland district of Badenoch and Strathspey has only 9000 people.

10.5 LOCAL GOVERNMENT IN NORTHERN IRELAND

Until 1972 Northern Ireland had its own devolved government with its own Parliament at Stormont. The structure of its local government developed on much the same lines as that in England and Wales. However, as a result of the Northern Ireland troubles and the sectarian violence between the Catholic and Protestant populations, the then Conservative Government prorogued (suspended) the Stormont Parliament and direct rule from Westminster was imposed.

One major cause of the Catholic minority's discontent was the control of housing and jobs by the Protestant majority. The control of local government by the Protestant Unionist Party was a major means of maintaining the Protestant ascendancy. The Unionist-dominated local councils often discriminated against the Catholic citizens by manipulating boundaries (gerrymandering). In some instances houses were allocated to Protestants to keep the Unionists in power, and local authority jobs seldom went to Catholics.

For these reasons local government in Northern Ireland was stripped of many of its powers. In October 1973 the existing local authorities were replaced by a single-tier structure of 26 district authorities (Fig. 10.8). Responsibility for administering many of the more important services formerly provided by local government was transferred to central government departments or area boards.

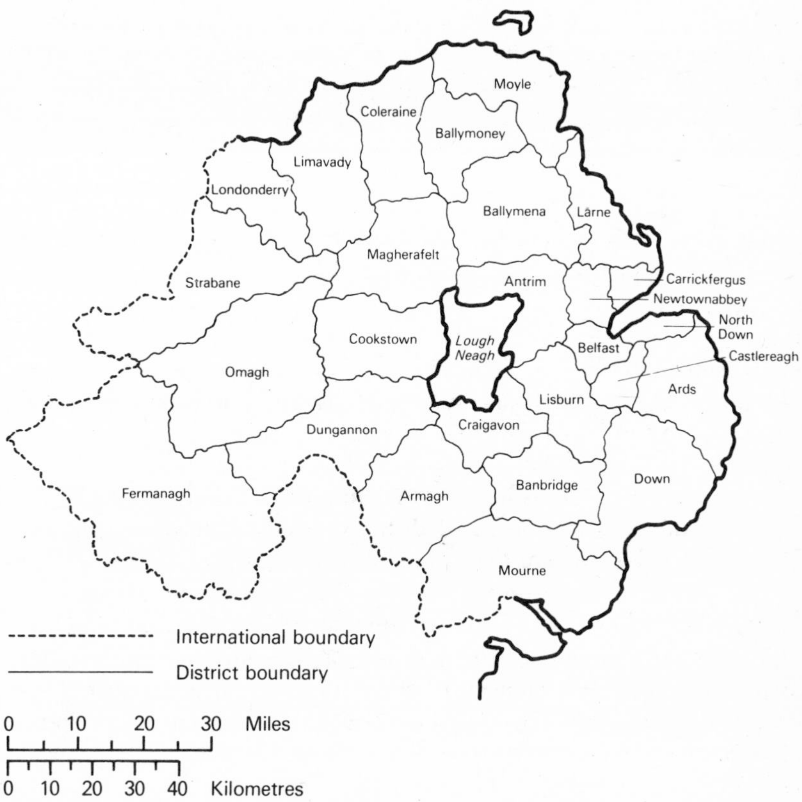

Figure 10.8 *District authorities in Northern Ireland. From Local Authorities in Britain, HMSO 1975. Reproduced with the permission of the Controller of Her Majesty's Stationery Office.*

District councils are directly responsible for public health functions, entertainments and recreation, parks, museums, refuse collection, cemeteries, building regulations and gas undertakings. They have a responsibility to represent local views and are consulted by the Department of Housing, Local Government and Planning.

Each district is based on a main town or centre and includes the surrounding urban and rural areas. The elections to the councils are held on the basis of proportional representation of the single transferable vote in order to ensure a fair representation of the minority Catholic population.

Functions relating to education and libraries, health and personal social services, housing, fire services, electricity, drainage and sport are exercised by area boards responsible to the appropriate Civil Service department. Most of the members of the area boards are appointed by the departments but include elected district councillors.

10.6 POLITICS IN LOCAL GOVERNMENT

Elections

Local councillors are elected for a four-year term of office. Elections take place on the first Thursday in May. The first past the post system is used except in Northern Ireland, where the single transferable vote is employed.

The electoral system is not uniform. In the GLC and all counties the county is divided into electoral districts, each of which returns one councillor. All seats are contested every four years. In the metropolitan districts voting takes place annually (except in the years of county elections), with a third of the members retiring in rotation. In the non-metropolitan districts there is even less uniformity. Under the 1972 Act districts are allowed to choose whether they are elected *en bloc* every four years or in thirds every year but one. In London boroughs voting takes place every four years for the whole council.

Local government electors

The franchise for voting in local elections is identical with that for Parliamentary elections. The average turnout, however, is much lower, averaging 35 per cent compared with 75 per cent for elections to Parliament. (The 1979 local elections were an exception, as the elections for local council and Parliament were held on the same day and the turnout for both was 76 per cent.)

The reform of local government has not stimulated the interest which its architects had hoped. There are a number of possible explanations for the lack of interest in voting for local councils, and they can be summarized as follows:

1. The electorate realize that local authorities are not the final controllers of local destiny. In a survey conducted for the 1973 Kilbrandon Commission on the Constitution most people interviewed agreed with the statement that 'The local council has very little power; it merely follows instructions from the Government'. Voting in local elections often reflects satisfaction or dissatisfaction with central Government rather than local issues.
2. There is no contest between well known personalities in the same way as there is in national elections, despite the coverage given to local personalities in local press and radio. In a study of attitudes towards the local council carried out for the London Borough of Southwark in 1980 by the Market & Opinion Research International (MORI) organization, 82 per cent of the respondents could not name one local councillor and only 2 per cent could correctly name three. Only 4 per cent could name the Leader of the Council, who had been the leader for the past decade (reported in *Whose Government Is It Anyway, Polls, Surveys and Public Opinion* by Robert M. Worcester – paper presented to the Royal Institute of Public Administration Conference 1981).
3. There is far less national mass media interest in local elections than in national elections.
4. The electorate are generally ignorant about the functions and powers of local government and about local issues. In 1967 a survey carried out for the Royal Commission on Local Government (Maud) showed that 20 per cent of the people interviewed were unable to name a single service provided at either county or local level.

Councillors

There are approximately 25 000 councillors in Britain, compared with about 34 000 prior to reorganization in 1974. Their qualifications for office are as follows:

1. They must be over 21 years of age.
2. They must occupy premises or land within the local authority's area or have worked in the area for at least 12 months.
3. They must not be an employee of the local authority for which they wish to stand for office. There is pressure from many local

government trade unions, especially the teachers' unions, for this ban to be lifted, as it effectively debars a considerable number of people who have direct knowledge of the workings of local services. The ban is imposed because of the legal notion that a person cannot be both master and servant. However, teachers do elect representatives to education committees.

4. Employees of certain government bodies are also barred from service by their employers. This category includes senior and middle-ranking civil servants and senior executives of certain public corporations.

The work of councillors

Councillors are part-time politicians in that most of them have full-time occupations. They are not paid a salary for their work, but they are paid expenses for their attendance at meetings. Under the Local Government Act 1980 responsibility allowances can be made to the leader of the council, the leader of the opposition and the chairmen of committees. The maximum total sum available in any one year is £9000 (the Leader of the GLC received £4000 in 1981). The Robinson Committee on the Remuneration of Councillors (1977) found that ordinary councillors spend on average 71 hours a month on council business and leaders of the council may work up to 122 hours a month. The work of councillors can be categorized into four main areas of activity:

1. The making of broad policy decisions.
2. Taking an interest in the welfare of constituents.
3. The management of the local authority's services and operations.
4. Controlling and limiting a local authority's expenditure.

Party politics in local government

The argument is often advanced that politics has no place in local government and that independent local councillors should make decisions on the merits of a case in the interests of the local community and not on the basis of party dogma. Despite the prevalence of this view, party politics nowadays dominates local government. However, this has not always been the case, especially in rural areas where party labels, if used at all, were little more than labels for electoral convenience. Since the turn of the century party organization at a local level has been an increasing influence over local government, and it was given a great stimulus by the 1974 reforms. The removal of the separation of the rural and the urban brought to the country the party traditions of the towns. In 1974 some 25 per cent of all councillors were independents, but this number had fallen to less than 20 per cent by the late 1970s. Some 80 per cent of all local authorities were controlled by councillors from one of the two main political parties. The arguments advanced against party politics in local government are:

1. Only party-sponsored candidates have any chance of success when political parties dominate local politics. In particular areas, where there is single-party domination, the selection of a candidate by a local party is tantamount to election.
2. Electors tend to vote on strict party lines when presented with candidates with party labels, and this means that relatively little weight is given to the personal qualities of candidates.
3. When party politics dominates, elections cease to be about issues and are merely an opportunity to register opinions about national politics.
4. Non-partisan candidates are discouraged from coming forward to serve the community.
5. Decisions about local issues may be made in private party meetings and the public debates in the council chamber become a sham. This causes decision-making to go on behind closed doors.

The following are some of the arguments used to justify party politics at a local level:

1. Local authorites are essentially *political* organizations. They make decisions about the allocation of resources and welfare which will be of advantage and disadvantage to various groups. It is not surprising, therefore, that political parties are involved in an essentially political process. Issues in housing, education and social services are subjects of political debate and cannot be treated as purely administrative.
2. Party dominance in local government brings a coherence to decision-making. Political parties bring together people of like minds who can iron out their differences of opinion and can therefore plan policies which have the agreement of a fairly broad base of views.
3. The electors know in advance the kind of local government which they are likely to receive when political parties enter the arena. Parties produce manifestoes which lay down policy and allow the electorate a clear choice of alternatives. (This does not imply that

Table 10.3 *Three models of the operation of political parties in local government*

Parliamentary Model	*Loose Party Dominance Model*	*Independent Member Model*
1. Party organization on the council is based on the organization of parties in Parliament. 2. The majority party elects a leader of the council who is seen by the party as a 'local prime minister'. 3. A system of party whips operates which ensures that councillors follow decisions made in the meetings of party groups. 4. The majority party takes all committee chairmanship. 5. The leader of the council and the committee chairman form a policy group which acts as a kind of 'cabinet'. 6. The minority party operates as a 'shadow government'. 7. This model is most closely reflected in local government in large urban areas, particularly in areas where the Labour Party dominates or where control alternates – the 'marginals'.	1. Members are elected on a party basis and usually vote for their party, but have substantial opportunity to desert. 2. Party groups meet irregularly. 3. Committee chairmanships are not always distributed on a party basis, although the majority party may dominate. 4. Individual councillors are seen to be entitled to freedom of thought and action. 5. This pattern is usually found in the Conservative Party dominated councils.	1. Members are elected on a party basis, but once elected tend to act as individuals. 2. No group meetings are held. 3. Committee chairmen are chosen irrespective of party politics. 4. This pattern is usually found in rural and non-industrial areas, especially in those where party politics was absent in the past.

election manifesto pledges are always kept.)

4. The growth of party political contests in local government has reduced the number of uncontested elections, and so the electorate has been given a greater choice of representatives and policy choices.

Despite the growth of party politics there are considerable differences in the way in which political parties operate in different parts of the country. In certain areas party labels are of little significance: the individual councillors act very much as independents once elected, and party organization is largely confined to winning elections. At the other extreme, there are areas, especially in large urban authorities, in which party organization is strong and party loyalty and discipline are tightly maintained in order to carry out the policy of the manifesto. Three models of the organization which political parties can take are given in Table 10.3. They are:

1. The Parliamentary model.
2. The loose party dominance model.
3. The independent member model.

It is true that in recent years there has been a considerable shift away from the third towards the first model.

10.7 DECISION-MAKING AND MANAGEMENT

The management of local authorities is based on the theory that elected councillors make policy while appointed officials administer and execute those policy decisions. In reality, however, it is impossible to make such a clear-cut distinction between policy and administration. In investigating the planning and management of local services the roles of both councillors and officials must be discussed.

Council committees

The formal structure of decision-making in local authorities takes place via a system of committees composed of the elected councillors. Senior officers of the council are usually in attendance to give advice and provide information. On certain committees, such as education committees, co-opted members representing various local interests may be included and have voting rights. Committees are organized along two lines:

1. *Vertical committees.* These are committees which manage a single service, for example education or housing. In the past they were the most common type of committee. Some of these committees are statutory, i.e. councils are required by law to set them up. For example, the 1944 Education Act specifies that those local authorities which are education authorities must set up an education committee.
2. *Horizontal committees.* These are committees which decide policy on areas of activity which affect a wide range of services across the council. Examples of horizontal committees include finance and personnel committees.

Council meetings

Committees are ultimately responsible to the full council, which is the final decision-making body in local government. However, the degree to which the council delegates decision-making powers to its committees varies from authority to authority. There are essentially three models of the role which the full council meeting plays:

1. At one extreme there are council meetings at which reports and minutes of all committees are received and at which councillors are at liberty to debate any matter they wish. In this model the council meeting acts as the final policy decision-maker.
2. In the second model councillors receive reports from their committees at the full council meeting, but they are limited to debating only the subject matter of the reports and cannot bring up matters unconnected with them. Issues of current importance have to be raised first in the appropriate committee.
3. At the other extreme there is the situation where virtually nothing comes before the council unless councillors specifically request that it does. In this model delegation of decision-making powers to committees is at a maximum. Decisions are made in committee and the function of the council meeting is to rubber-stamp them.

The Maud Report 1967

In the past, committees in local authorities tended to proliferate, and as a consequence full council meetings tended to lose their function as a review body and the body which could co-ordinate and plan the authority's operations as a whole. After the publication in 1967 of the Maud Report on the Management of Local Government, the number of committees in many authorities was drastically reduced. Maud had suggested a reduction in the number for reasons of efficiency and in order to improve co-ordination.

The Report argued that the large number of vertical committees led to an absence of unity in an authority's work and to excessive 'departmentalism' rather than a unified approach to local policy-making. This lack of unity was heightened by the fact that vertical committees usually served a single department with its own professional hierarchy of officers.

Maud recommended a reduction in the number of committees and the substitution of horizontal for vertical committees to allow for greater co-ordination. In addition, the Report made the case for the setting up of a management board of between five and nine leading councillors. The purpose of this board would be to unify the council's work, and it would be the body which would have an overview of decision-making.

The corporate approach: the Bains Report

So that the management structure of local authorities could be updated at the same time as their structure was being reformed, a study group under the chairmanship of M.A. Bains, Clerk to the Kent County Council, was set up in 1971. In 1972 the group presented its report, entitled The New Local Authorities: Management and Structure. The Bains Report followed the lead given by the Maud Report and proposed that local authorities should take a *corporate approach* to management and the provision of services. There was felt to be a need in local authorities for a structure which would unify decision-making and set objectives which the various parts of a local authority would then set out to achieve.

The idea behind corporate management is that a local authority's services should *not* be seen as separate entities each with its own purposes and objectives and vying with the others for scarce resources. The corporate view emphasizes that services are interlocking and that the solution to problems usually involves inputs from a range of departments and services which need to co-ordinate their activities.

In order to implement such an approach a number of elements are essential. First, councillors need a means by which they can set objectives for their authority. Bains proposed the setting up of a policy and resources committee (Fig. 10.9), which would have the functions of:

1. Giving the council full and co-ordinated advice on the implementation of decisions.
2. Setting objectives and priorities.
3. Co-ordinating the implementation of council decisions.
4. Playing a key role in the formulation of structure plans for the local authority's area.

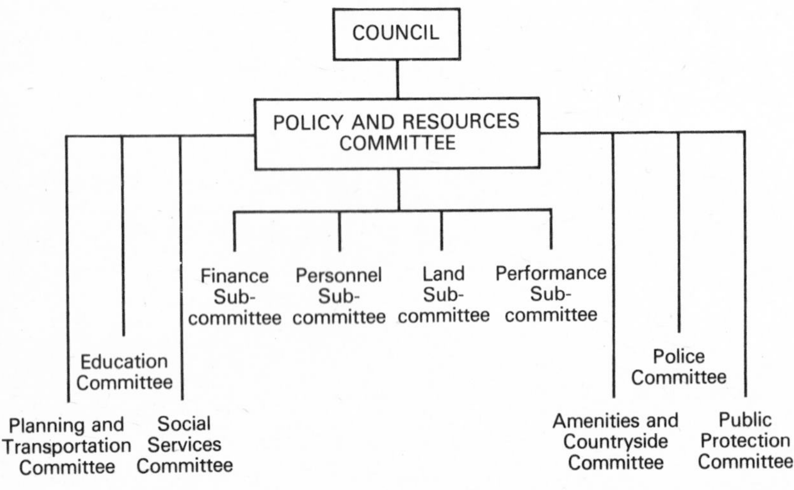

Figure 10.9 *Committee structure of a non-metropolitan county council. From New Local Authorities and Management and Structures (Bains Report), HMSO 1975. Reproduced with the permission of the Controller of Her Majesty's Stationery Office.*

Additionally, a performance review subcommittee was recommended by the Report. This committee would have the function of *monitoring* on a regular basis the performance of the council's programmes. It would review performance in order to see whether the original objectives of the programme had been met and whether value for money in the use of resources had been achieved. The results of the review system would be fed back into the policy-making process.

Second, the corporate approach involves changes at the level of senior management. The Bains Report recommended that local

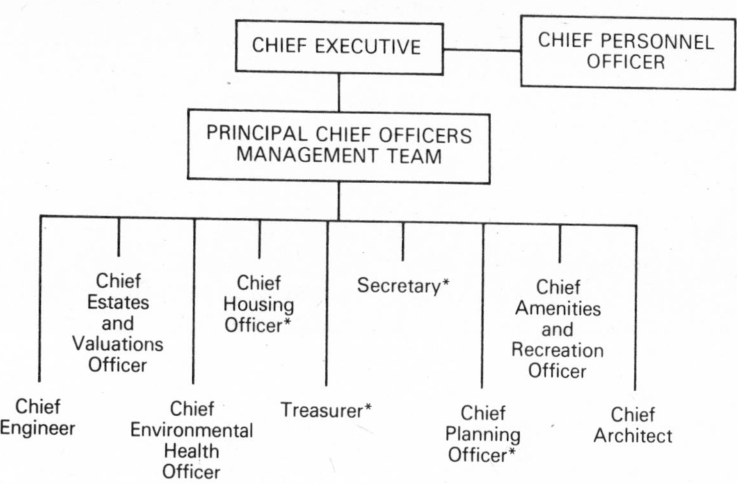

Figure 10.10 *Departmental structure of a non-metropolitan district. From New Local Authorities and Management and Structures (Bains Report), HMSO 1975. Reproduced with the permission of the Controller of Her Majesty's Stationery Office.*

authorities establish a post of chief executive (Fig. 10.10), whose role would be to co-ordinate the ideas and the work of a *management team* of chief officers. The management team would be the counterpart of the councillors' policy and resources committee. It would bring chief officers together and it was suggested that it would involve making decisions in the light of the authority's objectives rather than from the standpoint of the needs of particular departments. This, it was hoped, would lead to greater efficiency, as duplication would be prevented and resources use could be planned against stated objectives.

The corporate approach which was the central theme of the Bains Report has its critics. The criticism has come mainly from professional groups within authorities, who see an unwarranted interference in areas of professional concern by others in the authority who are not in that profession. For example, a central personnel function is an obvious need if a corporate approach is to be taken to manpower planning, but it is debatable whether a personnel officer or a personnel committee should specify to, for example, the education service or the social services the number and type of teachers or social workers that they employ. In some authorities youth and community functions nominally associated with the education service have been taken over by recreation and amenities committees.

In an era when local authorities are finding it more difficult to find a desired level of resources, the corporate approach has made headway. It has certainly been used to break down some of the narrow departmentalism which had been a feature of authorities in the past. In local government, unlike in the Civil Service, the specialist rather than the generalist administrators are the ones who reach the top. As specialists they are members of professions, each of which has its own codes of practice and methods of working. It is, therefore, only too easy to put the needs of the profession before the policy objectives of the council as a whole, or to see problems from only one perspective. The corporate approach is a way of reducing the narrowing aspects of professionalism and looking at the community's problems in the round.

Table 10.4 *Local authority manpower in England and Wales by service*

	Full-time	*Part-time (full-time equivalents)*	*Totals*	*Change (%) September 1979 to September 1980*
Education:				
lecturers and teachers	530 780	24 852	555 632	− 1.7
others	196 158	203 246	399 404	− 5.6
Construction	131 038	237	131 275	− 2.2
Transport	22 241	182	22 423	− 1.0
Social services	136 971	70 769	207 740	0.6
Public libraries and museums	24 519	8 088	32 607	− 1.5
Recreation, parks and baths	70 292	8 902	79 194	2.8
Environmental health	21 305	810	22 115	− 1.0
Refuse collection and disposal	49 911	136	50 047	− 0.9
Housing	45 561	5 631	51 192	3.1
Town and country planning	21 605	364	21 969	− 1.1
Fire services	40 024	861	40 885	− 0.4
Miscellaneous services	243 240	20 866	264 106	− 1.3
Law and order	171 863	4 962	176 825	2.8
Agency staff	471	128	599	− 13.2
Total	1 705 979	350 034	2 056 013	− 1.7

Source: Monthly Digest of Statistics No. 425 May 1981, Central Statistical Office. Reproduced with the permission of the Controller of Her Majesty's Stationery Office.

10.8 LOCAL GOVERNMENT MANPOWER

The local government service, taken as a whole, is the largest employer in the UK, with over 2.5 million employees, or one worker in ten, in the labour force. Not only is it the largest employer, but the range of jobs within it is more diverse than for any other employer (see Table 10.4): in the Greater London Council alone there are over 300 different manual occupations. But it is not only occupational diversity which characterizes local government employment; in several other respects it differs considerably from the national picture. For example, a majority of local government employees are female, and a considerable proportion of the employees are part-time workers, particularly in the education service (Table 10.5). In addition, a very high proportion, some 85 per cent, are members of trade unions.

Table 10.5 *Characteristics of local government employment*

	Local Government (%)	*National Average (%)*
Female employees	55	35
White-collar employees	57	43
Part-time employees	35	17

Employment in the local government service grew considerably between 1965 and 1976 (see Table 10.6), as central government placed more and more responsibilities at the door of local government.

Table 10.6 *Numbers employed in local government in Great Britain*

1952	1962	1972	1979
1 448 291	1 820 811	2 583 799	2 928 348

Employment in local government has been curtailed since it reached its peak in 1976. The changes in employment in England and Wales from 1976 to 1980 are as follows:

September 1976 to September 1977, − 1.1 per cent
September 1977 to September 1978, + 0.9 per cent

September 1978 to September 1979, + 0.6 per cent
September 1979 to September 1980, − 1.7 per cent

The 1.7 per cent decrease in employment between September 1979 and September 1980 represents a decrease of 36 424 employees (full-time equivalents).

10.9 INDUSTRIAL RELATIONS IN LOCAL GOVERNMENT

Some 20 per cent of all trade unionists in Britain work in local government, and about 85 per cent of local government staff are unionized. The local government service has been very willing over the years to foster the role of the trade unions and to negotiate with them. The need for sound industrial relations in local government is underlined by the fact that 70 per cent of local government expenditure is on manpower.

Unions in local government

The complexity and diversity of employment means that a large number of unions represent members in the local government service. They can be categorized as follows:

1. Unions which organize exclusively in local government: *The Fire Brigades Union* (30 000 members); *The Police Federation* (100 000 members); The Greater London Staffs Association (20 000 members).
2. Unions which have a majority of their members in local government, including the following.

   National Association of Local Government Officers (NALGO) (membership 709 000, of whom about 450 000 are in local government). NALGO's membership includes the majority of non-manual staff in local government in clerical, administrative, professional and technical occupations. It is the largest white-collar union in Britain. Its other members are in the NHS, gas, electricity, water and new towns.

   National Union of Public Employees (NUPE) (membership 693 000, of whom 357 000 are in local government). NUPE has 55 per cent of its members in local government, 36 per cent in the

NHS, 5 per cent in the universities and colleges and 4 per cent in the water services.

3. Unions with a substantial minority of members in local government. These include the following.

   General and Municipal Workers' Union (GMWU) (membership 945 000, of whom 300 000 are in local government). The majority of the GMWU's local government membership are in manual occupations.

   Transport and General Workers' Union (TGWU) (membership 2 022 000, of whom some 200 000 are employed in local government). The TGWU is the largest union in Britain. Its members in local government are employed in passenger transport services, building construction and engineering, and in supervisory grades.

4. Other unions have a minority of their members employed in local government. They include the Confederation of Health Service Employees (COHSE), the Union of Construction, Allied Trades and Technicians (UCATT), the Amalgamated Union of Engineering Workers (AUEW) and the Electrical, Electronic, Telecommunication and Plumbing Union (EETPU).

5. Teachers' unions can be said to form a distinct group, as teachers form the largest single occupational group in the local government workforce, amounting to 25 per cent of the total. The main teachers' unions are: *National Union of Teachers (NUT),* membership 290 000; *National Association of Schoolmasters/Union of Women Teachers (NAS/UWT),* membership 122 000; *National Association of Teachers in Further and Higher Education (NATFHE),* membership 61 000; *Educational Institute of Scotland (EIS),* membership 45 000; *National Association of Head Teachers,* membership 19 000; *Professional Association of Teachers (PAT),* membership 10 000; *Association of Polytechnic Teachers (APT),* membership 3500.

Employers' organizations

The existence of national wage and salary scales and conditions of service in local government is one reason for the existence of local authority associations. Additionally, they act as pressure groups for putting forward collective views to central government. The three main associations are:

1. *Association of Metropolitan Authorities,* which consists of the

metropolitan districts, the Greater London Council and the London boroughs.
2. *Association of District Councils,* which comprises all the non-metropolitan districts.
3. *Association of County Councils,* which comprises all the non-metropolitan counties.

All three associations aim to protect their members' interests, especially where changes in the law and the financing of local government are concerned. The associations all have seats on the national negotiating bodies for local government employees. In industrial relations matters they are advised by the *Local Government Conditions of Service Advisory Board (LACSAB).*

Collective bargaining in local authorities

Most of the negotiating bodies in local government are based on the style of Whitley councils. The Whitley Committee was set up in 1919 to improve employer/employee relationships. It recommended the introduction of national collective bargaining machinery. Since the Second World War there has been national negotiating machinery for most groups in local government, and there are now about 40 such bodies. The employers' side is advised by LACSAB, which provides a comprehensive range of advisory, research and secretarial services. Each national negotiating council has a similar format: each side of a national council elects its own chairman, and the chairmanship usually alternates in joint meetings year by year. In some bodies, such as the Burnham Committees for Teachers, an independent chairman presides. In the course of negotiations there are usually informal discussions in order to identify areas of possible agreement, but any offer and its acceptance must take place in the council or committee with both sides signifying their acceptance. As each side is usually made up of a number of parties, decisions on both sides are usually the result of majority voting. By voluntary agreement local authorities accept agreements made nationally.

In addition to national councils there is a system of provincial and local negotiating councils with a similar structure to the national bodies.

Pay settlements made in local government have a considerable effect on the national economy and on pay policies of national government. Industrial disputes in the local government sector, as in the 'winter of discontent' of 1979, have had a major effect on the fate of governments.

10.10 THE RELATIONSHIP BETWEEN LOCAL AND CENTRAL GOVERNMENT

If local government is to be true to its name then there has to be a sense in which local authorities truly *govern* the services which they provide rather than merely acting as agents for central government. Local *government* implies democratic accountability to the local electorate and a responsiveness to their wishes. Taken to an extreme the notion would imply local *autonomy,* with each local authority providing different levels and styles of service provision. Nationally this is seen to be unacceptable by central government. It has always been one of central government's responsibilities to ensure an adequate minimum provision and standard of service which must be maintained by every authority. It is argued that the young, the disabled, the homeless, the disadvantaged and the elderly are entitled to the same minimum standard of care regardless of the area in which they live. This leads to a tension between local and central government caused by the idea of local government being responsive to local needs contrasted with the requirement of a national standard of service provision. This is just one area where strains exist between central and local government.

Central government controls

Central government has at its disposal several means by which it can monitor and control the activities of local authorities. Included among them are the following:

1. Local authority accounts must be audited annually.
2. A range of local services are subject to inspection to make certain that they conform to minimum standards. These include the fire service, the police, education and social services.
3. Local authorities' development plans have to be approved by the appropriate central government departments.
4. Central departments can, in the last resort, take local authorities to court for failing to carry out their duties.
5. Central government can lay down what an authority ought to spend and can reduce the size of its block grant if it exceeds its cash limit.
6. Parliament can change the law to force local authorities to carry out particular policies.

In September 1979 the Secretary of State for the Environment announced the abandonment of over 300 central government controls over local authorities. Matters which are now left to the discretion of local councils include the levels of licence fees for dog breeders, the levels of library fines and charges, the establishment of pedestrian crossing schemes and the appointment of directors of social services. This was seen by the Government as an extension of local authority freedom, although many commentators saw it as merely freedom from unnecessary minor controls.

Accountability for local spending

Possibly the most important control exercised by central government is over money. Local government accounts for over one quarter of total public expenditure. In the recessionary period of the late 1970s and early 1980s governments of both parties have felt the need to put strict controls on public and hence local expenditure. The imposition of cash limits (which lay down maximum levels of expenditure) was the major means of controlling local expenditure until the passing of the Local Government Planning and Land (No. 2) Act in 1980. This Act has a block grant formula which lays down spending limits and has financial penalties for authorities which overspend. Earlier in this chapter it was noted that a major source of the *authority* of local government was the existence of an independent source of revenue from the rates. The declining contribution of the rates to local income and the strict limits to be placed both on the level of rate increases and on the level of the block grant give to central government a large degree of control over local spending and hence over the level of services which can be provided. 'He who pays the piper calls the tune' has been a phrase used by many authors to describe this aspect of the relationship between central and local government. If central government decides how much an authority can spend and on what, it must be asked whether local politicians can genuinely put forward alternative policies to the electorate, and whether the electorate in turn can make choices about the level of service provision in their locality. These questions were taken up by the Committee of Inquiry into Local Government, chaired by Frank Layfield QC, which reported in 1976.

The Layfield Committee found a lack of clear accountability for local spending. The reason for this they believed was the confusion between central government and local authorities about who is responsible for decisions to spend money. Central government includes local services in its expenditure plans but local authorities are *not* involved in the planning process through the Public Expenditure Survey Committees. The Layfield Committee found that local authorities felt that the bulk of their expenditure was determined by decisions in which they had no part. Central government, on the other hand, had no effective means of ensuring that local spending conformed to its plans until the introduction of the block grant in 1981. Layfield saw the resulting situation as one in which neither central government nor local authorities feel fully accountable for the level of spending.

Three models of local/central relationships

Clear accountability for spending implies that *either* local authorities are accountable for their service provision and expenditure to their local electorates, *or* central government is accountable to the national electorate for the total provision of local services.

In order to study this issue of accountability for local services it is useful to look at three models of the relationship between local and central government (Fig. 10.11).

The present system of local/central relationships in Britain most closely resembles the mixed accountability model, which is like the situation described by Layfield, where confusion exists over the issue of control and accountability. One of the prime motives behind the reform of the structure of local government was to increase the freedom of action which could be enjoyed by local authorities. It was suggested that the new and enlarged local government units would be large enough to allow central government to relinquish detailed control of their operations. But in recent years the reverse has occurred. The severe economic situation since the mid-1970s has led to a shift in the balance of power towards greater central government direction and control.

The passing of the Local Government Planning and Land (No. 2) Act 1980 has led to an altering of the relationship and a move to a situation bordering on Model 3. The effects of this Act are still to be felt, but certain commentators do see local government being transformed into an agent (albeit with a degree of local discretion) for central government. (See McAllister and Hunter, *Local Government: Death or Devolution*? and Burgess and Travers, *Ten Billion Pounds: Whitehall's Takeover of the Town Halls*.) At the time of the passing of the Act the leader of the Conservative group on the Association of Metropolitan Authorities is reported to have said that the Bill repre-

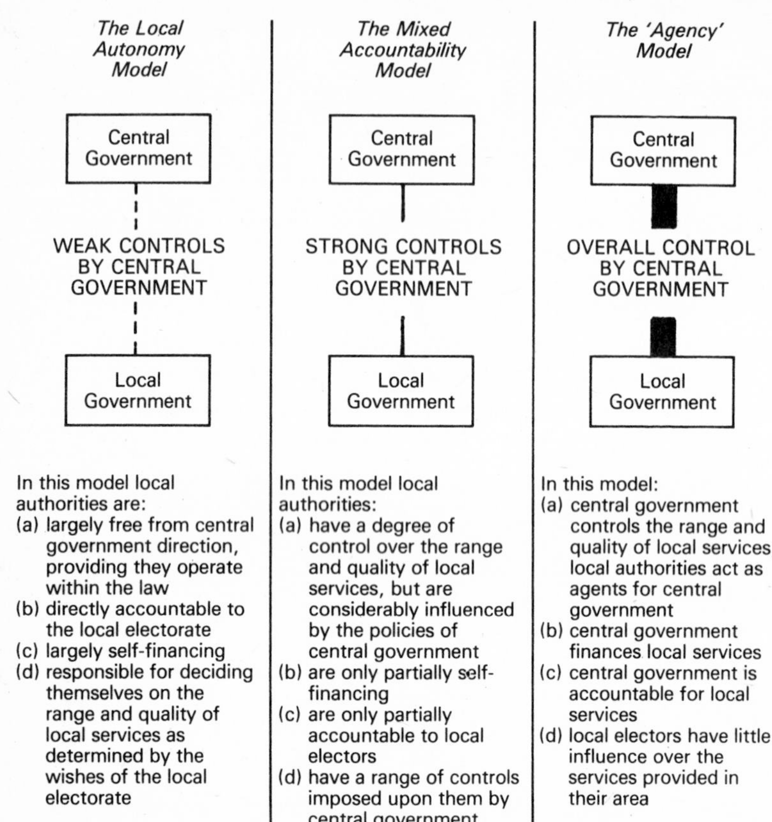

Figure 10.11 *Three models of local/central relationships*

sents 'the biggest threat to the constitutional independence of local government in this country since the nineteenth century . . . It would enable any Environment Secretary to override the democratic right of local electors to decide for themselves the kind of government they want to see in their own area' (reported in the *Guardian,* 13 July 1980).

When the Layfield Committee considered the drift towards central control, it argued that if central government controls the funds for local services then it should accept the accountability for them. In such a situation local authorities would become mere agents for central government; local government becomes local administration. Obviously this would destroy the rationale for democratic local government, which is that it is responsive to the wishes of local people. On the other hand, the agency relationship undoubtedly makes it easier for central government to carry out its task of economic management. Additionally, central government should be able to ensure a uniformity of standard of service over the whole country. (However, this is doubted by many commentators, even if they see it as a desirable aim. It is argued that there is no reason why civil servants should possess greater wisdom on the provision of local services than local government officers.)

The Layfield Committee looked at the other alternative, which is outlined in Model 1, the Local Autonomy Model. In this model local government is still subordinate to central government but the latter exercises only weak controls and allows local authorities to make their own decisions. If this were to take place, the Layfield Committee argued that authorities would have to be responsible for raising their own revenue. This would ensure that amounts spent would be under democratic and single control. Underlying this idea is the need for the introduction of a local income tax which would greatly increase the freedom of action of local authorities. Accountability to the local electors would be substantially increased. What would be altered would be central government's control over the level of public expenditure. The result would be a dramatic shift in the direction of local autonomy.

There seems little likelihood of Layfield's preference for local autonomy being taken up. Economic management and the control of public expenditure are seen by central government as greater priorities than the encouragement of local democracy. In July 1981 it was widely rumoured that the Government was considering introducing a new Local Government Bill which would considerably extend its control over local authorities. Its contents could include the limitation of powers to increase business rates and to throw the whole burden of extra spending on the domestic rate payer, and the only way that local authorities which wish to raise rates above a set norm could do so would be to gain their electorate's approval via a referendum.

In Scotland, the Secretary of State for Scotland has strong powers under the Local Government (Miscellaneous Provisions) (Scotland) Act 1981. These powers include the ability of the Scottish Secretary to cut a Scottish authority's rate support grant if he or she thinks that planned spending is 'excessive or unreasonable'. Scottish authorities are not allowed to levy supplementary rates or to make good the loss by borrowing. This Act provides for much stronger Government controls over Scottish authorities than over English and Welsh authorities.

ASSIGNMENTS

A10.1 As a local resident, you have complaints to make about the following matters. To which department and at which tier of authority should you make your complaint?

(a) unemptied dustbins;
(b) the choice of books in your local library;
(c) a refusal of an application for an improvement grant for your property;
(d) the refusal to grant you planning permission for an extension to your property;
(e) a refusal to put your name on the housing waiting list.

A10.2 Draw an organization chart of the main departments of one local authority with which you are familiar.

A10.3 Imagine that you are an old age pensioner who has been refused 'meals on wheels' by your local social services department. Write a letter to your local councillor stating why you feel that you are entitled to the service and asking for his or her help. What action do you think your councillor can take on your behalf? (When carrying out this assignment you should research the 'meals on wheels' service and find out who is entitled to it.)

A10.4 Draw a chart showing the grading and remuneration structure of local government officers.

A10.5 (This assignment is designed for students working for local authorities.) Write a report on the local authority in which you are employed. The report should contain the following information:

(a) the political composition of the council;
(b) the names of the committee chairmen;
(c) an organization chart of the main departments;
(d) the names of the various directors of services;
(e) the number of people employed;
(f) the type of authority it is;
(g) details of its income and expenditure;
(h) any special features of the authority or any special

problems it has (e.g. whether it is a member of an inner city partnership scheme);

(i) the main policies and priorities of the council.

A10.6 Describe the functions of the following:

(a) the London Boroughs Association;
(b) the Association of Metropolitan Councils;
(c) the Association of County Councils;
(d) the Association of District Councils.

11

Public Economic and Financial Policy

11.1 PUBLIC FINANCE

Public finance is an important topic not only because the Government requires income to pay for its expenditure, but also because of the impact which it has on the economy and on the lives of the citizens in

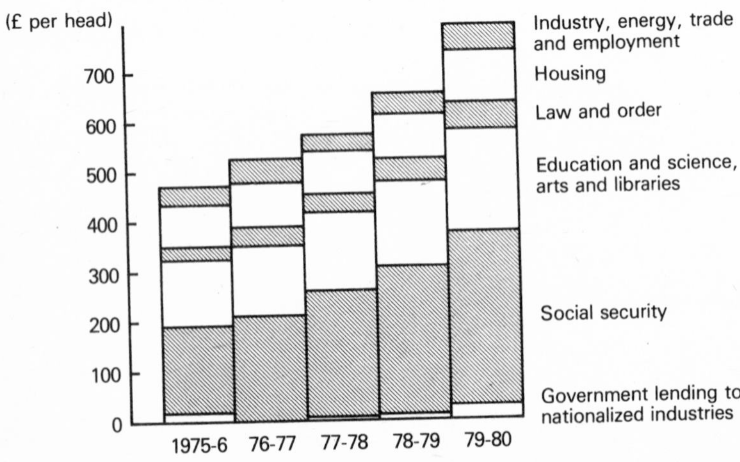

Figure 11.1 *Public spending. From New Society, 9 April 1981. Copyright © New Society, London. Reprinted by permission.*

British society. The latter point is an important area of political debate. The Conservatives see the high level of public expenditure as a major cause of Britain's economic ills, whereas the Labour Party believes that a high level of public spending is both socially necessary to sustain an adequate level of public services and is a means of stimulating the economy in recessionary periods.

Public expenditure has risen considerably in recent years (Fig. 11.1), from £34 000 million in 1974–75 to over £78 000 million in 1979–80.

11.2 CURRENT ACCOUNT

In 1980 expenditure by central and local government on goods and services amounted to over £48 000 million, or over 20 per cent of the Gross Domestic Product. But this figure does not include transfer payments made to individuals and organizations, including grants, pensions, unemployment benefits, social security benefits, etc. Transfer payments in 1980 amounted to over £32 000 million and this, together with the interest on the National Debt, gave a total level of current expenditure of £91 886 million (see Table 11.1). General Government expenditure is divided between the amount spent by Central Government, which is over 68 per cent of the total, and the amount spent by local government, i.e. the remaining 32 per cent. Local government finance is dealt with separately in this chapter.

Table 11.1 *General Government expenditure (current account) 1980*

Receipts	*£s m*	*Expenditure*	*£s m*
Taxes on income	30 893	Spending on goods and services	48 113
Taxes on expenditure	36 843	Subsidies	5 236
National Insurance contributions	13 977	Current grants	27 253
Other receipts[a]	8 758	Debt interest	11 284
Financial deficit	1 415		
	91 886		91 886

[a] Includes surpluses, interest, dividends, etc.

Source: *Financial Statistics,* Central Statistical Office No. 230, HMSO June 1981. Reproduced with the permission of the Controller of Her Majesty's Stationery Office.

Table 11.2 *Total public expenditure by programme*

	1981–82 £ billion projected cash spend	*1979–80*	*1980–81*	*1981–82*	*1982–83*	*1983–84*
			estimated £ million at 1980 survey prices			
Defence	12.3	9 294	9 746	9 750	10 050	10 350
Overseas aid and services	2.1	2 069	1 648	1 592	1 530	1 530
Agriculture, food, fisheries and forestry	1.3	1 010	1 150	1 005	980	920
Industry, energy, trade and employment	5.3	2 929	3 899	4 023	3 080	2 460
Transport	3.6	2 967	2 824	2 736	2 670	2 670
Housing	4.2	4 928	4 256	3 143	2 720	2 230
Other environmental services	4.0	3 210	3 064	2 976	2 880	2 860
Law, order and protective services	3.6	2 698	2 833	2 886	2 960	3 000
Education and science, libraries and arts	11.7	9 236	8 909	8 544	8 360	8 190
Health and personal social services	12.5	9 003	9 067	9 234	9 400	9 480
Social security	27.4	19 106	19 775	21 161	21 600	21 440
Other public services	1.3	931	941	973	930	920
Common services	1.5	1 103	1 106	1 183	1 180	1 230
Scotland	5.7	4 530	4 399	4 271	4 170	4 100
Wales	2.2	1 788	1 737	1 676	1 630	1 600
Northern Ireland	3.2	2 437	2 472	2 436	2 410	2 410
Government lending to nationalized industries	1.9	1 857	2 050	1 435	350	– 150
Nationalized industries net overseas and market borrowing	−0.7	– 322	– 500	– 530	– 400	– 550
Special sale of assets	−0.2	– 999	– 325	– 175	– 125	– 125
Contingency reserve	2.5	–	193	1 650	2 000	2 000
General allowance for shortfall	−1.0	–	–	– 500	– 500	– 500
Planning total	104.4	77 776	79 245	79 465	77 900	76 000

Source: *Economic Progress Report* No. 131, March 1981, HM Treasury. Reproduced with the permission of the Controller of Her Majesty's Stationery Office.

Central government expenditure goes to finance a very wide variety of services. These services are divided according to programme. The projected expenditure for the early 1980s is shown in Table 11.2.

11.3 CAPITAL ACCOUNT

In addition to the *current* expenditure (expenditure which is mainly regular or recurring, such as wages and salaries, fuel, social security payments, etc.) the Government also spends money on *capital* projects. Capital spending produces items of long-term benefit – roads, school buildings, etc. – which provide a stream of benefits over a number of years. In 1980 total capital expenditure by both central and local government was £8042 million.

It is often argued that all capital spending is necessarily good, since it adds to the productive capacity of the nation. Though this is true of certain capital projects, such as motorways or new power stations, it is not always the case. Investment in new prisons or parks, however useful, cannot be said to add to economic capacity. Certain items in the current account, such as research and development work, or industrial training, are of long-term benefit economically, although they are classified as current expenditure.

11.4 GOVERNMENT AND THE ECONOMY SINCE 1945

William Keegan and Rupert Pennant-Rea, in their book *Who Runs the Economy?* (1979), divide British economic policy-making since the Second World War into four periods:

1. Reconstruction 1945–51.
2. The period 1951–60.
3. 1961–73.
4. 1974–79.

To these must be added the period of economic policy-making since the Conservative Government came to office in 1979. As politics so often reflects the state of the economy, and political issues are about how the economy ought to be managed, a brief summary of some of the main economic events since 1945 is given here as background to economic policy-making.

Post-war reconstruction 1945–51

Policy-making during these years was concerned both with the return of the economy to a peacetime footing and with laying down the conditions for a prosperous society. It was a period which saw a considerable extension of public ownership, with the nationalization of a number of major industries – coal, gas, electricity, the railways and a number of other parts of the transport system.

The major element of the policy of the Labour Government of these years was the avoidance of the poverty and mass unemployment which had been a feature of the 1920s and 1930s. The Government had a major weapon in the new economics which were the result of the writings of John Maynard Keynes, particularly his *General Theory of Employment, Interest and Money* (1936).

Keynes put forward the view that unemployment could be almost eliminated by positive Government intervention in the economy. Government finance could be used to regulate the level of spending (aggregate demand) by altering its own expenditure or the level at which individuals or firms are taxed. At its simplest, if the economy were suffering unemployment then Government could boost the demand for goods and services and hence for labour (the demand for which is *derived* from the demand for goods and services) by increasing its own spending or reducing taxation. And, in reverse, if the economy were 'overheated' with inflationary levels of demand then taxes could be increased or public expenditure reduced in order to reduce the level of total demand in the economy. It was assumed that both the level of employment and the level of inflation were functions of the level of demand (spending) in the economy, and that unemployment and inflation were opposite phenomena and would not occur together.

The wartime coalition Government had committed itself to full employment with the publication in 1944 of the Beveridge Report *Full Employment in a Free Society*. This report committed the Government to using demand management, Keynesian style, 'in order to maintain the highest possible level of employment'. The definition of 'full employment' was 3 per cent unemployment. The 1945 Labour Government carried out this commitment to Beveridge and, with it, its other recommendations on social policy and the need for a comprehensive system of national insurance and social security.

The 1945–51 period was marked by a piecemeal replacement of wartime controls on the mobility of labour, on prices and on the supply of goods (rationing), although this was not fast enough for many citizens. The wartime controls were retained to avoid an inflationary consumer boom at the end of the war, when most industries were still directed towards wartime production. Government policy emphasized new investment and Britain was heavily dependent on financing from the United States via the Marshall Plan.

1951–60

During this period there was a Conservative Government in power. The economy went through a period of sustained growth (although not at such a fast rate as those of our main competitors). Unemployment was at the very low rate of between 1 and 2 per cent of the labour force. In many sections of the economy there was a severe shortage of labour, and the period saw an immigration of labour, with many people entering the country from countries of the new Commonwealth. Government policy was centred around Keynesian demand management, or what is known as *fiscal* policies. There was persistent inflation, but at mild rates, and there was little real attempt by the Government to deal with it. The *real* incomes of consumers (after the effects of inflation have been accounted for) rose by 50 per cent in this period.

1961–73

Although the 1950s saw a period of unparalleled increase in prosperity for ordinary people in Britain (what Harold Macmillan termed 'you've never had it so good') this did not lead to a sense of satisfaction with the country's economic performance. Britain's growth rates compared unfavourably with those of leading competitors, particularly West Germany (see Table 11.3). Levels of investment in new plant, equipment and methods by British industry compared unfavourably with investment by other western industrial nations. Economic policy in the early 1960s concentrated on faster economic growth and the use of longer-term economic planning. Active Government intervention in stimulatory growth through 'indicative planning' was taken from the French model, in which the French Government had taken a leading role in the economy. In 1962 the then Chancellor of the Exchequer, Selwyn Lloyd, set up the National Economic Development Council

Table 11.3 *Real gross domestic product growth 1951–1976 (1970 prices)*

	UK	*France*	*W. Germany*	*Italy*	*USA*	*Japan*
Average rate of growth 1951–1976	2.5%	4.8%	5.5%	4.9%	3.1%	8.5%

Source: *Economic Progress Report* No. 100, July 1978, HM Treasury. Reproduced with the permission of the Controller of Her Majesty's Stationery Office.

(NEDC). This was a bringing together of the Government with representatives of industry and the trade unions in order to advise on economic matters. One result of the setting up of the NEDC was the notion of growth targets for the economy to achieve.

The early part of the period also saw the first of a series of temporary *incomes policies,* when Selwyn Lloyd introduced a pay pause. This was an attempt to halt the upward drift of wages which was adding to inflationary pressures at the time.

When Labour came to power in 1964 it was committed to faster economic growth, technological change ('the white heat of technology', in Harold Wilson's words) and economic planning. In 1965 the Department of Economic Affairs was set up by the Deputy Prime Minister, George Brown, and it produced the short-lived *National Plan* in 1965.

The National Plan rested on the notion of the achievement of an annual growth rate of 3.8 per cent and a growth of exports of 5.25 per cent. The plan lasted only until the middle of 1966. The external situation of a balance of payments crisis made many of its assumptions untenable. At the end of 1967 the pound was devalued, and the momentum built up for economic planning since 1962 was lost.

The end of the Labour Government's period of office was marked by a tight budgetary policy while attempts were made to turn the external deficit.

The Conservatives, who came to office in 1970, initially took a doctrinaire approach to economic policy in their 'Selsden' programme. They were committed to less government, a reduction in taxation, increases in incentives in the economy, and a reduction in public expenditure. They were also committed to growth. In 1971 unemployment reached the million mark and the Government took to growth as a way out of its policy dilemma. In place of a purely fiscal policy the

Government also adopted a monetary policy to provide incentive for industry. In 1971 the Competition and Credit Control Policy removed many restrictions on bank lending and borrowing. In 1972 the pound was allowed to 'float' in line with market forces in order to remove the restraints which the external situation had placed on policy in the past. However, the expansionist monetary policy adopted in 1971 and 1972 to stimulate demand and growth in the economy accelerated the level of inflation in the economy. The Government attempted a series of incomes policies to hold down wage demands which were the response to rapidly rising prices.

1974–79

The Conservative Government fell after a confrontation with the miners over pay in 1974. The economic boom created by the Government in the early 1970s had brought about a high rate of growth (about 5 per cent annually) but this was led by monetary acceleration and so a high rate of inflation (over 25 per cent in 1975) followed it. This bout of monetary expansion was linked to an external situation which saw a dramatic increase in oil prices following the Arab-Israeli war in 1974. The quadrupling of oil prices by the OPEC producers added to both costs and prices. The effect was a fall in demand and production of many goods, and an increase in their prices.

The Labour Party faced a dilemma when they were returned to office in February 1974. As a party it was committed to the policy of free collective bargaining (as opposed to incomes policies), but it needed to control wage inflation. Its solution was the 'Social Contract', the author of which was the General Secretary of the TGWU, Jack Jones. This policy involved an agreement between the trade unions and the Government for voluntary wage restraint in return for the Government's providing increases in the 'social wage' (pensions, social benefits, etc.). Nevertheless, the period 1974–76 saw the persistence of high rates of inflation.

From 1976 the direction of economic policy took a new turn, with the emphasis being placed on monetary policy. The Government saw an expansion of the money supply in advance of productivity growth as essentially inflationary, and produced the first attempts to limit monetary growth. Additionally, another turnaround in economic policy took place with regard to public expenditure. Until 1976 public spending annually took a rising share of the gross domestic product. Government expenditure on goods and services took 20 per cent of the GDP in 1974 and 27 per cent in 1975. A run on the pound in 1976 required a massive loan to be secured by the Government from the International Monetary Fund. One condition of the loan was a reduction in the level of public expenditure. The end of the period of the Labour Government was marked by rising unemployment, planned reductions in public spending and a stagnant economy. By 1979 the annual rate of inflation was down to single figures via the introductions of incomes policies.

The Conservative Government 1979

When the Conservative Government came to power it was faced with a series of major economic problems – a worldwide recession, high but falling inflation rates, unemployment at about the million mark and falling manufacturing output.

The approach of this Government differed from that of other post-war Governments. It brought to an end the Keynesian consensus to which both major political parties had broadly subscribed. Instead of positive Government intervention in the economy, Mrs Thatcher and certain of her leading Cabinet colleagues, notably Sir Keith Joseph, the Industry Minister, and Sir Geoffrey Howe, the Chancellor of the Exchequer, followed the view of the Keynesian critic, Milton Friedman, and his monetarist philosophy. Friedman viewed positive state intervention as an economic evil and praised unfettered free enterprise. He saw inflation as being caused by excessive public expenditure and the Government fuelling of the money supply to finance their spending plans.

The Conservatives' economic and industrial strategy was based around the need to reduce the rate of inflation and to provide incentives for industry. Their method of tackling inflation rejected the idea of incomes policy, and they set themselves the task of reducing public spending and cutting the public sector borrowing requirements. Interests rates rose to encourage savings and to reduce inflationary demand. The reduction of expenditure allowed an initial cut in income tax in the Chancellor's first Budget, but value added tax, national insurance contributions and income tax (not directly, but by abolishing the index-linking of allowances) were increased in subsequent Budgets. The public spending cuts and high interest rates had a number of effects on the economy. The interest rates, which were high until mid-1981, attracted a great deal of foreign funds, which raised the exchange rate and made for considerable difficulties for exporters. The general deflationary effect of public spending cuts and tight money policies caused a substantial rise in the level of unemployment. In June 1981 the jobless total stood at 2 552 000 (registered unemployed, seasonally adjusted and excluding school leavers), or 10.6 per cent of the employed labour force. If school leavers, 60 per cent of whom could not find jobs in that year, were added, the number totalled over 3 million, a figure much higher than at any period since the 1930s. For this Government the alleviation of unemployment was seen as secondary to curing inflation and, unlike other post-war Governments, it saw this as a problem not open to Government solution. Ministers answered that only efficient industry operating in an economy with a low inflation rate could provide additional jobs. Fig. 11.2 shows the employment trends since 1970.

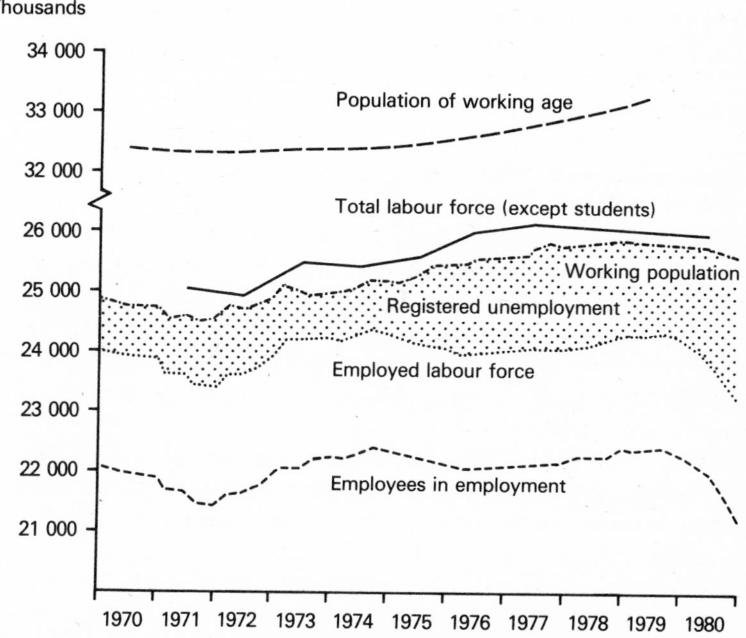

Figure 11.2 *Employment trends 1970–1980 (males 15 to 64, females 15 to 59). From HM Treasury's Economic Process Report No. 155, July 1981. Reproduced with the permission of the Controller of Her Majesty's Stationery Office.*

A degree of unemployment was part of the monetarist policy. Prior to the 1979 election Sir Keith Joseph had argued vigorously that British industry was overmanned and that increased efficiency required a shedding of labour.

At the time of writing it is not possible accurately to assess the consequences, successes or failures of this policy. But what can be noted is the sharp break in the style and objectives of economic policy which occurred with the return of the Conservatives in 1979.

11.5 THE CONTROL AND PLANNING OF PUBLIC EXPENDITURE

The modern system of controlling and planning public spending originated in 1961 with the publication of the Plowden Report. Until the implementation of the report's recommendations most expenditure plans, with the exception of those for certain areas, like defence, covered only the period of the coming financial year, despite the fact that the programmes themselves might take several years to complete and could incur costs over a long time. The Plowden Report argued that 'decisions involving substantial future expenditure should always be taken in the light of surveys of public expenditure as a whole, over a number of years and in relation to the prospective resources'.

Regular surveys began in 1963 and became known as PESC, after the initials of the interdepartmental Civil Service committee involved, the Public Expenditure Survey Committee.

The PESC cycle

The aim of PESC is to make an annual survey of public expenditure covering a period of four to five years rolled forward a year at a time. The cycle begins in the spring of each year, when individual Civil Service departments cost out the various items on which Government money is to be spent – salaries, tanks, urban aid, etc. Until 1982 this was done at the prices prevailing in the previous year, which were known as survey prices; i.e. the 1981 survey prices were those prevailing in 1980. The advantage of the survey price method, also known as 'volume', was that the figures had a constant base and they were a reasonably good measure of the inputs of programmes – fuel for heating, salaries for social workers, number of hospitals to be built, etc. But this method of costing in 'funny money' had been criticized because it did not show what a programme would cost in, for example, three years' time. Since 1982 public expenditure planning has been conducted in cash terms so that projections for expenditure will be directly related to the amount of cash available for the programmes. Changes in costs can also be brought into the discussions.

In late March each year the Treasury has talks with the individual departments about their projections. These initial discussions take place under the supervision of the Public Expenditure Survey Committee. PESC is chaired by the Deputy Secretary of the Treasury and is made up of the finance officers of the various departments. The Committee reports on its deliberations and sends its projections for expenditure to Ministers for their consideration. It is interesting to note that local authorities, who in 1979–80 spent £25 thousand million of public money, are not included in these discussions, although of course they can make recommendations. This aspect has been heavily criticized, as it means that in areas where the local authorities are the service providers, e.g. in education or the social services, the expenditure plans cannot be precisely geared to programme needs.

In late June and early July there are the first rounds of Cabinet discussions on future expenditure. The next stage, in the autumn, entails Treasury forecasts of the state of the economy being made available to the Chancellor so that he or she can calculate the possible size of next year's public sector borrowing requirement. At this stage the Cabinet has to look at the surveys again and decide on the size of the expenditure for the coming year and the effect it will have on the public services and on the economy. Decisions have to be made on such matters as the size of the PSBR, the rate support grant for local authorities, and the cash limits for various heads of expenditure. Cash limits are the maximum sums available for, say, public sector pay rises. They do not cover all areas of expenditure; there are areas (e.g. unemployment benefit) where it would be impossible to set a limit because the volume of expenditure is 'demand determined'.

The decisions made by the Cabinet in the autumn are translated into the public expenditure White Paper, which until 1981 was published in January. However, this publication date was heavily criticized, as it meant that expenditure decisions were published before decisions of how money was to be raised in the Budget, which was announced in March/April. In 1981 the White Paper was published at the same time as the Budget.

The function of PESC

When PESC was first set up it was seen as a means of planning public expenditure, but as Maurice Wright has suggested (see 'From planning to control: PESC in the 1970s' in *Public Spending Decisions* (1980)), by the end of the 1970s it had become a means of restraining and controlling public spending. The emphasis has switched from using PESC as a means of trying to make the most effective use of resources to its use as a means of cost control. Maurice Wright suggests that the changeover date was 1972–73, when higher unemployment and inflation and stagnant production provided different problems and restricted opportunities. This set of circumstances demanded a different approach from that of the growth years of the 1960s. Maurice Wright has argued that PESC comprises elements of five processes: planning, allocating, controlling, evaluating and accounting.

Planning

This happens over a four-year to five-year period. Forecasts and costings for both current and capital spending are produced.

Allocating

In this role PESC has to come to conclusions about competing claims for resources and their allocation over the period of the plan.

Controlling

1. Commitment. This process ensures that allocated resources are committed by spending authorities at the time stipulated by the plan.
2. Monitoring. This involves the controlling of cash flow to finance the use of prescribed volumes of resources.
3. Verification. This process involves the comparison of actual and planned expenditure at programme and sub-programme levels and accounting for differences.

Evaluating

1. Output. Identifying and measuring the output of the use of allocated resources.
2. Impact. Measuring the impact of the outputs.

3. Effectiveness. Evaluating the output and its impact in terms of their effectiveness in achieving broad policy objectives.

Accounting

1. Audit. Auditing cash flows to finance expenditure programmes in accordance with Parliamentary appropriations.
2. Efficiency audit. Examining the economical and effective use of resources.
3. Accounting to Parliament and the public. Explaining and justifying the planning, allocating and use of resources.

11.6 THE BUDGET

Traditionally the raising of Government revenue via taxation is considered separately from the planning and control of public expenditure, and for this reason the term 'Budget' is a misnomer. The Budget is essentially concerned with the income side of the Government's accounts. This has altered to an extent with the publication of the Public Expenditure White Paper at the same time as the Budget in March/April. Nevertheless, the Budget can still be considered to be a tax budget. Public expenditure is projected four to five years ahead, but taxation is still considered on an annual basis.

Although the Budget is a means of raising revenue to finance Government expenditure, it has other objectives – both social and economic – which a Government attempts to achieve through change. Some objectives may be long-term, such as attempting to alleviate certain types of poverty, while others are short term, such as the curing of a temporary balance of payments problem. Because of the need to make periodic alterations to the economy, there are often mini-budgets in the summer or the autumn in addition to the main Budget.

Different Governments will have different objectives and priorities but, regardless of what their objectives are, the Budget is a major means of trying to achieve them.

Some of the major budgetary objectives of successive Governments since the war have been:

1. To maintain full employment (or to reduce unemployment).
2. To maintain a stable currency (or to reduce the rate of inflation).

3. To maintain a stable balance of payments.
4. To increase incentives.
5. To reduce poverty.
6. To provide support for industry.
7. To provide assistance to particular regions (regional policy).
8. To promote savings and investment.
9. To decrease (or increase) the size and provision of the public services.
10. To alter the distribution of income and wealth (either to make the distribution more equitable or inequitable).
11. To control the growth of the money supply.
12. To give assistance to particular disadvantaged groups in society (e.g. one-parent families, the blind, etc.). Changes in social security payments are announced in the Budget.

In the March 1981 Budget the Chancellor of the Exchequer, Sir Geoffrey Howe, said that his central Budget objectives were:

1. To maintain success in the battle against inflation by carrying forward the medium-term financial strategy.
2. To correct two major imbalances in the economy:
   (a) between consumers and industry; and
   (b) between the public and private sectors.

Obviously, not all Governments will have all the above objectives as their priorities and not all of them will be seen as appropriate or legitimate objectives by all Governments. Many of the objectives in the above lists are in conflict and clearly could not all be achieved at the same time, however desirable they may be.

11.7 TAXATION

Taxation in Britain is divided into two types: direct and indirect.

Direct taxation

Direct taxes are taxes which fall directly on incomes and are administered by the Board of Inland Revenue. The main direct taxes are shown in Table 11.4

Table 11.4 *Main direct taxes*

	Net receipts 1980–81 (£s m)
Income tax	24 305
Corporation tax	4 645
Capital gains tax	508
Development land tax	26
Estate duty	28
Capital transfer tax	425
Stamp duties	635
Petroleum revenue tax	2 410
Total	32 982

Source: *Financial Statistics,* Central Statistical Office No. 230, HMSO June 1981. Reproduced with the permission of the Controller of Her Majesty's Stationery Office.

Income tax

This is charged on incomes of individual citizens whether they are employed or self-employed, and whether their income is earned or unearned. (An example of unearned income is interest on bank deposit accounts.) It is also charged on the profits of unincorporated businesses.

Britain, like most other countries, has a 'progressive' income tax structure, which means that the rate of taxation rises as income rises. For example, in 1979–80 single people paid no tax at all on incomes up to £1075 per year, and above that level paid tax at rates rising from 25 per cent to 65 per cent (or 83 per cent on unearned income). There are many allowances which can be claimed against income tax and which reduce the amount that a taxpayer has to pay. These allowances include the married man's allowance, allowance for interest on mortgage payments, allowances for blind people, for maintaining a dependent relative, etc. The existence of allowances and different tax rates makes income tax complex, but it does allow the Government to pursue social and economic objectives through it. For example, in the 1981 Budget additional help was given to blind people by doubling their special allowance.

Corporation tax

This is a tax on the profits of limited companies which was introduced in 1965. In 1981 it raised over £4500 million.

Capital transfer tax

This tax was introduced in 1975 and replaced estate duty, which had taxed the wealth of people on their death. The major loophole in estate duty was that wealth could be given away before the death of the owner and so tax was avoided. The new tax covers all large gifts made at any point during a person's life.

Capital gains tax

Capital gains tax is levied on the proceeds of the sale of capital assets, for example property and shares. Certain assets, such as houses, motor-cars and first homes, are exempt.

Petroleum revenue tax

This is levied on profits made from the exploitation of North Sea oil and is charged in addition to corporation tax.

Indirect taxation

Indirect taxation is administered by the Board of Customs and Excise. The Board is accountable to Parliament through the Chancellor of the Exchequer. In March 1980 it employed 27 273 people. In 1979–80 the Board collected taxes to the value of approximately £18 000 million at an administrative cost of £245 million, which represents about 1.35 pence in the pound (see Table 11.5).

Indirect taxation is taxation on expenditure. The vast majority of goods and services are taxed, with the exception of items such as heating, children's clothes and foodstuffs. Indirect taxation represents about 40 per cent of the total central government revenue. Indirect taxes are said to be regressive, in that they fall heaviest on the poorest section of society.

Table 11.5 *Net receipts by HM Customs and Excise 1979–80*

	£s m
Beer	916.4
Wines, cider, perry and spirits	1 526.0
Tobacco	2 579.1
Betting and gaming	406.2
Hydrocarbon oils	2 928.2
Customs duties	1 177.1
Value added tax	8 187.6
Car tax	516.2
Shipbuilders' relief	−9.2
Other	8.3
Total	18 235.9

Source: *Financial Statistics,* Central Statistical Office No. 230, June 1981, HMSO. Reproduced with the permission of the Controller of Her Majesty's Stationery Office.

Value added tax

VAT is the main indirect tax and is charged on all goods and services, except necessities, at a rate of 15 per cent. The introduction of VAT was a condition of Britain's membership of the European Community. In 1979–80 it yielded a revenue of just over £8000 million. It is a useful tax, as it is the only tax whose yield automatically keeps pace with inflation (as prices rise, a fixed percentage of the price yields a larger sum).

Excise duties

These are specific duties on specified goods and are charged in addition to VAT. They are charged on goods for which the demand is thought to be 'price inelastic' (that is, the demand for them remains fairly constant despite price changes). However, there is often a point at which the imposition of an additional duty leads to a fall in demand and revenue.

11.8 LOCAL GOVERNMENT FINANCE

Local government has the power to levy its own tax – the rates – to finance its services. This taxing power has long been regarded as essential to the maintenance of a degree of independence from central government. However, in recent years this independence has been diminished: local government is increasingly financed by central government via the rate support grant and is less and less financed by the rates. In England in 1979–80 local authorities spent a total of £27 166 million, of which £12 889 million was contributed by central government.

Revenue expenditure and finance

This represents expenditure on current items which are not regarded as assets. The main items of current or revenue expenditure are wages and salaries, but this heading also includes the running costs of buildings and equipment, heating, lighting, stationery, etc. In 1979–80 the current expenditure of all local authorities was £14 565 million, a figure which represents nearly 20 per cent of total current public expenditure.

There are three main sources of finance for current expenditure – the rates, the rate support grant and other revenue such as council house rents, bus fares, etc. (see Table 11.6).

Table 11.6 *Local government finance: current account 1979–80*

Source	*£s m*	*Percentage of total*
Rates	6 772	30
Rate support grant (from central government)	11 756	51
Rent	2 713	12
Gross trading surplus, dividends and interest received, etc.	1 603	7
Total	22 844	100

Source: *Financial Statistics*, Central Statistical Office No. 230, HMSO June 1981. Reproduced with the permission of the Controller of Her Majesty's Stationery Office.

The rates

The rates are a local property tax paid by all occupiers of residential, industrial and commercial property. The amount of income received by an individual local authority from the rates depends on:

1. The rateable value of properties within an authority's boundaries. The valuation of properties is carried out by the Inland Revenue. The value of properties can vary enormously from area to area; for example, the London Borough of Hillingdon in 1975–76 had a rateable value per head of the population of £230, compared with mid-Glamorgan's £63.
2. The rate in the pound which the authority decides to charge to its ratepayers. For example, if an authority decides to charge a rate of 60 pence in the pound, the occupier of a property valued at £200 will have to pay £120 a year.

In theory the decision about the rate in the pound to be charged by a local authority is its own decision, but in recent years there has been an increase in the amount of control exercised from the centre. As local authorities spend one fifth of all public expenditure, control of their spending is seen as a crucial aspect of policies to reduce the rate of inflation. The proportion of income collected from the rates has fallen from 40 per cent of total incomes in the mid-1960s to under 30 per cent in 1981.

Appraisal of the rating system. The advantages of the rating system are:

1. The tax base is localized.
2. The rates are simple and easy to collect.
3. It is a difficult tax to evade.
4. The yield from the rates is predictable, stable and largely unaffected by changing economic conditions.

Its disadvantages are:

1. There are inequities in the system of valuation; for example, flats tend to be overvalued compared with houses.
2. The rates are an inflexible tax and it is difficult to increase the yield to meet the demand for increased spending in a period of inflation.
3. The rates are regressive, since the amount an individual has to pay bears little relationship to the amount earned by the household.
4. Rates are an unpopular form of taxation, as they fall unevenly and some people with income do not contribute at all.

Alternatives to the rating system. The current system of rating has come in for a great deal of criticism. There is no geneal agreement about alternatives to the present system, but listed below are some possible ways of financing local services:

1. The introduction of a local income tax (discussed in more detail in the next section, on the Layfield Committee Report).
2. The introduction of a local sales tax, i.e. a local VAT.
3. The introduction of charges to consumers of certain local services. This could include charges for refuse collection or the payment of full economic fees for attendance at evening classes, etc.
4. The transfer of certain present local government services to central government. The service most discussed in this context is education. The remaining services could, because of the amount spent on education, be financed out of local authorities' own incomes. A move in this direction was proposed in 1981, i.e. the transfer of the polytechnics and other local authority colleges of higher education to a national body with direct central government funding. The transfer of services is an unpopular idea in local government, as it reduces authorities' local influence and the scope of their provision.

The Layfield Committee and the reform of the rates. The present system of rating has been the subject of considerable controversy both because of its unpopularity with the general public and because it has been yielding a diminishing share of local government finance. In 1976 the Committee of Inquiry into Local Government Finance (the Layfield Committee) made its report. It proposed a number of changes to the system of financing local services. Its recommendations have been ignored by Government, but nevertheless it remains an important document for students of local government both for its discussions of local finance and for its analysis of the relationship between central and local government. (The latter aspect is examined in Chapter 10.) The main conclusions of the report on finance were as follows:

1. The rating system, with some modifications, should continue to provide a substantial amount of local revenue. However, the report did consider that rating could not finance a larger share of local spending. It put forward the argument that in future rates should be based on the capital value (market value) of property and not on the notional rental value, which is the current basis of valuation.

2. A local income tax should be introduced. This would abolish the need for the rate support grant and so would provide local authorities with an extra degree of independence. The introduction of a local income tax would not necessarily increase the total level of income tax, as one of its purposes would be to replace the existing rate support grant from central government. The report admitted that the system would be administratively complex, requiring an additional 12 000 staff and costing an extra £100 million a year (1976 prices), but it argued that this additional expenditure could be more than justified if it led to more decisions being made locally.

The rate support grant

The RSG made by central to local government is needed to meet the shortfall in local authorities' rate income. Until 1981, when a new system of calculation was introduced, the grant was made up of three elements:

1. A subsidy to domestic ratepayers (and from 1981 to business ratepayers).
2. A resources element, which was a subsidy to authorities with lower-than-average rateable values in their areas.
3. A needs element which was introduced in 1971 as a subsidy to those authorities with pressing social needs, e.g. above-average numbers of homeless families or immigrants in their areas. This element came under a great deal of criticism, as its calculation was based on the previous year's spending and so it was said to encourage high-spending authorities.

As a result of the 1976 Layfield Report the then Labour Government published a Green Paper (1977) on local authority finance. The Layfield Report had argued for a 'localist' approach to provide local government with more freedom in their spending. The Green Paper put forward a 'centralist' approach to give central government greater control. Though the recommendations of the Green Paper were not implemented, the Conservative Government followed much the same path in its reform of the rate support grant in its Local Government, Planning and Land (No. 2) Act 1980. The 1980 Act introduced a new system of calculating the grants which became effective from April 1981. Under the new system the needs and resources elements have been replaced by a *block grant,* with the following formula being applied to assess the amount to be received by an individual authority:

1. The Government assesses how much each authority should spend in order to bring its services into line with the national level of service provision.
2. A calculation is made of the national average level of rates. (This figure is worked out by the Department of the Environment.)
3. The gap between a local authority's assessed level of spending and the total it could raise from the rates if it charged the national average level is calculated.
4. The difference between the two figures is the amount of grant an authority will receive.

Local authorities are allowed a degree of freedom to overspend up to a level of 10 per cent before their grant is affected. In fact they can spend exactly what they wish, except that over this 10 per cent threshold their grant diminishes progressively. Local ratepayers then have to foot the entire bill.

The block grant formula was introduced to provide substantially greater control over local spending. It was argued by the Government that its introduction would provide greater accountability by authorities to their electorates: substantial rate increases would be seen by ratepayers as evidence that the authority had decided to spend more than the national average on its services. Its critics argue that it removes much of the independence from local authorities by dictating national standards for services and the amount that they are able to spend. The new system allows the Government a far greater degree of control over local authorities' expenditure than the previous system.

The initial evidence of the workings of the block grant system shows that the Government's intention to hold down local authority spending has not been met. The 1981–82 estimates of spending were £1000 million over targets. In addition, certain authorities – mainly urban Labour-controlled councils – deliberately exceeded their notified targets and lost their grants. These included the Inner London Education Authority and the London Boroughs of Hackney, Camden and Lambeth. To compensate for the loss of grants these authorities' rates for 1981–82 rose by between 40 and 50 per cent.

The issue comes down to whether or not central government wants full control over local authority finance. Central government could, of course, simply set the level of rates for all authorities or abolish separate local taxes altogether and finance local services directly from the centre. Or it could, as a half-way measure, go for greater rate control by putting a limit on non-domestic (commercial and industrial) rates, from which £5000 million was raised in 1981. This would leave authorities free to determine only their domestic rates. The Environment Secretary proposed legislation in the autumn of 1981 to exercise greater control by proposing a local referendum before an authority could charge a supplementary rate or make additional borrowings if it lost its block grant, an idea which he was forced to drop in December 1981 due to a threatened revolt by Conservative backbenchers. The Secretary of State instead proposed a measure to prevent certain supplementary rate demands by high-spending authorities. Whatever the solution to local government financing in the future is, it is not just one of finance, for the control of local authority revenue is the key to the independence of local government.

Other receipts on current account

The other income available to local authorities can be divided into three categories:

1. *Trading income* from bus fares, swimming-bath charges, evening class fees, etc.
2. *Rental income* from council housing.
3. *Interest received* from loans made on, for example, local authority mortgages.

Capital expenditure and finance

This is the money which local authorities spend on the purchase of assets. Assets are durable items which have a life and use of a number of years. Examples of capital assets include buses, buildings, roads, council houses and computers. In 1979–80 the capital expenditure of local authorities amounted to £3711 million.

The cost of capital expenditure is spread over the life of the purchased assets, unlike that of current expenditure, which must be met in the year in which it is incurred. As a result the bulk of capital expenditure is financed by borrowing and repaying the amount borrowed over a period related to the life of the asset. This transfers the burden to ratepayers of the future, who can be expected to derive benefits from the assets. Half of local authority capital expenditure is on housing.

The Local Government Planning and Land (No. 2) Act introduced a new system of central or local authority capital expenditure. Under the old system authorities received permission from central government for capital expenditure on individual projects. From 1981 each authority receives an annual capital allocation for housing, education, personal social services and other services. Each local authority has the freedom to aggregate these allocations into a single block and decide its own priorities.

The purpose of the new system is to provide central government with control over total spending and to ensure that spending is consistent with national plans, while providing local authorities with freedom to pursue their own priorities.

Local authorities can borrow money from the following sources (see Table 11.7):

1. From central government via the National Loans Fund. (In addition to lending money to local government and the nationalized industries, the Fund meets the interest and management charges of the National Debt.)
2. From the private banking and financial sector.
3. From companies and individuals via the sale of bonds.
4. From financial markets overseas.

Table 11.7 *Local authority finance: capital account 1979–80*

Source	*£s m*	*Percentage of total*
Current account surplus	1133	25
Capital grants from central government	335	7
Direct borrowing from central government	817	17
Borrowing from other sources (banking sector, overseas, etc.)	2210	49
Miscellaneous receipts, etc.	83	2
Total	4578	100

Source: *Financial Statistics,* Central Statistical Office No. 230, June 1981, HMSO. Reproduced with the permission of the Controller of Her Majesty's Stationery Office.

11.9 LOCAL FINANCE AND SERVICES, A CASE STUDY: THE LONDON BOROUGH OF EALING

(The information, figure and tables in this case study are reproduced by permission of the Director of Finance, London Borough of Ealing.)

The London Borough of Ealing has a population of 250 000. Being an outer London borough, it is its own education authority. For 1981–82 the Council made a General Rate of 131 pence in the pound. This is an

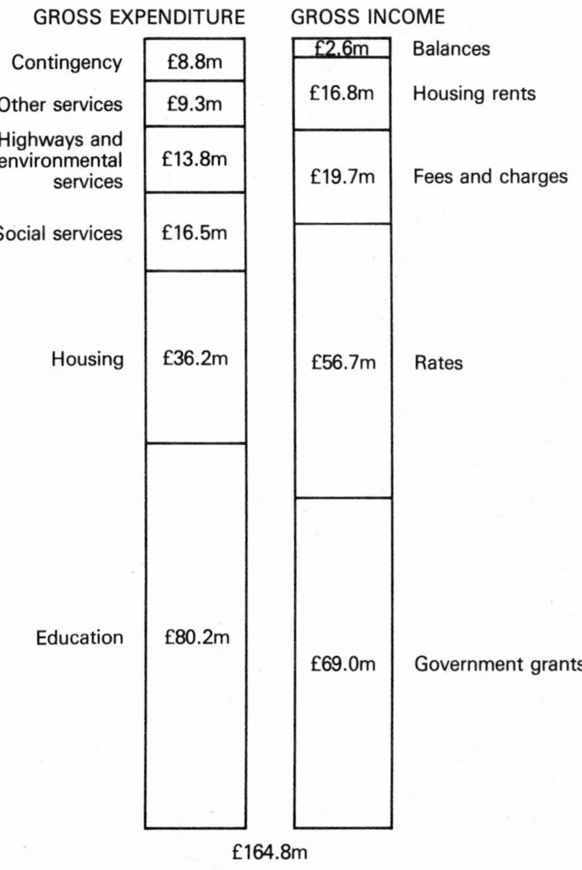

Figure 11.3 *Analysis of expenditure and income*

increase of 16.5 per cent on the 1980–81 figure. Because the Government subsidy to domestic ratepayers remains unchanged, at 18.5 pence in the pound, the rate for domestic properties will be 112.5 pence in the pound, an increase of 19.5 per cent.

Of the total rate levy for 1981–82 of 131 pence, 28 pence relates to precepts payable to the Greater London Council and to the Metropolitan Police. The remaining 103 pence relates to services provided by the London Borough of Ealing and shows an increase of 15 pence or 17 per cent over the last year. Fig. 11.3 gives an analysis of expenditure and income.

Table 11.8 *How the ratepayers' money is spent*

	Per annum		*Per week*	
	£	*£*	*£*	*£*
Ealing Council requirements				
Education, libraries, etc.		379		7.29
Housing		87		1.67
Highways and environmental services		73		1.40
Personal social services		80		1.54
Other (including contingency)		66		1.27
		685		13.17
Less specific government grants				
Housing	74		1.42	
Other	49		0.94	
		123		2.36
Net cost of Ealing services		562		10.81
Less block grant		253		4.87
		309		5.94
Other authorities, requirements (net of block grant)				
Greater London Council	54		1.04	
Metropolitan Police	30		0.58	
		84		1.62
		393		7.56
Less domestic rate relief		56		1.07
Total rates payable		337		6.49

How the ratepayers' money is spent

Assuming a house with a rateable value of £300, the rate for 1981–82 at 112½ pence in the pound will be £337 or £6.49 per week. This is made up as shown in Table 11.8.

Manpower

Table 11.9 compares the borough's manpower in 1981–82 with that in 1980–81.

Table 11.9 *Manpower*

	Total full-time equivalent	
	1980–81	*1981–82*
Education	5 854	5 789
Housing	432	439
Highways and environmental services	1 141	1 117
Social services	1 496	1 452
Town planning	125	127
Other services	309	302
Direct labour	645	645
Capital projects: design, etc.	136	136
Total	10 138	10 007

Capital expenditure

In 1981–82 the council's capital programme provides for an expenditure of £24.9 million (see Table 11.10). Of this capital expenditure about £7 million was financed from internal sources. The remaining capital expenditure will be financed by external borrowing and will be repayable over varying periods of up to 60 years.

Table 11.10 *Capital expenditure*

	£s m
Projects in progress	11.8
Housing projects	5.8
House purchase and improvement and to housing associations	2.8
Town planning projects	1.3
Education projects	2.2
	23.9

ASSIGNMENTS

A11.1 As Chancellor of the Exchequer you have been instructed by the Cabinet to prepare a Budget which will drastically reduce the level of unemployment in time for the next election, to be held in two years' time. Draw up a memorandum to the Cabinet outlining the possible measures which you could take to achieve this objective and the effects that the measures will have on the other parts of the economy.

A11.2 From the Treasury's Economic Progress Reports make a list of the main items in the Government's last Budget. What were the main social and economic objectives being pursued in the Budget and what measures were being taken to achieve them?

A11.3 Imagine that you are a backbench MP and that you have decided to make a speech in a debate on local government on the desirability of the introduction of a system of local income taxes to replace the present rating system. Write the speech, giving your arguments in favour of the change. Assume that the Secretary of State for the Environment is not in agreement with your suggestion and draft his reply to your proposal.

A11.4 What is the role of the Treasury in the controlling and co-ordination of public expenditure? Assess its importance in the overall control of public spending.

A11.5 You have recently been appointed Economic Adviser to the Chancellor of the Exchequer. In three weeks' time there is an Organization for Economic Co-operation and Development (OECD) meeting on the prospects for the world economy which he will be attending. In order to be fully briefed he needs an assessment of the current performance of the British economy for the coming year. Prepare an economic forecast for the Chancellor. You should illustrate your statement with statistics, graphs and charts where appropriate.

12

Public Accountability and Control

12.1 CITIZENS' GRIEVANCES: MEANS OF REDRESS

The vast increase in the size, scope and function of Government in Britain this century, particularly since the Second World War, has led to greater and greater contact between members of the public and Government bureaucracies. Much of this Government activity has considerably and positively increased the rights of many social groups in society: to mention but a few, the introduction of old age pensions in 1908, the provision of a free health service in 1948, the provision of a comprehensive range of social security benefits, health and safety at work legislation, etc. But the growth of Government has disadvantages as well as benefits for citizens, frustrating their actions in a number of ways. Many pieces of legislation reduce freedom: social services necessitate high taxation, properties may be compulsorily purchased for desirable community schemes, planning legislation affects how homes may be improved or where businesses may be located. People often feel bewildered by their contacts with bureaucracy and consequently many never claim benefits to which they are entitled.

Despite many of the undoubted benefits of the welfare state its operation can and does lead to frustration and anger on the part of many. It is therefore important in a democratic society to have some means by which people can complain if they feel that their interests have been harmed or their rights denied. Most complaints will be about *maladministration,* that is, poor, inappropriate or unfair actions on the part of administrators. Most complaints on issues of policy are dealt with through the ballot box at election time, when a Government's record comes up for public examination.

12.2 MEMBERS OF PARLIAMENT AND LOCAL COUNCILLORS

The means of redressing grievances which springs most readily to people's minds is to write to their MP, and dealing with constituents' complaints is a major part of the work of most Members of Parliament. MPs hold *surgeries* in their constituencies where the public can bring their problems direct, and there are various means open to MPs of helping constituents if they believe that there is a case to answer or a problem to solve. A Member of Parliament can write to the Government department which is the source of the complaint. This is usually a very effective means of redress, as letters from MPs have top priority in Government offices. If this means is not successful, or if the remedy of the grievance lies in the hands of a Minister, then the MP will usually bring the matter up in Parliament. This can be done in the form of a written question to the Minister, the reply to which will be published in Hansard, or it may take the form of an oral question at Question Time. If an MP is not satisfied with the reply, then he or she can use the daily Adjournment Debate to push the case. This is a debate during half an hour set aside for MPs to raise matters of concern to their constituents. Matters can also be raised in general debates and of course they can be pursued through the media.

If a complaint is complicated and requires detailed research then a Member of Parliament may pass it on to the Parliamentary Commissioner for Administration for investigation. (We will consider the role of the PCA later in this chapter.)

Members of Parliament usually find that as many as half of their complaints from the public are about local government. Though MPs can of course make contact directly with local authorities, they are *not* the elected representatives for local government and so they cannot ask questions on it in the House of Commons, unless of course it affects national policy. For this reason, MPs work closely with local councillors, who are elected to represent the public on local councils. MPs and local councillors of the same political parties will often hold joint surgeries to avoid delay in dealing with problems, as members of the public are often unaware of who provides which service.

Councillors act in much the same way as MPs with regard to complaints. Matters can be raised at committee meetings or in the council chamber, officers may be written to or visited, and, like MPs, local councillors have Commissioners for Local Administration who can make detailed investigations of cases on their behalf.

12.3 ADMINISTRATIVE LAW

Administrative law is the branch of law concerned with the Government's powers of regulation and control, and with its provision of social services. A major objective is to protect the citizen from the unwarranted use of power by the state, and to ensure that the powers granted by Parliament are not exceeded. It is a major means of regulating the relationship between the governed and the government in our society.

The British system of government is often said to rest on the *'rule of law'*, meaning that no person, however powerful or influential, is above the law. Authority and power flow from legal sanction and not from people. Administrative law seeks to ensure that the rule of law remains paramount in the dealings between the public and officials and politicians. Ministers have considerable powers under Acts of Parliament, but courts have the power to determine whether they have been correctly exercised and whether a Minister has stepped outside those powers. Individual citizens may wish, for example, to dispute the ruling by officials about their entitlement to social security benefits or the amount of income tax they have to pay. In Britain there is no separate system of administrative courts to deal with these relationships. Most disputes between officials and the public are dealt with by special *ad hoc* tribunals, but in matters of law the ordinary courts deal with them.

Certain other countries use the French system of *droit administratif,* in which there is a separate branch of administrative law with its own court system to deal with disputes between the government and the governed.

Ultra vires

In British administration all powers are derived from law. Statute law lays down the extent and limit of these powers, where and when they can be used and who can exercise them. Therefore anyone who operates outside these legally defined powers is acting unlawfully or *ultra vires*. If it can be shown that an action is not justified by the law then it will be questioned by the courts. In fact by so acting the courts are enforcing the *rule of law*.

Ultra vires not only governs the exercise of power, but also covers the abuse of power. Parliament often gives Ministers or public bodies a great deal of *discretion* in order to allow them to carry out their duties. The procedure or process by which these duties are carried out is also subject to *ultra vires*. In December 1981 the House of Lords ruled that the Greater London Council had acted *ultra vires* in implementing the ruling Labour group's election manifesto promise to provide Londoners with cheaper fares under its 'fares fair' policy on London Transport. Under the Transport (London) Act 1969, which governs the operation of London Transport, the London Transport Executive is charged with providing an economic service. It was held that the GLC was acting beyond its powers in subsidizing the operation of London Transport when those services should run on a commercial basis.

Administrative tribunals

The growth of Government activity and regulation has seen a similar growth of tribunals to deal with disputes that arise between citizens and government bodies, as well as between citizens and private organizations where aspects of the latter's operations have been made subject to government regulation. There are over 2000 tribunals in existence in the United Kingdom, including agricultural land tribunals, rent tribunals, national insurance local tribunals, National Health Service tribunals, General Commissioners of Income Tax, transport tribunals, industrial tribunals, medical appeal tribunals and supplementary benefits appeal tribunals.

Tribunals have been set up to deal with the type of disputes which otherwise would overwhelm the ordinary courts (see Table 12.1). The aim is to provide a simple and cheap procedure, but one which nevertheless can be fair, independent and objective. They are informal in their operation.

In most tribunals decisions are made by a panel, which consists of a

Table 12.1 *Administrative tribunals in the social field: cases dealt with in 1979*

	000s
Immigration adjudicators	9.1
Industrial tribunals	37.5
Local valuation courts (England and Wales) and valuation appeals committees (Scotland)	100.5
Mental health review tribunals (England and Wales)	0.7
National Health Service family practitioner committees and service committees	1.1
Rent tribunals	5.6
Supplementary benefits appeals tribunals	51.4

Source: Social Trends HMSO 1981. Reproduced with the permission of the Controller of Her Majesty's Stationery Office.

chairman, who is legally qualified but who may do this work in a part-time capacity, and two lay people. In certain cases these may be technical experts, while in others they may represent certain interests. For example, in industrial tribunals there will be an employer and a representative of a trade union. Although tribunals can usually decide their own procedure and are not required to follow legal rules of evidence, nevertheless they must follow common law rules of natural justice. The two rules of natural justice are:

1. The rule against bias: 'no man be a judge in his own cause'. This means that decisions must be made by independent assessors.
2. *Audi alteram partem*: 'hear the other side'. This rule allows a person the right to be heard, and implied in it is the notion of a fair procedure in which both parties to a dispute are allowed a fair hearing.

Despite the fact that tribunals have been given a good deal of discretion over their procedure and operation they are supervised by the courts in two ways. First, they are supervised in the matter of appeals. The statutes setting up tribunals usually allow appeals to the High Court or to some special appeal body. There is no general right of appeal against decisions: it depends on the statute which created the tribunal. Certain tribunals have their own special appeals mechanism; for example, appeals from industrial tribunals are heard by the Employment Appeal Tribunal. In certain instances there is then a right of appeal to the High Court and so to the House of Lords. Appeals are usually on questions of law and not on matters of fact.

The second type of supervision is exercised by the Queen's Bench Division of the High Court. This is a general supervision of all administrative acts where they are acts of tribunals, public bodies or Ministers. This supervision is exercised via a number of *prerogative orders*. These are designed to ensure that public bodies do not exceed their powers, make errors of law, or refuse to exercise powers when they should. The three prerogative orders are mandamus, certiorari and prohibition.

Mandamus

This prerogative remedy compels a public body to perform one of its duties. It may be taken out by a private citizen or it may be used by one public body against another. For example, in February 1976 the then Conservative-controlled Tameside Council refused to comply with the Secretary of State for Education's instructions that the council's schools should be made comprehensive. The Secretary of State sought an order of mandamus in the Divisional Court to force the council to comply with his directive. The Secretary of State finally lost the case on appeal to the House of Lords on the grounds that the 1944 Education Act had not given him the necessary power to direct the council to 'go comprehensive' (that is, the Secretary of State was acting *ultra vires*).

Certiorari

This is an order removing the record of the proceedings of a lower court to the High Court, so that the High Court can quash the lower court's proceedings. It is used in cases where a tribunal has exceeded its powers, or has failed to follow the rules of natural justice. It can be used where the tribunal has made an error of law on which a decision was based.

Prohibition

This is a similar remedy to certiorari, but it is used to prevent an authority from continuing to act contrary to the law or where it is feared that in the future it might continue to do so. For example, if it were thought that a tribunal was going to act *ultra vires* then an order of prohibition would prevent it from doing so.

The Franks Report

The Committee on Administrative Tribunals and Enquiries (the Franks Committee) was set up in 1955 to survey the work carried out by tribunals. As tribunals had been set up in an *ad hoc* fashion there were considerable differences in their procedures and methods of working. The Committee reported in 1957 and its central proposal was the setting up of a council on tribunals to provide the machinery for the general supervision of tribunals and their procedure. Such a body was set up in 1958. The Committee concluded that tribunals should adhere to the standards of 'openness, fairness and impartiality' in the conduct of their functions. The main problem with the operation of administrative tribunals is the bewildering complexity of the 'system' as seen by ordinary members of the public. The majority of the general public have neither the knowledge nor the confidence to present a case.

12.4 DELEGATED LEGISLATION

Although Parliament is the sovereign law-making body in the United Kingdom, it does not have the time or the expertise to make law on the detail and content affecting every regulation. For this reason Acts of Parliament tend to lay down the general framework or principles and then *delegate* to the appropriate Minister or public body the power to make regulations concerning details. This is known as delegated or subordinate legislation. The justifications for it are:

1. The technical nature of much legislation requires prior consultation with experts and pressure groups before suitable regulations can be made.
2. There is often a need for flexibility to meet unforeseen circumstances.
3. Parliamentary time is limited and Parliament would become completely overwhelmed if it had to consider the technical aspects of every piece of legislation.

Delegated legislation takes the following forms:

1. *Orders in Council.* These are made by the Queen in Council. The draft for the orders originates from the appropriate Minister.
2. *Statutory instruments.* These are made by the appropriate Minister and have to be laid before Parliament before they can come into force.
3. *By-laws.* These are made by local authorities and other public bodies on the basis of powers given in Acts of Parliament. Ministerial approval must be given before they can come into operation.

The amount of delegated legislation has increased considerably since 1945, with the development of the welfare state. In some circles its growth has been a cause for concern, as it gives extended powers to the executive. Obviously the reconciliation of the necessity for delegated legislation with the idea of democratic accountability is a problem. Delegated legislation is controlled in the following ways:

1. Consultation with pressure groups and interested parties. The technical nature of much delegated legislation makes it necessary for Ministers to consult a wide range of interested bodies and pressure groups before making an order.
2. Control by Parliament. A committee of both Houses of Parliament scrutinizes regulations made by Ministers and submits to each House any order that deserves special attention.
3. Control by the courts. Ministerial actions can be challenged in the courts on the grounds that an action is *ultra vires* (acting beyond legal powers). The courts cannot declare an Act of Parliament to be *ultra vires,* but they can so declare statutory instruments.

12.5 THE 'OMBUDSMAN SYSTEM'

Although MPs and local councillors do a good job of looking after citizens' interests there is a limit to their effectiveness. British MPs do not have the facilities, the money or the staff to investigate in detail the dozens of complaints that they can receive each week. Local councillors are unpaid and part-time, and so the time that they can give to this kind of work is limited. Also, in many areas of administration the procedures, regulations and rules may be extremely technical and may require a great deal of research before it can be ascertained whether a constituent's complaint is justified.

The need to protect the rights of citizens was one which required remedy and led in 1967 to the establishment of a Parliamentary Commissioner for Administration (PCA) or the 'Ombudsman'. The term 'Ombudsman' comes from Sweden, where such a system was set up in 1807 to assist citizens with complaints against the Government. The word means 'speaker for the people'. The powers of the PCA are not nearly as broad as those of the Swedish Ombudsman. The general public cannot approach him or her directly: only MPs can refer cases for investigation. This is because some MPs feared the loss of their traditional role if the public had direct access. In Britain the Ombudsman is seen as strengthening the role of MPs rather than as an independent 'speaker for the people'.

The powers of the Parliamentary Commissioner for Administration

The 1967 Parliamentary Commissioner for Administration Act gives the Ombudsman the power to investigate complaints referred by Members of Parliament. These complaints come originally from members of the general public who claim to have sustained injustice as a consequence of *maladministration* in connection with actions taken by or on behalf of Government departments. The crucial word here is 'maladministration', meaning quite literally 'bad administration'. This can occur where a civil servant has not properly followed a rule or procedure. It does *not* refer to Ministerial discretion or to whether a particular policy is good or bad, right or wrong, fair or unfair. Thus the PCA cannot look at the justice of a decision, only at whether that decision was properly arrived at or whether the proper procedure was used to implement it.

In addition, the PCA is barred from investigating the following areas, which fall outside his or her jurisdiction:

1. Local government and the Health Service, which have their own commissioners.
2. Matters which the citizen has the right to remedy in a court of law or before a tribunal.
3. Actions taken by nationalized industries, which have their own consumer 'watchdog' bodies.
4. Actions taken by the police. There is a separate police complaints procedure.
5. Most matters concerning the armed forces.
6. International relations.

7. Extradition.
8. Passports.
9. Government contracts.
10. The grant of honours and privileges by the Crown.

Though this is a long list of things that cannot be investigated, the PCA can investigate all other Government departments (with the exception of the Cabinet Office, as this might breach Cabinet secrecy). He or she has the power of a High Court judge 'to call for people and papers' while making investigations, and there is a staff to help carry out these investigations.

Government departments must provide papers and documents and witnesses if necessary. All complaints must be made within 12 months of actions about which a person feels aggrieved.

After the PCA has investigated a case he or she produces a report to the MP who referred it in the first place. The PCA cannot prosecute even if evidence of criminal activity is found. It is up to the Attorney General whether or not to prosecute in a particular case. The mere fact of the PCA's having found evidence of maladministration is usually sufficient for the Government department concerned to remedy the situation, but if for any reason it does not, there are no remedies for the citizen other than the publicity which usually surrounds PCA reports and the embarrassment which the Government will face in the House of Commons.

In 1979 the PCA received 758 complaints, of which 541 were rejected as being outside his jurisdiction and 22 were discontinued after partial investigation. Of the remainder, 84 were found to contain elements of maladministration leading to injustice.

The Ombudsman's powers have been criticized as being too weak and, where delicate matters are concerned, having no substantial powers. Ministers can refuse to give the PCA papers and witnesses if they feel that this is in the national interest.

The majority of complaints involve those departments with which the public has a great deal of contact, i.e. the Inland Revenue, the Department of Health and Social Security and the Department of Employment.

The local ombudsman

A local ombudsman system was set up in England and Wales after local government reorganization in 1974. A separate local Commissioner for Administration for Scotland was established in 1975.

There are three Local Commissioners for Administration for England (one each for London and the South East; the South West, the West Midlands and East Anglia; and the North and the East Midlands) and a separate Commissioner for Wales.

They have powers to investigate maladministration in local government, with the exception of parish councils, water authorities and police authorities. Examples of injustices dealt with include: neglect and unjustified delay; failure to follow the council's agreed policies, rules or procedures; malice, bias or unfair discrimination; failure to have proper procedures or to review procedures when they need reviewing; failure to take into account matters which should have been taken into account; the use of faulty ways of doing things; and failure to tell people their rights.

Complaints about administration in local government are usually first directed to local councillors, who may then decide to pass the complaint to the commissioners. However, unlike the Parliamentary Commissioners, individual citizens may complain directly to the local commissioners. The investigation of complaints is carried out in a very similar way to that by the Parliamentary Commissioner, and a great deal of emphasis is put on conciliation by the local commissioners. After the investigation of cases of alleged maladministration, reports are published which go to the local authority concerned. It is up to individual authorities to remedy grievances.

In 1979 the Local Commissioners for Administration in Great Britain (England, Wales and Scotland) received 2584 complaints. Of these, 1765 were rejected as being outside their jurisdiction. They reported on 256 cases containing elements of maladministration leading to injustice.

The following areas are outside the jurisdiction of the local commissioners.

1. Complaints about events which occurred more than 12 months ago.
2. Complaints which have other means of remedy, e.g. before the courts or tribunals.
3. Complaints against the police.
4. Complaints concerning personnel matters in local government, including appointments, dismissals, pay, pensions, redundancy and discipline.
5. Complaints about the running of schools and colleges.
6. Complaints about commercial transactions by local authorities.
7. Complaints about public passenger transport, docks, harbours, entertainments, industrial establishments and markets.

Too many ombudsmen?

In recent years the scope of the machinery for the redress of grievances has been substantially increased. Citizens have means of complaining about injustices created by Government administration and about certain practices in other areas of business and social life. This has provided the citizen with substantial areas of new rights, but there is a major difficulty with the way the machinery operates. That difficulty is that the complaints machinery has been set up in an *ad hoc* fashion over the past 15 years, and so to the ordinary citizen the complaints procedures are often bewildering and complex.

Listed below are some of the 'ombudsmen' and complaints bodies to whom the citizen may complain, either directly or through an elected representative.

1. *Parliamentary Commissioner for Administration,* set up in 1967.
2. *Commissioners for Local Administration* (England), set up in 1974.
3. *Commissioner for Local Administration* (Wales), set up in 1974.
4. *Commissioner for Local Administration* (Scotland), set up in 1975.
5. *Commissioner for Complaints* (Northern Ireland), set up in 1969. The duties of the Northern Ireland Ombudsman cover a wide range of public bodies, both central and local government. The Commissioner not only has the power to produce reports, but also has specific powers of conciliation.
6. *Health Service Commissioner,* set up as part of the National Health Service reform in 1974. The PCA is also the Health Service Commissioner. He can deal only with complaints about the Health Service administration and not with complaints about clinical matters. In 1979, 562 complaints were received, of which 80 contained failures in the service or elements of maladministration leading to injustice.
7. *Commission for Racial Equality,* set up in 1977 following the Race Relations Act 1976. The Act makes discrimination unlawful in employment, training, education and the provision of goods and services. It makes it an offence to stir up racial hatred. The Commission replaces the Race Relations Board (set up in 1966) and the Community Relations Commission (1968).
8. *Equal Opportunities Commission,* set up under the Sex Discrimination Act 1975, which outlaws discrimination on the grounds of sex in all aspects of employment, education, insurance, credit, etc. The Commission's work involves promoting equality of

opportunity for men and women and eliminating discrimination. The Commission also deals with complaints under the Equal Pay Act 1970. In 1979 the following inquiries were dealt with:

Employment inquiries (under the Sex Discrimination Act)	905
Employment inquiries (under the Equal Pay Act)	375
Educational and training inquiries	239
Goods, facilities and service inquiries	477
Other discrimination inquiries (not covered by the Sex Discrimination Act)	521
Advertising inquiries	626
	3143

Source: *Social Trends,* HMSO 1981. Reproduced with the permission of the Controller of Her Majesty's Stationery Office.

9. *Community Health Councils,* set up following the National Health Service reorganization in 1974. They represent the clients and patients of the service in each health district. Complaints about administrative procedures and service failures can be made to them, but they cannot deal with clinical matters.
10. *Police Complaints Board,* set up under the Police Act 1976. It deals with complaints against the police by members of the public.
11. *Office of Fair Trading,* set up by the Fair Trading Act 1973 and presided over by the Director of Fair Trading. It deals with complaints about unfair trading practices, individual consumers' rights and monopolies and mergers.
12. *National Consumer Council,* set up in 1975 to represent a wide range of consumer viewpoints.
13. *Consumer Councils for Nationalized Industries.* The statutes creating the various nationalized industries have set up a variety of consumer and consultative councils. Their function is to receive complaints from the public about the service being provided and to bring them to the attention of the corporations. Reports are usually made public.

12.6 OPEN GOVERNMENT

British Government is surrounded by secrecy. The most important means of maintaining silence about a great deal of what goes on inside

Government is the Official Secrets Acts of 1911, 1920 and 1939. These Acts confer considerable powers which, though originally passed to prevent foreign espionage, are used mainly to prevent comment on matters of public interest. The definition of an official secret is 'any sketch, note, document or knowledge which relates to or is used in a prohibited place or anything in such a place'. It is wide enough to prevent any official information being disclosed even if it is in the public interest that it should be.

The Official Secrets Act has to be signed by all civil servants, military personnel, policemen and employees of nationalized industries, and covers any discussions which a Government employee might have with members of the press. Quite obviously the Act is breached regularly or there would be no sources of information about the workings of Government or press 'leaks'.

In many other countries the position is different and citizens have a right to information, especially information about themselves which is held by the Government. In the USA the Freedom of Information Act gives citizens and groups access to information held by Government. Such access allows for greater accountability, as the process of decision-making and the information on which decisions were made can be assessed by outside observers. Britain is one of the few democratic countries without a freedom of information Act. In favour of such an Act it has been argued that:

1. It would make the public bureaucracies more accountable to the citizen, as it could be ascertained easily where proper procedures had been followed in making decisions.
2. It would allow for greater research into public administration, which could uncover areas of inefficiency, waste or neglect, and it would be in the public interest to expose such areas.
3. It would strengthen the democratic process by giving pressure groups greater access to information.
4. It would ensure that information held on the citizen was not abused, since the citizen would have access to his or her own files. This right is particularly important in the age of the computer and the data bank.

Against the introduction of such an Act it has been argued that in Government secrecy is essential in many fields, particularly defence. The case has also been put that the quality of decision-making would suffer if particular Ministers and civil servants involved in decisions could easily be identified. This could lead to a particularly cautious approach to decision-making. Another argument is cost. In 1977 the cost of the US Freedom of Information Act was £13 million, and in Britain, though estimates vary, figures of between £5 million and £10 million have been estimated.

In 1979 Clement Freud, the Liberal MP for the Isle of Ely, introduced a Freedom of Information Bill which would have allowed public access to records in many areas of Government. However, the measure was killed by the timing of the 1979 general election.

The debate on the measure continues, but in terms of extending the accountability of Government to the electorate and providing citizens with a more informed means of participating in government, such a measure is of crucial importance.

ASSIGNMENTS

A12.1 Choose a tribunal within easy travelling distance of your home or college (e.g. a rent tribunal, an industrial tribunal, General Commissioner of Taxes) and make arrangements to visit it when it is in session. You can make this a group visit. Before the visit obtain from your college library information about the operation of the tribunal. After the visit write a report covering the following areas:

(a) the status and objectives of the tribunal;
(b) the powers of the tribunal;
(c) the composition of the tribunal;
(d) the procedure for making representation at the tribunal;
(e) details of the case(s) which you heard while you were on the visit.

A12.2 From your college library find out the addresses of the Parliamentary Commissioner for Administration, the Health Service Commissioner, and the Local Commissioner for Administration. Write to each of them requesting information about their role and responsibilities. From this information write a report on the role of 'ombudsmen' in Britain. Include in it any suggestions you have for improving the system.

Select Bibliography

General works

Birch, A.H. (1973) *The British System of Government.* London: George Allen & Unwin.

Butler, D. & Sloman, A. (1980) *British Political Facts,* 5th edition. London: Macmillan.

The *Economist* (1980) *Political Britain.* London: The Economist Newspapers Ltd.

Gladden, A.N. (1972) *A History of Public Administration.* St Albans: Frank Cross.

Hanson, A.H. & Walles, M. (1976) *Governing Britain.* London: Fontana.

Hartley, T.C. & Griffith, J.A.G. (1975) *Government and Law.* London: Weidenfeld & Nicolson.

Punnet, R.M. (1980) *British Government and Politics,* 4th edition. London: Heinemann Educational.

Rose, R. (1980) *Politics in England.* London: Faber and Faber.

Sallis, E.J. (1981) *The Machinery of Government: An Introduction to Public Administration.* A Workbook of Notes and Assignments for BEC National Level and Related Courses. Eastbourne: Holt, Rinehart and Winston.

Stanyer, J. & Smith, B.C. (1976) *Administering Britain.* London: Fontana.

Political concepts

Coxall, W.N. (1973) *Politics: Compromise and Conflict in Liberal Democracy*. Oxford: Pergamon Press.
Crick, B. (1964) *In Defence of Politics*. Harmondsworth: Penguin.
Dunsire, A. (1973) *Administration: the Word and the Science*. Oxford: Martin Robertson.
Finer, S.E. (ed.) (1979) *Five Constitutions*. Harmondsworth: Penguin.
Heater, D. (1974) *Contemporary Political Ideas*. Harlow: Longman.
Marshall, G. & Moodie, G.C. (1967) *Some Problems of the Constitution*. London: Hutchinson.
Miller, J.D.B. (1962) *The Nature of Politics*. Harmondsworth: Penguin.

The process of participation

Higgins, G.M. & Richardson, J.J. (1976) *Political Participation*. London: Politics Association.
Maclean, I. (1980) *Elections,* 2nd edition. Harlow: Longman.
Macpherson, C.B. (1977) *The Life and Times of Liberal Democracy*. Oxford: Oxford University Press.
Parry, G. (1972) *Participation in Politics*. Manchester: Manchester University Press.
Pateman, C. (1970) *Participation and Democratic Theory*. Cambridge: Cambridge University Press.
Skeffington Committee (1969) People and Planning: Report of the Committee on Public Participation in Planning. London: HMSO.

Political parties

Bealey, F. (ed.) (1970) *The Social and Political Thought of the British Labour Party*. London: Weidenfeld.
Beer, S.H. (1969) *Modern British Politics,* 2nd edition. London: Faber and Faber.
Blondell, J. (1976) *Voters, Parties and Leaders*. Harmondsworth: Penguin.
Cook, C. (1976) *A Short History of the Liberal Party 1900–1976*. London: Macmillan.
Coxall, W.N. (1980) *Parties and Pressure Groups*. Harlow: Longman.
Gilmour, I. (1978) *Inside Right*. London: Quartet Books.
Hogg, Q. (1947) *The Case for Conservatism*. Harmondsworth: Penguin.

Mackenzie, R. (1963) *British Political Parties,* 2nd edition. London: Heinemann.
Pelling, H. (1976) *A Short History of the Labour Party,* 5th edition. London: Macmillan.
Russel, T. (1978) *The Tory Party*. Harmondsworth: Penguin.

Pressure groups

Coxall, W.N. (1980) *Parties and Pressure Groups*. Harlow: Longman.
Kogan, M. (1975) *Educational Policy-making*. London: George Allen & Unwin.
Wotton, G. (1975) *Pressure Groups in Britain 1720–1970*. Harmondsworth: Allen Lane.

Parliament

Central Office of Information (1977) *The British Parliament*. London: Central Office of Information No. 33.
Coombes, D. & Walkland, S.A. (ed.) (1980) *Parliament and Economic Affairs*. London: Policy Studies Institute.
Davies, A. (1980) *Reformed Select Committees: The First Year*. London: The Outer Circle Policy Unit.
Lidderdale, Sir D. (ed.) (1976) *Parliament and the People*. Harlow: Longman.
May, E. (1976) *Erskine May's Treatise on the Law, Privileges, and Proceedings and Usages of Parliament,* 19th edition. Sevenoaks: Butterworth.
Norton, P. (1981) *The Commons in Perspective*. Oxford: Martin Robertson.
Punnett, R.M. (1973) *Front-Bench Opposition*. London: Heinemann.
Richards, P.G. (1974) *The Backbenchers*. London: Faber and Faber.

Prime Minister and the Cabinet

Bagehot, W. (1963) (introduction by R.H.S. Crossmand) *English Constitution*. London: Fontana.
Gordon Walker, P. (1972) *The Cabinet*. London: Fontana.
Herman, V. & Alt, J. (1975) *Cabinet Studies: a reader*. London: Macmillan.

King, A. (1970) *The Prime Minister*. London: Macmillan.
Mackintosh, J. (1976) *The British Cabinet*, 3rd edition. London: Stevens & Sons.
Royal Institute of Public Administration Policy and Practice (1981) *The Experience of Government*. London: RIPA.

Policy implementation and Government administration

Beaumont, P.B. (1981) *Government as an Employer—Setting an example?* London: RIPA.
Birch, A.H. (1979) *Political Integration and Disintegration in the British Isles*. London: George Allen & Unwin.
Chapman, C. (1970) *The Higher Civil Service in Britain*. London: Constable.
Civil Service College (1980) *Industrial Relations in the Civil Service*. London: HMSO.
Civil Service Department (1980) *Staff Relations in the Civil Service*, 4th edition. London: HMSO.
Crowther Hunt, Lord (1981) *The Civil Servants*. London: Macdonald.
Fulton Committee (1968) *The Civil Service* Vol. 1 Cmnd. 3638. London: HMSO.
Garrett, J. (1972) *The Management of Government*. Harmondsworth: Penguin.
Garrett, J. (1980) *Managing the Civil Service*. London: Heinemann.
Hill, M. (1976) *The State, Administration and the Individual*. London: Fontana.
Mackenzie, W.J.M. & Grove, J.W. (1976) *Central Administration in Britain*. London: Longman.
Parris, H. (1973) *Staff Relations in the Civil Service: Fifty Years of Whitleyism*. London: George Allen & Unwin.
Pitt, D.C. & Smith, B.C. (1981) *Government Departments: An Organisational Perspective*. London: Routledge & Kegan Paul.
Russell-Smith, E. (1974) *Modern Bureaucracy: The Home Civil Service*. Harlow: Longman.
Thornhill, W. (ed.) (1972) *The Case for Regional Reform*. Sunbury-on-Thames: Thomas Nelson & Sons.

Public corporations and public bodies

Brown, R.G.S. (1974) *The Changing National Health Service*. London: Routledge & Kegan Paul.

Coombes, D. (1971) *State Enterprise: Business or Politics*. London: George Allen & Unwin.

Open University (1972) *Nationalised Industries*. Milton Keynes: Open University.

Outer Circle Policy Unit (1979) *What's Wrong with Quangos*. London: Outer Circle Policy Unit.

Pryke, R. (1971) *Public Enterprise in Practice: the British experience of nationalisation over two decades*. St Albans: MacGibbon & Kee.

Tivey, L. (1973) *Nationalisation in British Industry*. London: Jonathan Cape.

Tivey, L. (ed.) (1973) *The Nationalised Industries since 1960*. London: George Allen & Unwin.

Public administration and local government

Burgess, T. & Travers, T. (1980) *Ten Billion Pounds: Whitehall's Takeover of the Town Halls*. London: Grant McIntyre.

Greenwood, R. & Stewart, J.D. (1974) *Corporate Planning in English Local Government*. Tonbridge: Charles Knight.

Gyford, J. (1976) *Local Politics in Britain*. London: Croom Helm.

Haynes, R.J. (1980) *Organisational Theory and Local Government*. London: George Allen & Unwin.

McAllister, R. & Hunter, D. (1980) *Local Government: Death or Devolution?* London: Outer Circle Policy Unit.

Minogue, M. (1977) *Documents on Contemporary British Government Volume 2, Local Government in Britain*. Cambridge: Cambridge University Press.

Poole, K. (1978) *The Local Government Service*. London: George Allen & Unwin.

Redcliffe Maud, Lord & Wood, B. (1974) *English Local Government Reformed*. Oxford: Oxford University Press.

Richards, P. (1975) *The Reformed Local Government System*, 2nd edition. London: George Allen & Unwin.

Royal Institute of Public Administration (1980) *Party Politics in English Local Government: Officers and Members*. RIPA & PSI.

Seeley, I.H. (1978) *Local Government Explained*. London: Macmillan.

International organizations

Barber, J. (ed.) (1974) *European Community: Vision and Reality*. London: Croom Helm for the Open University.

Harris, P.B. (1975) *The Commonwealth.* Harlow: Longman.

Heater, D. (1976) *Britain and the Outside World.* Harlow: Longman.

Swann, D. (1975) *The Economics of the Common Market.* Harmondsworth: Penguin.

Public finance

Armstrong of Sanderstead, Lord (1980) *Budgetary Reform in the UK.* Oxford: Oxford University Press for the Institute of Fiscal Studies.

Brittan, S. (1971) *Steering the Economy: the Role of the Treasury.* Harmondsworth: Penguin.

Hepworth, M.P. (1976) *The Finance of Local Government.* London: George Allen & Unwin.

Kay, A.D. & King, D.D. (1978) *The British Tax System.* Oxford: Oxford University Press.

Keegan, W. & Pennant-Rea, R. (1979) *Who Runs the Economy?* London: Maurice Temple Smith.

Lethbridge, D. (ed.) (1976) *Government and Industry Relationships.* Oxford: Pergamon Press.

Marshall, A.H. (1974) *Financial Management in Local Government.* London: George Allen & Unwin.

Wright, M. (ed.) (1980) *Public Spending Decisions.* London: George Allen & Unwin.

Public accountability

Commission for Local Administration in England (1980) *Your Local Ombudsman Report for the year ending 31 March.*

Farmer, J.A. (1974) *Tribunals and Governments.* London: Wiedenfeld & Nicolson.

Hill, M. (1977) *Our Fettered Ombudsman.* London: Stevens & Sons.

Wade, H.W.R. (1977) *Administrative Law.* Oxford: Oxford University Press.

Wraith, R.E. (1977) *Open Government: The British Interpretation.* London: Royal Institute of Public Administration.

Wraith, R.E. & Hutchinson, P.G. (1973) *Administrative Tribunals.* London: George Allen & Unwin.

Index